For Karen Magee

Sidney Berg Neil

BY APPOINTMENT

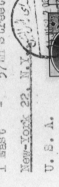
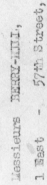

SECRÉTARIAT PRIVE
DE S.M. LE ROI

AIRMAIL
No. 507

Messieurs BERRY-HILL,
1 East - 57th Street,
New-York 22, N.Y.
U. S. A.

POSTES D'ÉGYPTE

POSTE AERIENNE — EGYPTE — 30 MILLIEMES

By Appointment

Sidney Berry Hill

VANTAGE PRESS
New York

Published by Vantage Press, Inc.
516 West 34th Street, New York, New York 10001

Manufactured in the United States of America
ISBN: 0-533-10014-3

Library of Congress Catalog Card No.: 91-92885

0 9 8 7 6 5 4 3 2 1

For Leona

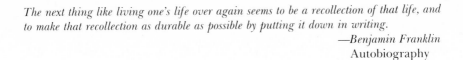

The next thing like living one's life over again seems to be a recollection of that life, and to make that recollection as durable as possible by putting it down in writing.

—*Benjamin Franklin*
Autobiography

Contents

Foreword

Unstudied, unpretentious, direct, and personal, Sidney Berry Hill's lively and amusing reminiscences of a lifetime spent in the art and antiques trade is like a great Victorian house, replete with curious antiquarian details, rambling corridors, grand staircases, innumerable rooms decorated in a variety of styles, and noisy plumbing, but ultimately well adapted to its complex function and presenting an imposing spectacle when viewed from a distance. Anecdotes about and conversations with the rich and famous, eccentric collectors, and the tragic victims of their own times and destiny satisfy the reader's obsessive ambition to step through the door and down the corridor. Wit, polish, formal elegance, unfeigned gusto, admirable bluntness, and a naturally happy and grateful response to the physical beauty of life, people, and works of art—these are some of the many excellent qualities that emerge from Mr. Hill's fluent and compelling account.

It is against this background that Mr. Hill's entertaining and thoughtful memoirs of the art market take on added significance. How people collected works of art in England and what they bought reflect on what one sociologist has referred to as "the custom and culture of a most peculiar island." Custom and culture certainly involve some of the deepest and most obscure forces at work in British society during these years, a complex web of history, tradition, and "myths ourselves," which are easier to describe than to explain.

—Wendell Garrett
Editor-at-large
Antiques Magazine

Preface

It was on one of those truly beautiful days that we all look forward to with such great pleasure one of those days when the skies are blue and there is no suggestion of a cloud. It was on such a day that while I was reclining lazily on my recliner chaise on the open deck of our summer cottage in Connecticut, my eyes closed. I started dreaming.

I began to ponder the days of my childhood and the years of my youth, as well as the long years I had spent in the business realms of art and antiquity. As these thoughts began to stream through my consciousness I seemed to be looking at myself as through a telescope of time. Naturally these recollections crowded apace through my mind without any semblance of order.

Then and there I decided that my lifetime of experiences, some of which were quite extraordinary, some amusing, and many tinged with historical interest, might be put together in some sort of order as footnotes to events of the past. Unfortunately, and I must say to my utter regret, I had never compiled or kept any sort of diary.

During the half century of my business life, there were fascinating incidents that by their outstanding or unique character have continued to hound my memory, through all of my lifetime. Some of these happenings might appear to be quite improbable, yet I must assure my readers that all that I have penned are in fact true. Even to this day, as I think back over the years, I find such occurrences as the Skeffington-Smythe story almost unbelievable, and yet, as I have written it, so it was. Many of the transatlantic journeys that I have made by sea, and later by air, were all in some way intermingled in my thoughts.

Thus it was the day following my daydreaming that I commenced to set down on paper some of the episodes and events to which I have referred, episodes that cover virtually all of the five continents and in which the cast ranges from crowned heads and movie stars to lesser known millionaires.

It was my wife, Leona Bowman, herself an international figure in the field of fashion reporting, who encouraged me. Over the past quarter of a century of our married life she had heard me relate some of my experiences and had always found them intriguing, and she always held that they would make interesting reading to others, particularly as they touch upon so many historical events of the past years. It is for this reason that I dedicate this book to her, with all the love and respect that I possess, as without her constant encouragement it would never have been written.

Acknowledgments

I wish to thank my two sons, Lawrence Charles Berry Hill and James Berry Hill, together with Frederick David Hill, Barbara Anderman, and Kristina Peterson Shak for the valued advice and encouragement in writing this book.

BY APPOINTMENT

Chapter 1

How I Came into the Business in London

"You are now going to be an art and antiques dealer."

It was with these words that my father greeted me immediately upon my arrival home in London from my boarding school in Brussels. In those days, back in the early twenties, it was usually accepted as an understood thing that a son would join in his father's business as soon as he had finished his schooling. This was the case unless he preferred to enter one or other of the professions and become a doctor, lawyer, engineer, or what you will.

It had been with this thought in mind that Father had contacted an old friend of his, a gentleman named Thomas Christie, not in any way to be confused with Christie's, the great international firm of art auctioneers. He had asked him whether perhaps he knew of any business that might be available for sale. At the time Christie was the manager of a business house dealing in antique jewels and other antiquities and was very well informed in many aspects of the antiquarian field. My father had explained to Christie that he wanted to buy a going concern for me. Christie had replied that curiously enough, he had just at that moment been told of a very old and well-established shop that was on the market. The owner was at the time still running it, but he was a very old man, well into his eighties, and wanted to retire as soon as possible. It was then arranged that Christie would look further into the proposition and be in touch with Father again in a few days.

The following week, Christie called and suggested that he and my father lunch together, at which time he would outline the matter in fullest detail. At this luncheon Christie explained that the business in question was being run under the name of Frederick Berry, the name of the owner, who was the last and sole survivor of his family, which dated back into the early seventeen-hundreds.

1

The business, he said, had been started by the old man's ancestor, named John Berry, a man who had risen to such very high eminence in his business that he had been elected to the high office of master of the famed Clockmaker's Company, which was one of the leading so-called "Livery Companies" of the day. These Livery Companies numbered in their group such great authorities as the Goldsmith's Company, the Mercer's Company, and the Haberdasher's Company, to mention just a few. Over the centuries these companies had acquired immense wealth and had endowed many hospitals, schools, and other institutions.

The Berry shop was located in the center of London's West End at the corner of Haymarket and the famed Jermyn street. It held an excellent lease on most favorable terms directly from the British Royal Properties, who actually received the rents.

After passing along to my father these details, Christie also told him that in the event he actually did buy the business, Christie himself would very much like to join the firm as an employee. Christie also explained to Father that he had been informed that "Old Fred," as he was always affectionately called by his friends and cronies, had one great fault—if fault it could be called—he was a very heavy drinker and each day consumed an entire bottle of Scotch whiskey. He also told Father that the old man spent several hours a day over at a pub, very conveniently situated over the road from the shop, where he would foregather with some other of his old pals, similarly to imbibe.

After hearing all this, Father said that he thought it would be a good idea not to waste my time, but to go round and look over the business. Christie agreed, and they strolled round to the premises. After looking the place over, Father asked the old man, who had just at that moment returned from his "pub crawl," how much he was asking for his business as it stood, together with its stock.

Old Fred mulled the matter over for a very short time and soon stated his figure. The amount that the old man mentioned turned out to be almost precisely what both Father and Christie had considered the establishment to be worth to them, and a transaction was soon agreed upon.

Having bought the business, Father told Old Fred that they would continue the business under its old name, and this pleased the old man enormously, particularly as he was handed a check for the amount on the spot. This, then, was possibly one of the fastest takeover transactions in all history. Thus I was to become the owner of a highly respected seventeenth-century business.

At the time of this takeover, there were two employees in the shop, and my father asked them whether they would care to continue on with the new management. In unison they both replied that they would be delighted, and that was that.

The elder of these two was a man in his early sixties named Frederick Andrews, a tall handsome man with what appeared to be a perpetual smile on his face. He explained that he had been with Old Fred for very many years and had acted at all times as a general overall factotum. By trade he was a watch and clockmaker, but he served as general manager during the old man's very frequent absences. Each morning, he explained, he would open the shop, and each evening he would close it. On occasion he would also act as salesman, and he was well liked by all the old customers, many of whom had traded with the shop for over half a century.

The second employee was a considerably younger man named Arthur White, at the time in his early twenties. He was known to all and sundry as "Arthur the Boy," a nomenclature that was destined to remain with him until his passing, when he was in his seventies and still active at the shop. Factually he had spent his entire life with the firm. From a visual point of view, he could easily have been a character out of one of Charles Dickens's novels.

From an antiquarian viewpoint, the shop itself was very interesting, as it was actually the lower portion of a Queen Anne mansion that over the years had been converted to commercial use, certainly over two hundred years before the takeover. In front it had a bow window, with a door to one side, and under this window there was a half-rounded divider of brass certainly dating back to the building of the shop front. This divider had originally been incised across its middle with the name BERRY. However, over the years this brass had been polished and repolished so many times that, at the time of our purchase, it was almost indecipherable.

In their extreme wisdom my parents had sent me away to a boarding school in Brussels named Belgium House, where I could learn to speak French. It was their thinking that an extra language was an extra arm.

The reason for their choice of this particular school was very sound indeed. The school only accepted about thirty students, and these came from all over the world. There were boys from the Arab states, from England, from Germany, from Austria, from Scandinavia, and as at the school the language was naturally French, all conversation had to be conducted in that tongue. Thus, in short order, the pupils all acquired facility in the French language.

It so happened that German was one of the subjects on the curriculum, so I was able to learn this language at the same time as I did French. When I started in the business, I asked Christie whether he would consider acting as manager, as obviously I had much to learn before I could even contemplate taking over. At this suggestion he was overjoyed, and he then told me that he had already arranged this with Father before he had made the purchase. Christie then at once started to run the establishment, and after this he remained with the firm until his retirement many years later.

It was after I had been at the shop for several weeks that I noticed many of the crowned heads of Europe had, over the years, been our customers; and although I had heard that we had done considerable business with the British Royal Family, I could no-where find any certificate of appointment hanging on the wall.

One day, in the course of a conversation with Andrews, I asked him about this. "Do you know of any reason why I do not see a Royal Appointment to the British Crown hanging anywhere on the walls?"

Laughingly, he replied, "Indeed, I do."

I then asked him whether he could tell me anything about the matter.

"Yes, I can tell you in precise detail." He then proceeded to relate the following story.

"Old Fred and King Edward VII were very old friends; in fact, they habitually called each other by their first names. Both of them were members of an exclusive fishing society named the Royal Piscatorial Society. This society was just about to celebrate its centennial. The king wished to mark this occasion by presenting to the membership a silver salver to be kept in their clubhouse, and he wished to have the facsimile signature of each of the members engraved on its surface. With this in mind, the king came into the shop and brought with him a piece of paper with all the signatures written on it and asked Old Fred to add his signature as well. He then apparently ordered a fine silver salver.

"As I was away on my vacation at this time, I knew nothing about any of this. It then appears that Old Fred told the king he would put the engraving in hand immediately and that it would be ready in about two weeks. The king apparently told the old man there was no hurry and that he could take his time. However, it appears that the king said that it was important that nobody know anything about the matter, especially up at the palace. He then said 'I shall come by in about two or three weeks and pick it up myself.' Old Fred then told the king that he understood perfectly and that he would keep the matter absolutely confidential. Whether Old Fred remembered what he had told the king or not is a moot point; however, he told me nothing about this when I came back from my holiday.

"Obviously, no sooner was the king out the door than the old man went over to the pub, obviously forgetting all about the royal order. About three weeks passed, and one afternoon King Edward arrived, as he had arranged to do, and asked to speak with Old Fred. But as usual Old Fred was over at the pub.

"Knowing nothing about the salver or about the order, I told the king that I knew where Old Fred was at the time, and I asked His Majesty whether he would care to take a seat while I went to fetch the old man. The king replied that he welcomed the idea, as he was rather tired, having walked all the way from Buckingham Palace. I then crossed over to the pub and told Old Fred that the king was over at the shop waiting for him.

"Unfortunately, by this time Old Fred was well in his cups and told me that he had completely forgotten all about the salver that the king had commissioned. This was the first time I had heard anything about the silver salver that the king had ordered.

" 'Go back and tell the king that the work is not quite ready for him, as it entailed rather more labor than I had originally figured, but that it will be finished definitely the following week.' Then, as an afterthought, he added, 'You can tell His Majesty that he can shove his royal order up his royal and very commodious asshole.' There was nothing I could do but return and explain to the king that his order was not quite ready, but it certainly would be completed by the following week. Naturally, I refrained from passing on to the king Old Fred's parting message regarding his royal person. The king said that this would be fine and that he would again come in by himself the following week.

"In due course the following week the king returned, and again Old Fred was over at the pub. I fibbed again and told the king that the old man had been called out on some important business, but I again said that I would go and bring him back. The king again said that this was fine, as he would enjoy spending a little time reading his *Times*, and that he was in no hurry.

"I then again crossed over to the pub and spoke with Old Fred, who had completely forgotten all about the order, and there was nothing that I could do but return with another ridiculous message.

"King Edward was by no means a simpleton, and as soon as I gave him some message or other, he said, 'I see that I can no longer rely on the old man and I shall have to go elsewhere to get my salver in time for the presentation.' As he was leaving the shop, he turned, saying, 'Isn't it a terrible shame that a sincere friendship such as ours has been over so many years should end in this way? You can tell Old Fred that I shall never darken his doors again.'

"It was quite soon after this incident that the king passed away, and I do not know whether or not the society ever received its salver. So you can well understand that we have no Royal Appointment hanging anywhere on the walls."

The shop itself was most interesting, with its very long basement that extended under the roadway and across to the other side of Jermyn street. Part of this basement, under the sidewalk, was inset with thick panels of glass, which allowed some glimmer of light to penetrate from above. Under this glass roof stood the toilet, an obvious adaptation from its antiquarian days. This had been, in fact, a "modern" addition at some time in the early Victorian days. The main area was quite fascinating and was actually a museum piece on its own, as it had housed a jeweler's workshop during the eighteenth century and was still equipped with its old-time workers' benches. Also, there was a wire drawing bench that extended from one side of the room to the other, in which a thick length of gold could be inserted at one end and which, by turning a handle, could be drawn into a length of gold wire of any required thickness.

Up until the time that I took over the establishment very few had ventured downstairs, as the place had become the home of innumerable rats, and indeed all had avoided use of the toilet facilities as much as was humanly possible. In a way this avoidance was of considerable moment to me as, being rather of an inquisitive nature, I did go downstairs into these nether regions, and as I did so I noticed a long series of shelves round the walls and under the ceiling. In the dim light I could not see anything particular on them, but I saw that the shelves were laden with "things." On the floor I saw several large barrels, all apparently overflowing with papers.

I went back upstairs and returned with a flashlight, and then I saw that the papers in the barrels were all old letters and bills. These barrels I then concluded must have been the filing system in earlier days. I tried to pick up some of the letters, but as I touched them, they disintegrated into dust in my hands. Without touching it, I noticed a letter that seemed to be signed by Charles Dickens lying on top of a pile. I would dearly have loved to read this, but similarly it fell apart in my hands. The old man had mentioned in conversation one day, when speaking with Andrews, that Charles Dickens had been a frequent customer of the shop in years gone by.

Then turning my flashlight onto the shelves, I noticed many pieces of broken ceramics and pieces of what looked like silver plate, presumably things that had been consigned to the shop for repair and never collected by their owners. I then noticed what appeared to be a statuette of some sort, about eighteen inches in height; however, it was so begrimed that I could not make out what it might be. Anyhow, I took it down and went upstairs with it and, after filling a large basin with water, commenced to clean it. To my utter surprise there emerged a black wood pedestal on which stood an early ivory figure of a sixteenth-century cavalier of musketeer type, wearing a large, traditional wide-brimmed hat

7

with flowing feathers at one side. Close examination revealed that the sword he carried had broken away at the top and had been repaired; obviously this was one of the objects that had never been collected by its owner. As I was sure that the item was of seventeenth-century ivory work, I decided to take it home. Many years later, when many of my household effects were shipped over to me in New York, where I was then living, this statuette was included in the shipment. Today it occupies a prominent niche in the wall going up the stairs of our duplex apartment and is considered by us as our "household god."

At the shop our manager, Christie, had one invariable rule. At approximately noon each day he would call Arthur the Boy into his private office and ask him to go round the corner and bring him back two of those very crusty rolls for which the British are so well known and a piece of Cheddar cheese together with a bottle of Bass ale. Christie would ask him to do this monotonously each day without fail, and each time as though it were the first time. It was an inviolable rule, most stringently adhered to by all, that he was never to be disturbed during this hour. Only after his lunch was over would the others each leave for their various lunch hangouts.

Chapter 2

I Leave School and Become a Freemason

It was just around the time when I was away at school in Brussels that inflation of many European currencies began to run wild. This was especially the case in Germany, but the Belgian franc was no exception. Street hawkers were offering to sell German marks at every street corner in London with the cry, "Be a millionaire for a penny!" This cry was soon to be followed by, "Be a billionaire for a penny!" The German mark had fallen with such great rapidity that it was to all intents and purposes absolutely valueless, and people had to take small hand carts with them to work to carry home their wages.

It was during this period that my father bought a raffle ticket on some boxing match or other at a small restaurant that he frequented for lunch, and, as a joke, when he paid his shilling for the ticket, he put it in my name. As luck would have it, the ticket drew first prize, and incidentally, this was the first and last time that I had ever won any money on such an operation during my lifetime. The prize money amounted to about sixty dollars in American money in those days, and my father, being a gentleman, mailed me a draft to school for this amount. For a schoolboy, those were the days of pennies, but now for the first time I was in possession of what was, to me, a small fortune. Overnight, and at the young age of seventeen, I became an international financier.

Immediately on receipt of this draft I went downtown to a currency broker and changed my dollars into Belgian francs. It was to my good fortune that just at that moment the Belgian franc had plunged to its lowest ebb, and I soon returned to school with my pockets overflowing with more cash than one of the teachers at the school would earn in an entire year. There was at this time a boy from Manchester, England, who had become my dearest buddy, and to this day I still remember him well and recall his name, Alex Nightingale. It may well be that it was because of our mutual dislike of soccer that I remember him so clearly.

9

At our school all the boys were automatically enrolled as members of the two outstanding sporting clubs in town. One was where we could play tennis and the other soccer, and it was to one or the other of these that we were always being taken and where we could play for as long or as short a time as we wished. These two clubs were named, respectively, the Racing Club and the Daring Club. It was to this latter that Alex and I both preferred to go because here we were able to play tennis and take tennis lessons. We both loved this game. It was also at this club that we were supposed to play soccer, which we both detested. In order to get to the club, we had to take a bus, which always made a stop in the center of town at the Bourse. This Bourse stop was quite close to the celebrated opera house, the great Théàtre de la Monnaie.

One day, while en route to the club, I noticed a sign over the opera house that announced there was to be a matinée performance of the opera *La Juive* during the following week. Being loaded with cash, I invited my friend Alex to be my guest and join me at this matinée—if I could get tickets. The idea delighted him and we arranged to play hooky on that day and go to the theater. I then went straight to the box office and reserved the Royal Box for the performance. In retrospect, this was very funny indeed, as the Royal Box was very large and could seat some twenty people with ease. As I recall, the cost of this box was to me the equivalent of about fifty American cents.

We then arranged with the teacher who accompanied us to the club, on the day of this matinée, that we would leave the bus at the Bourse stop and again meet the bus on its homeward journey after the opera would have ended and then return to school with the others; thus the headmaster of the school would not be aware that we had not been at the club. The teacher was not too happy about this arrangement, as he said that he was, in a way, compounding a felony; but after being in receipt of, to him, a very substantial bribe, he relented. The bribe gave him a very large amount of cash.

All then was neatly arranged, and as far as we were concerned would have worked out very well indeed. . . .

We left the bus, promising the teacher that we would be waiting at the stop later that afternoon, when we would go back

10

to school with the others. After leaving the bus, we went straight to the theater and took our seats in the center of the box. As we sat there, we saw that the theater was crowded to the rafters, and all eyes were on us. The audience wondering which princes or notables were seated there.

The performance was a true delight, and we both enjoyed it to the full; we both loved music. As is quite customary in Europe, and this was something that we had not counted on, nearly every aria met with high approbation and was encored, in some cases even twice. The clapping of hands and the cries of "Bis" seemed endless. Suffice it to say that we failed to meet the bus at five o'clock. We were still in the theater at six, and knowing that in any case we would be back late, we took our time returning.

Eventually the opera was over and we left and arrived back at school while supper was in progress and all of the other boys were on their second courses. At this school there was one very large refectory table in the dining room, which occupied its entire length. At the head of the table sat the headmaster, who was, incidentally, also the owner of the school, and as I was the oldest boy, I had been assigned my seat at his side. It was here that we sat at all meals. To be seated here was to me a very dubious honor.

Thus arriving late, as soon as we entered the room, I seated myself in my allotted chair quite nonchalantly and prepared to eat my supper.

For a while nothing was said, but after the passage of maybe ten minutes of absolute silence, the headmaster turned to me. "Mr. Hill, would it be inconvenient for me to inquire where and how you spent this afternoon?"

He said this with utter disbelief in his voice, as he expected me to lie. He was quite positive that both Alex and I had spent the afternoon shacked up with a couple of hookers and in their loving embraces. In those days the streets of Brussels were filled with such ladies of easy virtue, as it probably is today, being the center of the European Common Market.

Without the slightest hesitancy I told him the truth. "Not at all. We spent the afternoon at the matinée performance at the Théâtre de la Monnaie."

The headmaster was, quite naturally, not prepared to accept this statement and, considering himself very smart indeed, inquired, "And what were they offering there this afternoon?"

11

Without a moment's hesitancy, I replied, "*La Juive*."

"And who were the principal singers?"

Naturally I did not recall any of the singers' names, and I replied that I did not know. Now he was absolutely convinced that we had not been anywhere near the Théàtre de la Monnaie. I then continued. "I don't remember, but if you wish I can show you the program, which I bought at the theater, as I would like to take it home to London with me as a nice memento."

When he saw the program that I handed him, he had to accept that I had told him the truth.

Basically, I suppose that after such an escapade we both should have been expelled, but as far as the headmaster was concerned, the idea of losing the income from two pupils did not in the least appeal to him. He said and did nothing further.

Over the past many years, when I have often been in London, I have tried to contact Alex by telephone, but so far I have never been able to reach him. After the terrible bombings of the war years, I do now know whether he is still living, neither do I know whether he is still in Manchester. If he is still living and ever sees this book, I am sure that he will contact me.

After I had spent the better part of a year at the school, I wrote my parents that I thought I had learned as much French as I could there and that it would be silly for me to continue for another year. They were delighted when I wrote and told them that I could now converse with ease in both French and German, and they replied to say that they tended to agree with me about leaving school. It was thus arranged that after the end of the semester I would return home and at once enter the business that father had bought me.

Shortly after my arriving in England, the country became engulfed in what was to become known as the General Strike. Nothing moved. All was at a standstill. There were no telephones, no mails, no subways, and very few buses on the roads. Those few that were running were being driven by soldiers, with other soldiers riding shotgun at their sides. Thus the entire city of London slept.

Just prior to my leaving Brussels for home, I had written my sister asking her whether there might be anything she would like me to bring her from Brussels. She replied that she would dearly love to have a piece of Brie, which she had missed so throughout the years. I replied that this would present no problem whatsoever, but here I was sorely mistaken. I went to a local cheese shop where I knew the owner quite well and told him I wanted to buy a Brie cheese to take back with me to London. The man looked over at his wife, who was standing at his side, and both looked at me with amazement and commenced to laugh. As the lady was quite obese, her entire front appeared to throb as though she were made of Jell-O. The man then said to me, "Monsieur, have you ever seen a whole Brie cheese?" I replied that although I had eaten plenty of it on occasion, I had never seen a whole one in the "raw."

Going into his back room, he soon emerged and laid on his counter a Brie about sixteen inches across its middle, lying on a bed of wet straw with the cheese oozing out at its side.

"Now, do you still want to take this back with you to England?" he asked.

"Yes, I do," I replied. "Please pack it up as well as you can, and I shall carry it along as a separate package with my other luggage."

At the time, as I was returning for the Christmas holiday, it was naturally in the depth of winter, and I had been standing on the cross-channel steamer. It was so cold my fingers were almost frozen stiff. When I arrived at Dover, I had to pass through Customs at the port. Once at the Customs desk, I placed my valise and the large flat package of cheese on the table. The officer asked me to unlock my bag, but I told him my fingers were so frozen that I could not hold the key, and I tried to hand the key to him. The officer refused to take the key from me. "We will wait until you can unlock your bag yourself," he said. At this point the officer presumed that I must be smuggling something or other, particularly when I told him that the large package contained a cheese. This latter he obviously did not believe.

When in due course my fingers thawed sufficiently, I was able to unlock and open my valise. As I did this, he saw some white powder that had upset inside the bag. When he saw this white powder, he seemed quite positive that I was a drug dealer and that the powder was, in fact, cocaine. Asking me to wait a minute, he scooped up a small quantity of the powder and took it to an anteroom for examination. As he left, he had a funny smirk on his face. He obviously felt he was about to uncover a drug ring and would naturally become the hero. After he had tested the powder, which was my tooth powder, he returned and slapped down the lid of my valise with a bang, in a violent temper, leaving my clothes in a veritable shambles. He then did something to the package of cheese that made it quite inedible and dirty-looking when the package was opened. And then in a very imperious voice, he said, "Get the hell out of here with your lousy package," and I left.

After I had been home for several years after my return, I passed my twentieth birthday and decided I would follow in the footsteps of my two brothers and become a Freemason. Normally, I would have been too young, as I was under twenty-one, but as they were both Freemasons, I was permitted to take my seat in a Lodge.

In those days, as it probably still is in England, Masonic lodges had quite small memberships, and the Lodge that I joined was named the Playgoer's Lodge Number 2705. As its name suggests, there were many members who were in the theater. One of its members was an eminent critic; also there were several well-known legal luminaries. At our Lodge we held four meetings a year, and after each we sat down to what can only be termed Lucullan dinners. These Lodge meetings were always held at the old Hotel Cecil in London's Strand; however, this hotel no longer exists and the Shell Oil Corporation now occupies its site.

As a young and very enthusiastic Brother, I became entirely fascinated with the operation of the Lodge and its ritual, and for this reason and after a short while I was installed as a preceptor of Masonic ritual at what is known as a Lodge of Instruction. It was here at this Lodge that brethren desirous of doing so could learn about Masonic ritual and lore. These meetings of the Lodge of Instruction were always held on Thursday evenings at the hotel, and we would all congregate and dine at Simpson's Restaurant, which was next-door, and at these dinners we would discuss matters of moment that might have emerged during the preceding week and which might have been of interest to the membership.

14

It was during one of my very early years as preceptor that a quite famous judge of the High Court was admitted into my "class," since he proposed entering into some high office at our Lodge and required some indoctrination into his potential duties. I was selected to be his tutor. To me, the idea of being an instructor for so eminent a jurist seemed to be quite ridiculous. Nevertheless, I succeeded in my task. He was a very apt pupil and eventually took his high office with dignity.

After I had been a member of the Lodge for several years, and having passed through all the various stages of office, it became my term to be elected its Master. As I now recall, I was, at the time, probably the youngest person ever to have achieved so high an office. It so happened that my elevation to mastership was during the year 1936; this was the year that King Edward VIII abdicated the throne for "the woman I love," and as such was the case, his brother became King George VI.

George had been a very high-ranking Freemason before his coronation, but as king he could no longer remain a member of any secret society, which of course Freemasonry is. He therefore had to resign all association. All the Masters of their Lodges throughout England were then invited to attend an extraordinary meeting to be held at London's famed Freemason's Hall, at which ceremony the king was to announce his resignation. This meeting was perhaps the most historic event that ever occurred in the entire annals of British Freemasonry.

Being at this time Master of my Lodge, and as this Lodge was among the most prestigious and famous of all, I was invited to attend and assist and be seated in the front row, almost in the king's lap. After a formal introduction by the presiding High Masonic official, the king rose and, with tears in his eyes, announced his resignation. It was, in truth, a heartbreaking experience to watch His Majesty speak. As he had a severe stutter, his entire body seemed to vibrate as he spoke. But speak he did, and most eloquently and at some considerable length.

As soon as he had ended his speech, the king rose to leave the chamber, and as he passed along the front row where I was seated, he shook hands with each of us and said good-bye. With several of the members, he stopped and chatted for a few moments and thanked them individually for attending the ceremony.

This ceremony was certainly quite unique in the entire history of Freemasonry and such a one as may never again recur.

It was at one of our Masonic dinners that a somewhat amusing incident occurred when one of our members, Lord Justice Latham, was seated at my right. Lord Latham had for many years been a very heavy Scotch drinker, capable of consuming an entire bottle by himself at dinner. On this particular evening His Lordship had just returned from presiding at the Assizes up in the North Country, and while there I had read a report in the press that he had sentenced a young man to three years in gaol for committing some crime or other while under the influence of drink. During the dinner I discussed this case with Latham and I asked how, in all conscience, being so heavy a drinker himself, he could send the young man to prison for so long a time for doing something under the influence of drink. He replied quite simply, "My dear Hill, you should know that it takes an old drunk like me to realize the evils of drink."

It was at another of our dinners that we entertained as our guests two eminent judges. One was Lord Hewart, at the time lord chief justice of England, and the other a well-known jurist named Sir Alfred Tobin. After the dinner and after I had made my little speech of welcome to these two guests, they each stood to reply to the toast I had proposed.

Lord Hewart, without so much as blinking an eyelid, spoke for some little time extemporaneously, or so it seemed, in pure Latin and as he sat down, Sir Alfred then rose and similarly spoke in Latin. Of a certainty, not one of our members understood a single word that either of these gentlemen had uttered, and we were never able to discover whether or not they had arranged this between themselves as some sort of gag. As far as we were concerned, we all accepted the entire matter as a tour de force and one that none of us would ever forget.

Chapter 3

Dr. Maurice Sandoz and His Automata

It was toward the end of 1925, by which time I had already taken over complete control of my business, that an elegantly dressed gentleman, quite tall and svelte in appearance, passed the shop and glanced into the window display. The weather having turned beautiful, I had, just at that moment, taken the opportunity to stand outside our door and take a little air before leaving to see a client at his hotel.

The gentleman approached me. "I see from your display that you deal in just the type of objects that I would very much love to collect, but which, unfortunately, I cannot do just at this time."

"What precisely are the sort of items to which you refer?" I inquired.

And he replied, "I am a Swiss and I want to collect anything fine and rare of an horological nature, such as watches, little gold boxes with musical mechanisms, little automata, and such." He then continued, "As I am sure you know, such objects were made in Switzerland during the late eighteen- and early nineteen-hundreds."

I replied, telling him that I was very well acquainted with all these types of objects and that we were always on the lookout to acquire any fine pieces of all of these categories for many of our customers who collect them.

He continued to chat with me about other matters and then said that he had much enjoyed speaking with me but had to leave for an important meeting. Then, just as he turned to leave, he said, "One of these days you will be seeing a lot of me, when I shall have money to spend."

It must have been some three or four years after this meeting that this gentleman again came into the shop and, sending his card in to me, told an assistant that he wished to speak with me. The name printed was Dr. Maurice Sandoz.

I came out of my office to meet him, and as soon as I saw him, I recalled our meeting of several years back.

"Do you remember me?"

"Yes," I replied. "I recall meeting you outside our shop door, when we discussed antique horology and similar antiquities."

"Now I have just come into my inheritance and have all the money that I could ever possibly require, which puts me in the position that I can buy anything I wish to gratify my desire to assemble the greatest collection in the world of any of the objects that I mentioned to you. It is my great desire to be able to bequeath such a collection to my native Switzerland after my death and in the meantime have the pleasure of collecting."

He then told me that he was a member of the internationally renowned firm of Sandoz & Company, the great chemical corporation, and that there was absolutely nothing that he need deny himself in his collecting.

Obviously he was homosexual, and seemed to make no bones about the fact, which, for those days, was somewhat astonishing. We then discussed in greater detail the scope of the objects that he sought to acquire through us. "Primarily I am most anxious to buy those small musical boxes in gold that have animated figures of men and women, together with musical attachments."

I told him that I knew precisely the sort of things to which he referred, but that just at that moment we had sold everything we had had of that nature. I promised him that if anything came our way, we would promise to give him first sight. We then continued chatting, and after giving me his address in Geneva, he left.

It was just about a week later that I saw listed in a Christie's auction catalog an object that, by its description, was precisely of the type the doctor sought. It was a small, enameled gold box with a musical mechanism, and I decided to go round and view the object. At the salesroom I examined the box and decided that I would buy it.

Next day I attended the auction and bought it. Actually, it did not matter how much I had to pay for it, as it is always impossible to set a precise figure on any such item. Later that day I had the box in my office and noticed after study that it had a tiny lever at one side. I immediately moved this lever and activated the mechanism. A small panel then raised itself and revealed a garden scene with a lady in a crinoline skirt. When another tiny lever was moved at one side, that raised the skirt, displaying her nudity; at the same time a gentleman seated at her side was seen to be playing with her mound of Venus with one of his hands. All the while the music played. The entire scene was in beautifully enameled gold. Then as the music stopped the skirt went back into its original position and the man's hands went back into his lap and all became a picture of absolute innocence.

As soon as I saw what I had in my hands, I telephoned the doctor at his home in Switzerland and told him of my discovery. He said that he was delighted to hear from me and that just at that moment I had caught him as he was about to leave Geneva. However, as soon as I had finished telling him all about the little box, he said, "Now I can see that I am going to commence my collection with as delicious an object as I could ever hope to find. I am going to delay my present plans, and I shall be in London tomorrow. In any case, unseen, the box is mine."

Next day, as promised, he arrived, saw the box, and immediately paid for it. He then said, "I can see that you understand exactly the sort of things that I have in mind, and I know we are going to do a lot of business together."

From this beginning, the doctor was a very frequent visitor at our shop and purchased practically everything I showed him.

"You know," he once told me, "it is a very funny thing. Here in London I can buy objects that I never seem to see in my native Geneva, and whenever I do see anything there, the dealers ask prices that are quite out of line."

After this and the passage of three or four years, the doctor had been able to amass as superb a collection as anyone had ever assembled.

A few years after that, we moved our shop to a new location on Piccadilly, actually in one of the sides of the Piccadilly Hotel. (The Piccadilly home no longer exists and the Meridian Hotel has taken its place.) Here we occupied a frontage on the street. In the rear of the shop we had a winding staircase that led up to a very large gallery, and this space had two large wide windows that overlooked the street below. Despite the later Battle of Britain during the Second World War, the shop still stands almost undamaged, except, of course, that today it is occupied by some other business.

It was during these early years that my brother Henry and I were crossing over to Paris from London on an almost weekly basis. Either he crossed or I did. As this was the case, we arranged to have a suite at our disposal at the Hotel Castiglione on the Faubourg Saint Honore, where we arranged with the manager, Monsieur Montcomble, that the suite would be ours unless we telephoned him that we would not be crossing on any particular weekend. One prime reason for these weekend crossings was that Paris was at that time a very happy hunting ground for all types of rare objects that we bought and which were basically unobtainable in any quantity anywhere else in Europe, except on very rare occasions.

In those days the trip across to Paris started at nine o'clock in the morning and ended at four o'clock in the afternoon. We would invariably leave London on Friday morning and return on Sunday afternoon with whatever treasures we had been able to find and buy. Whenever we crossed in those days it would have been unusual not to find Nevil T. Chamberlain, at that time Britain's prime minister, seated on the cross-channel boat reading the *London Times* and engrossed in its crossword puzzle. It was he who, after visiting with Hitler, announced on his return, with a wave of his umbrella, "We are now going to have peace in Europe in our time." How wrong he was. Shortly thereafter the Nazi hordes began their rampage and war was in full spate.

It was during one of these trips to Paris that a friendly dealer, later liquidated by the Germans, told my brother that there was on view at the Musée des Arts Decoratifs, at the Musée du Louvre, a superb collection of automata that we should not miss seeing. The dealer knew how very interested we were in such items.

"You know, Mr. Hill, you will see there what is perhaps the greatest collection of musical automata that has ever been brought together. The collection has been placed there on loan by Madame Jonas, widow of the late Monsieur Jonas, the well-known textile merchant, but unfortunately, it is not to be sold. But in any case you should see it."

Taking good note of what the dealer had told him, my brother decided to stay over in Paris and see this collection. When he did see this group in its showcase at the museum, he was more than delighted that he had stayed over. After seeing it, he spoke to another dealer and told him about the exhibit. The dealer said that he already knew of the collection. My brother then said to him, "This Jonas collection is just the sort of thing that we would like to buy."

He said this in the same way as one might say that he would like to buy the renowned Mona Lisa that is one of the gems of the Louvre.

A few weeks then passed and this same dealer telephoned us in London. "Do you remember telling me that the Jonas collection is the sort of thing you would like to buy?" he asked.

My brother replied, "Yes, indeed, I do remember our conversation very well, and if the collection might ever be on the market we are prepared to buy and we would have the cash immediately available."

The French dealer then said that there was a possibility that the collection might well be on the market and that he would call back very shortly.

Later that same afternoon the French dealer again telephoned. "I have arranged for you to meet with Madame Jonas here in Paris, and you can then discuss the possible acquisition of her collection directly with her." He continued, "As a matter of fact, I know that the lady has to dispose of the collection as quickly as possible."

My brother then replied that he would be in Paris in a couple of days, when he would see the lady.

In due course he met with Madame Jonas and asked her what she was asking for the group, and she set a price on it. My brother then countered with a somewhat lower figure, but the lady was adamant. She did, however, agree to include the vitrine table in the deal, and this table was by itself a little dream of eighteenth-century French make.

My brother then agreed to her figure, and a deal was made. Next day we paid over the money, and the collection, as it had been shown at the museum in its vitrine table, was ours. Most of the objects included in the collection were precisely what Dr. Sandoz wanted to acquire.

Now many of these treasures were extremely fragile, and any extra movement could easily damage some of the very delicate mechanisms. However, we had to get the collection over to London and this as soon as possible. We decided that the best way would be for us to pack each piece in a separate box and carry them to London in two valises and then have the vitrine showcase shipped over by carrier. This was not too easy to accomplish, as we know that the items would have to be unwrapped and examined at the Customs at Dover.

We then decided to contact the British consul general resident in Paris and discuss our problem with him. We told him that we knew that Queen Mary would want to see these objects as soon as they were at our galleries, and this made him most anxious to assist us. The consul then told us that he himself would call at our hotel, see us pack each item into our two valises, and then he would seal each with a government seal. With these two bags so sealed, he said that we would have no difficulty in passing through the Customs at Dover. He then arranged that as soon as we arrived in London we were to contact the London Customs department and have them send their agent to our galleries to examine the seals, after which, if they were unbroken, he would allow us to work with the contents. The consul, however, did warn us that in the event the agent found that the seals had been broken, we would be subjected to heavy penalties. Thus as soon as we had the boxes in our galleries, we did contact the Customs agent, who, finding the seals intact, broke them, and we were then free to do what we wanted with our collection.

The following day the beautiful vitrine table arrived, and we were able to reassemble the collection in exactly the same way as it had been show at the museum in Paris. The collection comprised some fifty pieces, and each was superb and more beautiful than the next. We then telephoned Dr. Sandoz in Geneva and told him of our acquisition, and he said that he would make a special crossing on the following day. He also said that he hoped we would not show the pieces to anybody else until he had had first sight. We promised we would keep the collection aside and intact until he arrived.

Next day he saw the collection. "I must say that I had never hoped to see such a collection, let alone be able to buy."

After a very short time the doctor selected and bought about half of the collection. "Unfortunately, just at this moment I cannot possibly buy all, as I have made a very large commitment in another area, but for the time being I must be satisfied."

In the group that he acquired there was one particular item that was one of the greatest of its type ever to come to light. It was a largish gold snuff box, about four inches by three, and for very obvious reasons we had named it the Magician's Box. Under its lid there was an enameled scene of a tiny magician wearing a conical hat and a long caftan type of robe. His whole robe was covered with tiny magical signs of the Zodiac. In the magician's right hand was a tiny wand, and when the mechanism was set in motion the music would play a somber dirge and at the same time he would raise his wand and tap with it on a tiny panel. As soon as he did this, the panel would slide aside and open to disclose a tiny window on which was inscribed, in French, a quotation: "What does a maiden desire more than anything else in the world?" After the passage of several seconds, the magician would again raise his wand, and immediately the panel would close back. He would then again tap the panel, which would open to reply: "A husband." Besides this question and answer, there were three other similar questions and answers. To our minds today such questions and answers might be considered sentimental mush, but presumably in those days they were not so considered.

Beyond this quite remarkable object there were at least some half-dozen pieces, all of enameled gold and each with an extremely rare horological mechanism. Today such objects are being sought worldwide by collectors, but they rarely indeed ever come onto the market. Similarly, in the group there were several tiny, enameled gold makeup boxes, known as *Boîtes a mouche*. These little gems contained compartments designed to hold all of a lady's makeup: kohl for the eyes, which would be today's equivalent of mascara, and tiny black silk patches that ladies used either for flirtation purposes or to hide little pimples or other facial blemishes. Also each contained a tiny gold-handled brush with sable hairs for applying rouge. Still another very fascinating object was a gold walking cane handle that held in its top a watch similarly with a tiny musical attachment, which could be operated and set in motion by moving a lever at one side. This handle was of gold of several colors of the type known as *quatre couleur* work.

Chapter 4

I Meet Young King Farouk

It was not long after we had concluded the purchase of the rather fabulous Jonas collection of antique gold automata in Paris that the young King Farouk of Egypt (he was just sixteen years old at the time) happened to be strolling through the Faubourg Saint Honoré in Paris while looking at the displays of many of the antique dealers along the way. It was at this time that he had decided he wished to collect antiquities with rare automata mechanism and other horological specimens. As he window-shopped, something in one of the dealers' windows caught his eye. Going into this shop, he asked the proprietor to show him anything that he had to offer in the way of rare watches and such things. In the course of conversation with this dealer, he told him he wanted to make an important collection of such material. The jeweler apologized and explained that just at that moment there was nothing he could offer, but he said that if the gentleman would leave his name he would be pleased to let him know when anything important came in. The young Farouk gave the jeweler his name, and when the jeweler dealer heard that he was King Farouk of Egypt, he became more and more interested in doing all that he could for the young gentleman.

In his attempt to please the king, he said to him, "Your Majesty, it so happens that I know of a very famous collection of just the type of things that you are asking for which was sold to a London dealer quite recently."

As soon as the king heard this, he asked the dealer for the name of the firm, since he would be in London within a few days and would like to go and see whether there might be anything that he would buy from them. The dealer could not very well avoid giving the king our name, although quite naturally he was rather reluctant to do so. The king then left, and no sooner was he out of the door, the dealer telephoned us in London to tell us that the young King Farouk of Egypt would be coming in to see us very shortly, as he was very interested in the Jonas collection. He suggested that we send Farouk a letter inviting him to come in to see us. The king had told him that he would be staying at the Ritz Hotel. No sooner was our French colleague off the telephone than we wrote a letter inviting the king in to see what was left of the Jonas collection. Needless to say, we sent the letter round to the hotel by messenger so that the king would have it in his hands as soon as he arrived.

Next day, we were very busy in the shop, with people seated at each of our four tables, when a young man entered. I noticed him out of the corner of my eye, but as he was bare-headed and holding a letter in his hand I presumed that he was a messenger. At the time he wore a camel-colored turtleneck sweater and a pair of gray flannel slacks, with an open-neck sports shirt, not at all the attire that one might associate with royalty.

My assistant, similarly thinking that he was a messenger, was just on the point of sending him downstairs when, looking up again, I quickly realized that the young man was carrying the letter that we had written to the king. Thus I quickly asked my assistant to take over with my customer and went over to the young king and welcomed him to our establishment.

I at once escorted him upstairs so that I could show him some of our things, but he said that primarily he was interested in seeing the Jonas collection, which he had been told about in Paris.

I then showed him the vitrine in which all that was left unsold was still lying in situ, and the moment that he saw what was there he commenced to make a selection of what he wished to buy.

The king then explained that he was very interested in anything that had some mechanical mechanism, such as the little automata, things that had automated figurines, objects that had musical movements, and things of great and rare horological interest. As some of the Jonas objects were of these types, they all seemed to fascinate him. He could not have been upstairs more than half an hour when he purchased some twenty-odd pieces.

"I understand that when you made your original purchase in Paris the Jonas collection had some fifty pieces."

I then explained to him that he was quite correct but that quite a number of pieces had already been sold to another collector.

He then asked, "What is the name of the other collector?"

I answered him, saying that the buyer was a Dr. Sandoz, who owned, as far as I knew, the greatest collection of such automata, possibly the greatest in the world.

The king then said, "Mr. Hill, I would like you to telephone the doctor and ask him whether he would resell any of his pieces, in fact, all that he has acquired from the Jonas collection."

I told the king that I would contact the doctor as soon as possible, but that I was quite positive he would not part with a single object.

Later that afternoon I telephoned the doctor, who I knew would still be at his hotel in London, and as expected I received a very blunt "No" to my question about his reselling any of his purchases.

I then spoke with the king and told him what the doctor had replied and he said that he understood very well the doctor's reluctance to even consider reselling.

Next day the king was in again to see us and explained that he was finding great difficulty in buying any of the sort of things that he had purchased from us. He also said that the pieces that he had bought from the Jonas collection were finer than anything else he had acquired so far.

I then told the king that when I had spoken with the doctor he had replied that far from reselling any of his pieces, he was sorry that he had missed some of the pieces that I had told him the king had bought.

Next day, having delivered the purchases to the king at the Ritz Hotel, we received our check in full payment. We then discussed the question of collecting in general with the king, and he told us that his father, King Fu'ād I, had been a great collector of coins, medals, and postage stamps, and he then said that he wished to continue his father's collections but that he himself wished to collect in many other areas.

Since he loved color, he had been buying some of the very lovely and colorful French glass paperweights that had been produced during the middle of the nineteenth century at the famous glass factories of Clichy, Baccarat, and Saint Louis. I told the king that we had purchased many fine examples from time to time, but only when they were extra special specimens. At his request

I promised to advise him of any further such paperweights that came through our hands.

"I see," the king then said, "that you understand exactly what I have in mind, and I wish you to make me offers of anything that you think might fit into one or the other of my collections."

The following day he was again in to see us and he then told us that he had been in touch with his embassies both in London and Paris and that he had instructed them to accept from us any shipments that were to be taken to him in Egypt and always use the "diplomatic pouch" that he said was taken to Cairo every day, and also upon arrival in Cairo they were to be taken to him wherever he might at the moment be traveling. Then just as he was about to leave, he said that he was returning to Cairo the next day and continued, "Before I forget, I must tell you that I also collect fine Lalique and Gallé glass objects."

Then saying good-bye he left.

From that day and until his abdication some twenty years later we were in almost daily contact with him, always directly with the king's private secretary, a gentleman named Husny Bey.

Some few years later when we visited with the king at the Abdine Palace in Cairo he invited us to a reception that he was giving at the palace. At this reception, held in one of the enormous reception rooms at the palace, they had set up a very long bar with every conceivable type of liquor or wine for the guests, although, he explained, as a Moslem he himself never touched a drop of anything other than lemonade. He explained that Moslems were not permitted to partake of any spirituous drinks. He also said that he had had the interior of the palace remodeled as a copy of Buckingham Palace in London. "I have been entertained at Buckingham Palace so many times by the king and queen that as far as possible I wanted to emulate them."

In fact, he said that he wanted to emulate even their collection propensities as far as possible, and also the manner in which they conduct the operation of their palaces. He then added, with a laugh, "People frequently send me barrels of rum from their distilleries, and these I love to receive because, although I do not drink any of the stuff, I love to run my hands through the brew and smell the aroma."

27

In the palace there was one basic difference from Buckingham Palace, as in the large reception room there were balconies set up high in the walls and these were curtained off in front, so that the queen and her ladies could sit and watch the proceedings from behind these curtains, since, being Moslems, they were in the strictest of purdah.

It was just a few days after this reception that we received a very imposing-looking certificate appointing us "Suppliers to the Throne of Egypt"; this certificate was number 3. The moment that the certificate was in our hands we had it framed in gold and hung in my private office.

This association with the king was, indeed, one of the most interesting of my entire business life, as it created the opportunity to travel, and this was for me quite fantastic. From the very first day that we commended to do business with the king and until his last day on the throne, all was conducted with extraordinary precision. Both the king and his secretary, Husny Bey, had explained there was never to be the slightest suggestion of any baksheesh, a situation that was almost unheard of elsewhere in the Near East.

Chapter 5

Alice Wickett

In accord with London's regulations, we were requested to close our establishment on one afternoon of each week, and, as did most firms in the West End, we elected to close at midday on Saturday; many of the suburban shops closed on either Wednesday or Thursday afternoon.

And so it happened that one Saturday in early spring when hordes of American tourists were beginning to flock into London, and just as our man Andrews was preparing to close our door for the weekend, a quite elderly-looking lady came up to him and inquired whether we were still at that time open for business.

As Andrews happened to be at the door just at that moment, he told the lady that we were on the point of closing for the day, but he was in no great hurry if there was anything he could do for her.

In a very querulous voice she said, "I have only just this morning arrived from Chicago, and while unpacking my bags at the Carlton Hotel, I bent to unlock one of them and in so doing I dropped my glasses on the floor and without them I cannot read. Unless I can get them fixed I shall be obliged to stay in my room until Monday and just stare at the walls."

Andrews, who was adept at all sorts of odd jobs, told her that he would try to see what he could do for her, at least if only temporarily. It took him about ten minutes to make a pretty fair repair for her, and when he handed her the eyeglasses she was most profuse in her thanks. When he refused to accept any money from her for the job she was overwhelmed.

The lady took her glasses and told him that she would be in again on Monday to tell him how she had managed over the weekend. On this note she left.

As she had promised that she would do, she was in again early on Monday morning. As I had just at that moment arrived,

I met her, and she told me how nice our man had been to her on the Saturday.

We then chatted for a short while, and she told me that she visited in London every spring and whenever she arrived she remained for about three months. She said that she had decided to make a collection of antiques. I inquired as to whether she had decided on any particular category, and she replied, "No, I just want to buy anything that takes my fancy."

I then told her that I would show her some of our things and I asked my assistant to bring out some antique silver pieces and also some antique jewels.

As soon as he had placed all manner of things on one of our long counters, she commenced buying. After about half an hour she had purchased some thirty or forty pieces in all areas. She then said, "I have to leave you now to return to my hotel for lunch, but I shall be in again later."

True to her word, she was in again later that same afternoon and commenced to buy all over again, buying all sorts of things, from saltcellars to necklaces. We then sat and chatted some more. It seems that she was quite lonely and had nobody to talk to except me. She explained that she lived on Lake Shore Drive in Chicago, where she had a very large apartment, and she wished to fill her rooms with "beauty."

She then, becoming confidential, told me, "My husband works for John D. Rockefeller as his troubleshooter."

I asked her what she meant by "troubleshooter," and she replied, "Whenever the men go on strike in the mines, my husband stands up on any old box that might be handy and tries to talk the men into going back to work." And as an afterthought, she added, "He is usually successful." Next day Alice—her name was Alice Wickett—was back again in the shop, and I sold her several beautiful antique gold snuff boxes of the Louis XV and Louis XVI periods and types. I then asked her whether she would like to have her acquisitions sent round to her at the hotel or whether she wanted us to ship them to Chicago.

"No, I want you to hold everything aside for me until I decide just how I want to handle the matter." She then opened her handbag and, taking a thick bundle of bills out into her hand, handed me a large portion to cover most of her purchases. She left a small balance owing.

The following day she was in again and, from that day on she was in every day, either in the morning or afternoon, and also, on several occasions, both times. At every visit she continued her buying. In fact, she always asked to see what we had acquired on that day, and as a rule she at once purchased whatever it might be.

On one day she was particularly talkative and asked me to change a pound note for her into sixpences. I asked her what she wanted so many sixpences for, and she replied, "I always follow Mr. Rockefeller's advice and never give a waiter more than a sixpenny tip, as he did with dimes." She also told me that she loved to come in and see me, as she knew nobody else in London. She also said, "If I don't talk with you, then I have to talk to the walls."

On several occasions I invited her out to dine with us, but she always refused to come. I could never understand her reluctance to join us.

One afternoon, while sitting in my private office, she suddenly opened up. "I feel that I must tell you something of my life and the life that I am living at this time. My husband is having an affair with his secretary, and he has made it quite clear to me that there must never be the slightest suggestion of this that could possibly come to the ears of Mr. Rockefeller. So we have made an arrangement that I can travel as much as I like and can spend as much money as I want to so long as I don't mention anything of his affair to anybody. Now I feel that I know you sufficiently well to tell you this and that my confidence will be respected."

Naturally I assured her that whatever she told me would be held in the strictest confidence and that as far as I was concerned nobody would ever hear a word from me.

She then continued, "You must have noticed that whenever I pay you for my buyings there is always a balance left over, and there is a reason for this. Whenever I need money, our arrangement is that all that I need to do is to write Chicago and my husband will cable me funds immediately, and sometimes I am temporarily a little short of cash."

I then told her that I understood perfectly. She then continued talking.

"Actually, as you can see, I am spending his money like a drunken sailor, not only because I love all types of antiques, but also because I want to punish him for his transgression." This latter she spoke with a half smile on her face.

After she had been in London for about three months, buying and buying, she came in one morning and told me that she was going home to Chicago the next day, but she said, "I want you to continue holding all of my things until I return in the spring of next year, when I shall recommence my buying, and I want you to hold aside for me, until I return, anything that you feel I would like to have."

I promised that I would do this for her, and she was off. After she had left we totaled up her purchases and found that it amounted to quite a staggering sum.

Next spring, on almost the same day as the previous spring, she was back again and as she arrived she said, "I am back again like the swallows over Capistrano." She then at once went through a number of things that had been put aside for her to see, and she bought all of them. Never once did she ask to see the things that she had purchased the previous year.

She then said, "Before leaving Chicago my husband commissioned me to find for his corporation a suitable apartment here. He said that he wished to have me furnish it as luxuriously as I possibly could so that whenever any of their personnel came to London they would be able to meet at the apartment and also hold their board meetings there. He told me that they preferred this to having to stay at any hotels." She asked us to assist her in finding a suitable place. We discussed the matter and we sent her to a realtor and very soon she had rented a very large apartment that she felt would be ideal for the corporation.

The apartment was in a house quite close to the famed home of the Duke of Wellington, today a museum devoted to the duke's memorabilia. The idea of this location pleased her enormously.

Alice then began discussing the furnishings and she commenced to buy all sorts of exotic items, after which, on the advice of an architect that she had employed, she had all of the rooms rebuilt to accommodate some of the pieces. Her idea was to have the apartment look like an old Italian palazzo.

While walking through one of London's side streets my brother Henry went in to visit with an old antique dealer friend of ours, and while there he saw standing an enormous overmantel that had surely been taken from an old Venetian palazzo. It was of heavily carved wood, painted all over with every sort of colorful detail. As soon as he saw this, he knew that it was precisely the sort of thing that Alice had in mind, so he had the piece put on a truck and delivered to the apartment.

As soon as it was standing against a wall in the apartment he telephoned Alice and told her what he had done, and she said that she would come right over. As soon as she saw the piece she fell madly in love with it and called her architect to come over to discuss it.

The architect was over within the hour, and as soon as he saw the piece they arranged to pull down one of the walls that had just been erected and rebuild another to accommodate the overmantel.

Actually, the piece was a gigantic white elephant, and I am sure that the dealer who sold it was delighted to get it out of his place of business.

After the passage of a couple of weeks Alice came in to see us and said, "The apartment is now quite ready for occupancy, and I am going to cable my husband that his people can begin using it." He then cabled her that he was coming over on the next boat, and Alice also told me that she wanted me to meet him. But she said, "Remember our arrangement," and I replied that I would be most happy to meet him, but that my lips would be sealed.

However, this visit was not to materialize. The next day there was the financial crash on Wall Street known as Black Friday, and instead of coming over on the next boat Alice showed me a cable from Chicago reading: "Stop making any further purchases, and return to Chicago on the next available boat."

As she showed me this cable her eyes were full of tears. She then requested that we continue to hold all of the things that she had purchased over the previous couple of years, until she could see clearly what was going to happen. She then said, "One thing that I can tell you is that you will not be the losers," although there was at that moment a fairly substantial sum owing to us.

At the time that she said this we knew that if her husband were wiped out financially there would be no money for us. However, we were not unduly worried, as there was a great value in the things that she had already paid for and which we still held. More than anything, during the time that we had known Alice we had begun to have a deep affection for her, and we were not worried for ourselves; rather we were worried about her situation when she arrived home in the States. A few weeks after her return we received a cable from a firm of attorneys in Chicago telling us that Alice had conferred with them and that if we would accept in lieu of full payment for the balance of our account that she still owed us, they would immediately send us a check for half of the sum and we could keep everything that she had purchased and which we were still holding. This proposition went far beyond anything that we could possibly have envisioned and as far as we were concerned was an excellent deal, particularly in light of the fact that the depression that had struck the States and its economy did not effect us too badly in England.

We at once cabled the attorneys, accepting their proposition, and in due course received their promised check.

After this, despite the fact that we tried on several occasions to contact Alice to find out how she was faring, we never received any response to our letters. As far as I know the apartment was never used even for one single night, although it was so lavishly furnished. What happened to it I never knew, and it may well have been destroyed in the terrible bombings during the last war.

Chapter 6

Maharaja Tagore and the Silver Plates

Among the multitudinous group of things that Alice Wickett had purchased from us was a superb service of twenty-four antique silver meat plates and a dozen matching silver soup plates; each piece was hallmarked and engraved with the armorials of a member of the Peerage. As these plates were included in the collection, we naturally reacquired them in our all-over settlement with her attorneys.

Soon after the service was again in our hands we advertised it for sale in the famous *Connoisseur Magazine*. Several weeks after the advertisement appeared, we received a long letter from the Maharaja Tagore, brother of the famed poet Sir Rabindranath Tagore, from India asking us for more complete information about this service and also inquiring the price.

In his letter, the maharaja wrote calling upon the Heavens to shower our establishment with every possible blessing and giving us notice that these blessings were to extend to any of our children either born or as yet unborn.

We replied to this letter thanking him for all his blessings and at the same time giving him all the information available to us and also quoting him our asking price.

After the lapse of several weeks we again received a reply from the maharaja similarly repeating his blessings, but this time even more fulsomely than before, if indeed that were at all possible. However, he ended his letter by saying that the figure that we had placed on the service was much too high.

Now by the time this letter was received, my brother and I had decided to withdraw the service from sale, as we then proposed including it in a shipment of antiquities that we were preparing to go to New York, where we had established our New York offices. We agreed between ourselves that as soon as we were settled in our New York apartments we would split the service into two equal parts, so that each of us could use the plates in his home.

We eventually did this, and to this day we have these silver plates in constant use, even as frequent guests in our dishwashers, where they cannot be in any way damaged, as they might well be were they of porcelain.

Previous to our shipping this service to New York we had written a further letter to the maharaja advising him that the service was no longer on the market. Despite this letter that we had written him, we received a further letter addressed to us at our London office, which was remailed to us in New York. In this letter the maharaja completely ignored the previous letter that we had written and stated that he had decided to purchase the service at our original price without any reduction. In this letter he refrained from his showering us with his "blessings" and simply addressed us as "Dear Sirs."

We then again replied to him and advised him that the service was no longer available for sale, particularly as by this time the value of such silverware had risen enormously.

After this we heard no more from the maharaja.

Chapter 7

Douglas Fairbanks, Sr., and Mary Pickford and
Later Lady Ashley

In those far off days of the twenties, and some time before the great financial crash of '29, when film stars were still film stars and not sellers on television commercials of such items as detergents, vaginal sprays, instant coffee, and other things of personal or home use, we had many of the famous and beautiful people coming through our doors; today we would probably be calling them jet setters. Thus it was on one particularly lovely spring day, on one of those rare occasions when England's traditional April showers were not in evidence, that our door opened to admit two people whom we recognized immediately. They were none other than the "World's Sweethearts": Douglas Fairbanks, Sr., and his charming wife, Mary Pickford.

As they entered, happening to be at that moment near the door, I greeted them, and they asked me whether they could sit and relax for a few moments.

She said, "We are both of us utterly exhausted."

I told them that they were welcome to sit and relax for as long as they wished, and Mary Pickford kicked off her shoes. She then said that although they were always flattered by being greeted so profusely on all sides, the hounding that they were receiving was becoming very onerous and tiring. She then remarked that while she sat she would love to discuss antiques with me, and I told her that this would give me much pleasure.

However, before I could even open my mouth about antiques in general she began telling me about some of the movies that they had in process and about others they had on the planning boards, which they would be starting to produce as soon as they returned to California.

Naturally all of this was quite fascinating to me, as in those days anything pertaining to the movie industry was something quite special. They then remained chatting with me for about an hour, and then after thanking me for our courtesy they left.

This then was the first and last time that I saw either of them. Some several years then passed, and one day I received a telephone call from a Lady Ashley who said that she wished to discuss some matter of business with me and asked me to visit with her at her hotel. We then made a mutually convenient appointment, and I went to see her at her suite at the Ritz Hotel.

When I arrived she told me that she had called me at the request of Douglas Fairbanks, Sr., whom she was about to marry in London. Douglas had written to her from the States that he wanted her to discuss any business with me because I had been so nice to him and Mary Pickford when they had been in London.

She then went on to say they would require a large service of antique Georgian silver flatware—knives, forks, spoons, and all the rest. I replied that finding such a service for them would present no problems whatsoever and that I would call her as soon as I had such a suitable service.

We then had a drink together and spoke of all manner of things. She told me that I should go to the States as soon as possible, remarking that I would be "bowled over" by all that I would see there. I told her that I had been planning a visit to the States and that I would go over "one of these days."

They had taken a townhouse in London's West End, and she was in the process of furnishing it.

It took me about two days to lay my hands on a service that I knew would be ideal for her, and I promptly telephoned her to this effect. She then asked that I have the service delivered to her at the townhouse and that as soon as it was there I should call her again and arrange to meet her there.

Our truckers then delivered the service to the house, and we arranged to meet there.

As soon as I arrived I rang the doorbell and the door was opened by a butler beautifully dressed in correct costume; he was the epitome of the proverbial Jeeves of P. G. Wodehouse fame.

As I entered I could see the entire house appeared to be devoid of any furnishings. There was nothing whatsoever in the entrance hall; there was no carpeting on the floor.

The butler then asked me to go into the living room. Here again there was no carpeting on the floor; there were no chairs, tables, or other normal furnishings. Seated on the floor in the center of the room was Lady Ashley, surrounded by the silver service that had been neatly laid out and which spread over quite a large surface of floor.

She invited me to sit down on the floor with her, as though this were the most normal thing to do. She loved the service and said they were going to buy it.

She did say that when next I visited with her there would be at least a chair to sit on, this latter with a laugh.

I thanked her and told her how wise she was to select the service, as it was indeed quite an exceptionally complete one.

She told me that she had already shown the service to Douglas, who had arrived the previous day from the States, and he had heartily approved it.

Douglas wished to have each piece engraved with his family crest. For the life of me I could not fathom what sort of family crest he could possibly have, but I said nothing.

Actually, she then said, "What he means is that he wants his initials, D.F., engraved on each piece."

The question then arose as to how these initials were to be engraved and I told her the correct traditional way, but she said no. Douglas said that he wanted to have them the other way round. This was to my mind upside down, but as the old adage goes, "the customer is always right." We had these initials engraved just as he wished. To my traditional thinking they were upside down, but then that was entirely his business.

Lady Ashley then asked me for my advice regarding the sort of furniture they should buy for the house, and I suggested that it be done in eighteenth-century Chippendale style, and she agreed that what I had advised made good sense to her.

The following week she was again on the telephone asking me to come over to meet with her at the house. She wished to discuss with me some further silver purchases, and we made an appointment to meet there the following day.

When I arrived I could see that she had already commenced furnishing the rooms and the house was beginning to shape up as a home. At least as far as I could see the downstairs was more or less in shape. What she was doing about the bedrooms upstairs I do not know, as I was never invited up there.

Laughingly she said, "Now you can take your ease and sit on a comfortable chair while we discuss our further business. Now that we have made a start there is no real hurry about any of the further things that Douglas wishes to get for the house."

That the Fairbanks had come to see us was in those days nothing unusual, as being where we were, we were virtually a mecca for many people in the theatrical world, both of England and the States.

Chapter 8

Elsie Janis and Her Silver Purchases

Being situated as we were in the heart of London's West End, we naturally had many notables from the theater through our doors. One morning the famous international comedienne of her day came in, the well-known Elsie Janis. Elsie always traveled with her mother. In fact, all the time that I eventually got to know her I never once saw her without this lady at her side. As a couple they were full of fun and games, and it was always a pleasure to be with them.

Both of these ladies loved exotic jewels, the rarer the better as far as they were both concerned, and I recall that the first thing that they bought from me was an enormous butterfly pin much larger than any such pin that I had ever previously encountered, certainly much larger than most butterflies; it measured about six inches across from wing tip to wing tip and was covered all over with colorful precious and semiprecious gems. It was something quite out of the ordinary, and I have never seen its like anywhere again.

If this jewel still exists somewhere today it must be worth an enormous amount of money.

Both of the ladies spent a goodly part of each year in England, Elsie performing at the various music halls across the country. She told me that besides being in constant demand for her services there, she loved living in London. She felt that England was more her home than back in the States.

After they had spent several months in London on this trip, Elsie came in to see me to say that they were returning to New York in a couple of weeks, as her agent had made a commitment for her to perform over there.

She then made of me what I considered to be a most extraordinary request. "I want you to buy for me as many enormous pieces of Victorian English silverware as you can possibly lay your hands on. Nothing will be too big for my purpose. I want wine coolers, candelabra, large tea trays, platters, tankards, in fact, anything, so long as it is enormous."

I told her that I would go into the market and pick up whatever might be available.

About a week later I telephoned her and told her that I had accumulated a large quantity of very large pieces for her to look at. I described the collection—wine coolers, very large tea trays, tea and coffee services, several teakettles, and two large well and tree dishes and dish covers, the sort of dishes that had compartments underneath to hold hot water and keep foods hot. Beyond these I had several very large complete services of table flatware.

She replied, "What you are telling me is music to my ears, and I don't really care a jot what you have found, so long as each piece is very large." She then said that really she did not even need to come round and see what I had for her, but that she just wanted me to send her the bill. She would be coming in the next day and tell me what she wanted done with the purchases.

The following day she came in and asked me to take her into my private office so that we could speak without being overheard.

We then went in and as soon as we were seated she explained. "As you know, all the silver that you have bought for me is today dutable into America as none of it is over one hundred years old or at least before 1830."

I confirmed that this was the case.

"Now," she continued, "I can tell you that I am getting a bit tired of the stage and want to go into the antique business in America, and I want all the things that you have sold me to blaze a window in the shop that I have already rented."

She then continued, "I don't want to pay any duty on the silver when it arrives in America, so I want you to have each piece painted with heavy whitewash, so that I can tell the boys at the Customs they are stage props, as I know most of the boys there, they will not question me." It was then arranged that we do this whitewashing for her and have everything delivered to the boat so that they could cross with her and on arrival be cleared without any problem with the Customs boys.

We did this for her, and a couple of weeks later she wrote that everything had gone as she had planned and that she hadn't the slightest trouble at the Customs. She also wrote that the opening of her shop was a great success and that she had done very well with all of the pieces that we had found for her.

She then asked that we pick up many more similar pieces that she would buy on some subsequent date.

We did this, but we never again saw either Elsie or her mother, nor did we ever hear from either of them again. From what I later discovered, Elsie's mother had passed away shortly after the opening of their shop. But what happened to Elsie herself I never did find out.

Chapter 9

Captain Lovelace and the Silver Purchases

It was one of those depressing very foggy days in November, when London was enveloped in one of its well-known and well-detested pea-souper fogs. Everything was at a virtual standstill, as it was almost impossible to conduct any business.

We were on the point of deciding whether or not to close for the day and allow our employees to make their way to their respective homes when just at this juncture—it was eleven o'clock—our door opened and a gentleman entered. By his dress he seemed to be an army man, wearing as he did a horsy hacking jacket with leather patches at the elbows and also on the shoulders. Under this jacket he sported a Tattersall waistcoat, and on his head he wore a brown derby hat. All of his costume certainly emanated from one of the workshops of a fine Savile Row tailor.

The gentleman was unknown to us and, as far as we could make out, had never previously been in our shop.

He introduced himself as Captain Lovelace. When we heard this name and title we knew that our assumption that he was an army man had been correct.

He then said in very cultured tones, "I am a collector of antique English silver of the Georgian periods, and I would like to see what you can show me; please show me as much as you can."

I asked him whether there was any particular object that he had in mind, but he replied, "No, I have not, but please show me anything."

Not knowing what to show, I called our manager, Christie, over and told him to place pieces of any type on our long counter. Christie at once set to work and placed piece after piece of all sorts and periods on the counter until there was no room for anything more.

While Christie was doing this the gentleman just stood and stared and did not open his mouth to utter a single word.

When Christie stopped, there must have been about a hundred items on the counter—tankards, teapots, salvers, entré dishes, candlesticks, etc.

The captain then took a short cane that he carried under his left arm and placed it through the approximate center of the items. "Please let me know how much all these things to the right of my cane amount to."

Christie then proceeded to make a total, and when he had finished he told the captain that the sum was somewhere in the area of ten thousand pounds.

"If you will add four pounds to your total I shall draw you a check for the lot and you can ship the goods out to me in due course," he replied. Although I had a funny feeling that his check might bounce, the whole matter was so preposterous that I nevertheless did as he requested and handed him the four pounds in bills.

The captain then left and we saw through the fog that he at once crossed the road and went into the pub.

To our, I must say, utter amazement, the check was honored, and we had all the pieces packaged for shipment to an address that the captain had given us somewhere in the heart of Exmoor in the west of England.

Next day the package was shipped out to the captain, and as we received no word from him, we presumed that he had received the goods in good order.

Several months then passed when the captain again reappeared at about the same time as he had done previously and again asked that we show him "silver." Christie, recalling the captain's previous visit, again proceeded to cover the countertop with all manner of pieces. Most of the things were similar to what the captain had purchased on his original visit.

While Christie was doing this, the captain, as he had done before, just stared and did not utter a word.

As soon as the countertop was covered and there was no room for another piece, even a small one, Christie stopped. Then as he had done previously, the captain again placed his short cane right through the middle and said, as he had done before, "Will you kindly let me know how much I owe you for all these things to the right of my cane, and if you will add five pounds, which I

45

would like you to give me in cash, I shall draw you my check for the lot."

Christie then at once totaled up the cost, and this time it was in the area of some fifteen thousand pounds. He then added five pounds to the total, which he handed the captain. The captain then wrote out his check and asked that we ship the things to the same address in Exmoor, and taking the five pounds in cash he left.

Just before he left, Christie said to him, "Is there perhaps any particular item that you might wish me to write you about?"

And the captain replied, "Yes, if ever you find a very fine tankard of the Charles period, please contact me." And saying this he left, going straight across the road into the pub. Again his check was honored.

We then noticed that at three o'clock in the afternoon and after the well-known and monotonous call of "Time, gentlemen, please" was surely made, we saw the captain leave the pub.

About three weeks after his visit we purchased what was as fine a Charles silver tankard as had ever come out of a silversmith's shop, and at once we had it photographed and we mailed proofs to the captain together with the price. After the passage of about a couple of weeks, we had no response to this letter, so we again wrote him, but still there was no word from him.

As the tankard was a very readily saleable item for us, I told Christie to drop the matter and place the tankard on general sale, which he did.

It so happened that about this time my brother Henry and I had to visit with a customer in Exeter and we decided that en route we would stop off at the captain's house and visit with him and perhaps find out why he had not replied to our two letters. On arrival by automobile at the edge of the moors, an area so well recorded in the novels of Thomas Hardy as one of the most desolate districts in all of England, we asked several yokels who were standing nearby whether they could perhaps direct us to Captain Lovelace's house.

Two of these men gave us precise directions, but while speaking to us they both had somewhat quizzical expressions on their faces. So after taking the directions that they had given us, we proceeded to drive across the very rocky terrain, strewn with pieces of rock, until we arrived at a solitary house standing in the middle of nowhere that, from the man's directives, had to be the captain's house.

Leaving our car, we went over to the house, where we saw pinned up on the door a very dirty card printed with the captain's name on it.

I rang a doorbell, and although I could hear reverberations of the bell ringing inside, it seemed that there was nobody there. I again rang, and still getting no response, we were just about to leave when the door opened. There stood in front of us what was certainly the most slovenly and most slatternly-looking female we had ever set eyes on. The woman must have been somewhere in her thirties. Her hair was straggling all over her seemingly unwashed face.

After looking us both up and down, she said, "What do you want?"

I replied, "We have come to visit with the captain."

Without a word she pointed across the very dark room at somebody seated in front of a roaring fire, despite the fact that it was now midsummer and quite warm outside. The woman then looked up. "There 'e is," and without a further word she left and disappeared into the depths of the darkened room.

We then went farther into the room and saw that the seated figure in front of the fireplace was, indeed, the captain! In front of his feet lay a pile of unopened mail, including both of the letters we had written him. All about the room and all over the floor we saw bottles of Scotch whiskey, some full and others empty, together with riding boots and a pile of brown bowler hats. Then looking at the top of a table in the rear we saw the two wood boxes of silver that had been shipped out to him, as yet unopened.

I went over to speak to the captain, but he was so drunk that any conversation was out of the question.

Realizing that we were getting nowhere very fast with the captain and since the heat and stench in the room were almost unbearable, we decided to leave. There was no visible sign of any kitchen or other toilet arrangements anywhere around the place. So, leaving the house, we decided to go straight on to Exeter, where we had to meet our client.

The drive over the moors with their stones was a nightmare, but eventually we arrived at our destination, where we saw our client, who was waiting for us to arrive. Being seated with the gentleman, we told him where we had been en route and asked whether perhaps he knew the captain.

"I doubt whether another such individual exists anywhere," he replied with a laugh. "From what I have heard," he continued, "the captain is the scion of a very old military family and over the past several years has been involved in some matrimonial difficulties that have driven him to drink, and as far as I understand, he goes up to London twice a year, possibly to visit with his children, but this is all possibly just a local rumor."

We then concluded our business with the gentleman and left to return to London.

We never heard from the captain again.

Chapter 10

Mrs. Vakeel and the Statue of Liberty Pin

Following closely on the heels of the terrible financial crash in the States of 1929, many jewelers crossed the Atlantic from England to see what bargains they might be able to pick up from jewelers in America short of cash. At this time they were, at least most of them, without funds. Jewels they had, but no ready cash, and all were most anxious to lay their hands on any money that they could get.

The transatlantic liners were quickly filled with buyers from England, all on the prowl for possible bargains. At the time conditions in England were not too good, but in no way could they be compared with the dire state of affairs in America.

Among the jewelers arriving in New York was a man named Abie Cohen, a wealthy jewel dealer, very well known to many of the jewel dealers across America. Over the years he had made it his business to cross over to the States, where he always did considerable business, both buying and selling.

As soon as he arrived he went to see an old jeweler friend of his, a man he knew had always designed and created some of the most exquisite pieces. The first thing that this jeweler showed Mr. Cohen was a piece that he had titled "the Statue of Liberty pin." This was a large pin carved of solid platinum, about three inches in height, and all that it required was the necessary diamonds to complete it, the body being readied to be paved with fine diamonds.

The moment that Mr. Cohen saw this piece he was struck by its great beauty and asked his friend how much he wanted for it as it was, unset with the necessary diamonds.

"Mr. Cohen," said the jeweler, "please give me as much as you think that it is worth to you, as at the moment I am entirely without funds and do not have enough money to buy myself the proverbial cup of coffee."

Mr. Cohen was a very fair man and at once made the jeweler a good offer, which was accepted. Mr. Cohen knew that there would be no difficulty for him to have the piece completed in London.

Mr. Cohen then went through the dealer's other things and made considerable purchases from him, but he felt that his old friend should be assisted in any possible way.

As soon as Mr. Cohen returned to London he came to our offices to show us what he had been able to pick up, and among these pieces he laid this unfinished Statue of Liberty pin on the table. We at once purchased it from him, as we were, all of us, similarly struck by its great beauty.

After we had made the purchases, it did not take us very long to get the necessary diamonds and to have them set into the body of the "Lady," and within a few weeks the piece was ready for sale.

As soon as we had it in our hands we decided that it would make an outstanding and exquisite central feature in our window display, where we had it placed on a blue velvet stand. To say the least, it looked simply stunning.

The jewel could not have been on display for more than a few hours when a very fat Hindu lady came in and asked to see it. She actually said to our assistant, "What is that figure of a nude girl that you are showing in the center of your window?"

"That," replied the young man, "is not the figure of a nude girl; it is a Statue of Liberty modeled after the famous 'Liberty' that stands in New York harbor." Saying this, he took the piece out of the window and handed it to the lady. Our assistant then went on to explain to the lady that the jewel was of solid platinum and inset with the finest quality of diamonds that money could buy. The lady, who incidentally spoke excellent English, then explained that she knew perfectly well what the jewel represented and that she had seen the statue on very many occasions when she had visited in New York City. She then inquired the price that we were asking. The moment that our assistant told her the price she countered, in true Hindu manner, that the price was much too high, although she admitted that it was a lovely piece.

The offer that she made was, of course, refused, but the assistant came into my private office and asked me to come out and speak with the lady.

As soon as I saw the lady I said to her, "Actually, rather than sell the jewel, we would much prefer to keep it in our display for a few weeks as a showpiece." I also told the lady that we were under no pressure to dispose of the piece.

Then saying, "Good day," she left. However, the next day she was in again, and from that day onward, she was in and out of the shop at least once a day, and on one occasion she again asked to have the piece in her hands, when after again holding it she upped her original offer, which we again refused. By this time the entire matter had become quite a laughing matter between us, as when she continued to come in she at every visit upped her offer, which we invariably refused to accept, as actually we did not wish to part with the piece until we had exposed it in our display for some time.

After she had been in to see us about five or six times I said to her, "If you really want the piece, then all that I can do is advise you to buy it, as otherwise you will certainly lose it, and then you will never forgive yourself for not taking my advice."

After this little speech she said, "You win. I simply must have it, and I shall pay your price."

This then was possibly the first time and also the last that she had ever paid an original asking price for anything she bought.

Having purchased it, she at once pinned it onto her very ample bosom, where against her very colorful sari and dark skin it looked amazingly beautiful. And then she confessed, "I must tell you that I am delighted that you made me buy it."

By this time we had become fast friends, and she told me that she had to be off to Paris the next day. I told her that I might very well be over there at the same time as well, in which case perhaps we might meet and have a drink together.

A couple of days later I was, in fact, in Paris, but while there we did not see each other. However, while waiting at the airport Le Bourget in Paris for my return flight to London, I noticed her waiting similarly in the crowd, but then I immediately lost sight of her and could not see her until when I arrived at the Customs at the London airport and again saw her at the Customs barrier.

While I was going through I noticed that she was being questioned and detained by the authorities and eventually being marched off by a woman Customs officer.

I could not for the life of me imagine why she should have been detained, but there was nothing that I could do about it, and I returned to town. Next morning I telephoned her hotel, asked to speak with Mrs. Vakeel of Bombay, and was at once put through to her suite. I then told her that I had seen her being detained at the Customs and asked what had happened. With a laugh she replied, "I was taken into an anteroom by a matron who looked and acted as though I were in jail. She completely undressed me, down to my skin, and since they found that I was not carrying any contraband, I was told to dress myself and leave. Fortunately, I have a good sense of humor, and I inquired what I had done to bring about this investigation and the matron said that as I was so very fat it looked as though I might have had several rolls of silk wound round my middle, and this was dutiable. When I heard this I again laughed and thought to myself that it was a good thing that I was not undressed by a man officer, as this might in some way contravene my religion."

Next day she was again in to see me and told me that wherever she had been in Paris her "Lady," as she called her, was much admired. She then continued talking, saying, "From now on she is going to be called Miss Liberty."

She then told me that she was returning home to Bombay in a few days and that I had to come and visit with her if and when I ever found myself in India. She then told me that she lived on Malabar Street in Bombay; until this time she had always appeared to be reluctant to tell me anything about herself. I never did visit with her in Bombay, and of course I have no idea whether she is still among the living, but if she is I am sure that she never moved from her house without Miss Liberty on her breast.

Chapter 11

Antique Silver Forgeries and Goldsmith's Hall

Suddenly there seemed to be on the London market, as if it were overnight, an enormous quantity of what appeared to be, at first glance, some eighteenth-century English silverware of the finest possible quality. Dealers up and down Bond Street were buying and selling pieces without any qualms whatsoever, in fact never for a moment suspecting that they might be selling forgeries. But actually they were selling many forged pieces, naturally quite innocently, and many of these items were being sold to collectors from America.

After this had been going on for several weeks, the authorities at famed Goldsmith's Hall were beginning to realize that something was wrong and that many forgeries were being foisted onto the market. All that they could do was warn the dealers and advise them to be very careful when buying further pieces. The authorities were worried that if the fact that tourists and collectors from America were buying fakes came out, the entire trade with such merchandise could dry up almost overnight. This was a serious problem for all.

It was just at about the time, when this trade was in fullest spate, that one morning a very well dressed and exceedingly personable young man came in to see me. He appeared to be quite prosperous. Speaking to my assistant, he asked to speak with me, and when I spoke to him, he was obviously so well bred and had such impeccable manners that I was completely put off my guard. After I had chatted with the young man for a short while, he told me that he was an international antiques dealer, just arrived from Germany, and that he had brought with him some fine antique English silver for sale. He inquired as to whether we might be interested in buying, and I told him that we certainly would be, subject to the goods pleasing us.

"I have with me a superb set of six Georgian silver saltcellars by the renowned woman silversmith Hester Bateman."

53

Now Hester Bateman as a silversmith had caught the imagination of many American silver collectors. I told him that I would very much like to see the set and that I was positive that I would want to buy from him. He then promised that he would bring it in next morning at ten o'clock. With true German precision, he appeared on the dot of ten next morning, and as soon as he arrived he placed the set on my table. At first glance they seemed to be quite superb.

Hester Bateman was a very fine silversmith, and her creations were always in great demand, not alone for their quality, but perhaps because she was a woman, which of itself was quite a rarity.

I studied the set for a short while, and after concluding that I wanted to buy it, I asked him for his price, and as soon as he told me this I suggested that we have a check drawn to him.

Seeing that we were prepared to buy the set, he then said, "Since you are going to buy these saltcellars, I must tell you that I have a further set of six at my hotel and that they would make a very handsome set of twelve, and I can bring the others round to you tomorrow morning at this same time."

To my mind a set of twelve was an almost unheard of rarity, and a little bell struck a note in my thinking. So before writing our check I said, "Yes. Please bring me the other six, and we shall then draw you a check to cover the twelve. In the meantime leave the present ones with me for study."

The young man did not seem to be too happy about leaving the six with me, but as I already had possession of them and had promised to buy the other six he could scarcely do anything but agree.

As soon as he was out of the door, and having heard about the very fine forgeries that were being sold, I decided that I would study these pieces in greater depth. Looking at the hallmarks with my eyeglass, I saw quite clearly that these marks had been struck over a series of scratch marks, such as one would normally find on old silver. I at once concluded that these hallmarks had been struck after the saltcellars had been in use for some little time.

Something then began to smell bad in the state of Denmark, as the saying goes. Silver that had been mined in the eighteenth century and during earlier periods has a slightly bluish color, as in those early days the smelters of the silver ore were not able to refine the metal as they do today, and for this reason there is a very small quantity of gold in it, which accounts for this bluish tinge. Now, if these saltcellars were forgeries, and by this time I was convinced they were, the forgers had gone so far as to produce the actual metal by melting down other old pieces of eighteenth century silver.

At this point, being positive, I at once telephoned and spoke with the master of the Goldsmith's Hall, and as soon as he was on the line I told him about my suspicions and also that I had arranged to have the young German at my offices the next morning at ten o'clock. Now Goldsmith's Hall is perhaps one of the oldest and wealthiest of all the so-called Livery Companies. These companies are all intensely proud of their fine reputations, and Goldsmith's Hall was very jealous of its record regarding antique English gold- and silverware. As a young boy I had been a student at the Haberdasher's School, and I can thus speak with some authority about the quality of the teaching. Anybody wishing to visit these company Halls in London, which themselves are in most cases miniature museums, will, I am sure, always receive a warm welcome.

Within the hour after my conversation with the master, and by arrangement, he was with me in my office. I at once showed him the six saltcellars, and it took him just a few moments to say, "Mr. Hill, you are quite right, these are superb forgeries, and I think that this is the angle that we have been waiting for to break up this most damaging trade."

He then continued, "Tomorrow morning two of my agents will be round at the shop. They will take off their jackets and wear aprons as though they are your assistants, and when the young German arrives they will be there waiting to speak with him."

Next morning, as we had arranged, the two agents were in situ walking about and polishing pieces of our silver, and as soon as the German came in they took from him the other six saltcellars, and after a very brief examination they were as convinced as we were that they were forgeries. I then came over to speak to the young man and told him that we were going to issue a check for the entire twelve, but before we could do this I needed to have his passport. With obvious pleasure he handed over to me the passport, which I at once gave to the agents.

The agents then proceeded to ask the German some seemingly innocent questions to which he gave them lying replies. The agents then inquired, as though out of curiosity, about his background in the antiques business and also about the business of antique silverware, and he replied to all their questions without the slightest suggestion of hesitancy.

As soon as the agents were satisfied that he was lying all the way, they told him that they were detectives and that he was under arrest and would be charged on several counts: first, with importing silverware into England without declaring it to Customs at the port; second, fraud; and third, attempting to sell forgeries.

The two agents then hailed a taxi and took the German away with them to the local police station, where he was formally booked and locked up.

Very shortly after this he was brought up in court, as such matters are handled in England with much greater rapidity than they would be over here in the States. Naturally I had to appear in court to give evidence against the young man, and the judge was, as I recall, very fair indeed. After advising the young man never again to attempt to bring any forged pieces of any kind into the country, the judge told him that he would allow him to return home without giving him a jail sentence, which, he said, he very much deserved. However, he told him that if he were ever to be caught doing again what he had done, a very long prison sentence would be imposed upon him.

The young German then promised the judge that he would never again do anything of a similar nature and thanked the judge for his leniency, and at once left the court.

The day following the trial the master of the Goldsmith's Hall telephoned me and told me that I had been instrumental in stopping the forgery trade and also that he would be sending me a letter of special thanks for what I had done for the trade in general. He also said he was positive that the entire antique silver trade owed me a debt of gratitude.

I replied, "If what I have done has had the effect of cleaning off this sore, then I am amply repaid."

As I think back, I shudder to think how many pieces of so-called Hester Bateman silver may be in some fine collections, especially here in the States, that are positively forgeries, but certainly quite unknown to their owners.

Over the years there have been many American collectors of fine antique English silver. There have been some who have concentrated on the productions of the great Paul Lamerie, a superb craftsman and a member of a small coterie of Huguenot silversmiths who had established themselves in London during the eighteenth century. Similarly, there were others who concentrated on the creations of Paul Storr, whose works are today much sought after. Also, there is a firm of coffee merchants whose collections of antique silver coffeepots is well established and which presumably they use for publicity purposes.

In this regard there is a story told about the great American banker Pierpont Morgan, who while visiting the shop of Crichton of London Silversmith, while seated in the office looking at a wall, saw in front of him a very large showcase of silver. In this showcase Mr. Crichton kept his personal collection of what was possibly one of the finest groups extant of pieces that dated from the early periods of King Henry VIII and on through that of Queen Elizabeth I and then on through those of Charles.

After glancing at the showcase for a short while, Mr. Morgan said, "Mr. Crichton, how much do you want for that entire showcase collection?"

Mr. Crichton replied, "But that is my personal collection and is not for sale."

Completely ignoring the dealer's reply, Morgan said, "Just work out the cost to me, including the showcase, and send round a note to my hotel; then after receipt I shall tell you what I want you to do for me." Then, without a further word, he rose and left the dealer's shop.

Next morning there was a letter from Mr. Crichton in Mr. Morgan's mail at the hotel establishing what must have been for those days a colossal figure.

Mr. Morgan then telephoned Mr. Crichton and said, "I am buying your collection, at your figure, and I want you to have the showcase with its contents photographed as it stands at present, and then as soon as you have this done I want you to have it shipped over to me in the States, and I shall need the photograph so that the collection can then be arranged exactly as I have seen it in your office."

Naturally, the dealer accepted these conditions and had the collection shipped as directed.

Whether or not this story is apochryphal I cannot tell, but as Mr. Morgan did establish the great Morgan Library on New York's Madison Avenue, where they have on display one of the greatest collections in America, it is well within the bounds of possibility that many of the fine silver pieces are still being exhibited there.

Chapter 12

Theodore Gary and His Jewel Purchases

It was at some time during the early thirties that a good friend of ours, a Mr. Charles Leighton, came round to our offices to see us. Leighton was a gentleman who loved to dress in exquisite taste and, as we all thought, always looked as though he were on the way to a wedding.

He had one small quirk, which was to us rather amusing; he would never place anything in his jacket pockets lest it make a slight bulge.

In other words, he was what one might term a well-dressed English gentleman. Professionally he acted as a sort of escort to the very wealthy, and especially to the very wealthy from America, who in those days were beginning to flock in hordes into England, especially into London. Among his particular clients was an elderly gentleman named Theordore Gary, who came from the Middle West. He had spoken with Leighton immediately upon his arrival and had arranged that they meet at his hotel as soon as possible. Mr. Gary told him that he had a very important commission that he wished him to fill for him. They arranged an appointment for the following morning, and as soon as Leighton arrived he was closeted with Mr. Gary for quite some time.

Mr. Gary was an industrialist and probably the first to be involved with the then new automatic telephone, and he explained to Leighton that in view of the financial crash of 1929 in the States he wanted to protect his wife and sister-in-law, who were traveling with him, as far as he was able to do.

In this regard he told Leighton that he wished to be introduced to a firm of gem dealers who would be in a position to supply him with some of the finest gems that money could buy, so that when he returned home to the States he could lock the gems up in a safe deposit box where they could remain as insurance should there be any further financial crash.

Leighton told Mr. Gary that he was very well acquainted with such a firm of gem dealers, Hill & Sons, whom he could recommend with all confidence. Mr. Gary then instructed Leighton to put our firm in touch with him so that he could discuss with us his special requirements. He then made it quite clear to Leighton that he did not wish him to either accept or ask for any renumeration from us, as he would himself take care of any such matters directly.

Leaving Mr. Gary, Mr. Leighton came up to our offices and told my brother all about his client and his desires. It was then arranged that my brother Henry telephone Mr. Gary and arrange to meet with him at his hotel, as soon as possible.

At this meeting Mr. Leighton explained that Mr. Gary was an enormously wealthy gentleman and could easily pay for anything that he might wish to buy. He also explained that we were not to give or even offer him any commission on this introduction, as Mr. Gary had arranged to pay him directly.

Next day my brother contacted Mr. Gary and arranged to meet him at his hotel later that same day.

As soon as Henry was with Mr. Gary at the hotel, the gentleman asked the two ladies who were at the time in an adjoining room to come in. As soon as they were there he said to them, "Girls, I want you to meet Mr. Hill, who will be able to get you anything that you might want to buy while you are here in London." He then asked the ladies to leave the room. as soon as they had exited, he said to my brother, "Mr. Hill, after all, I am not as young as I look, and if anything should happen to me while we are in London, I want you to look after my 'girls' for me.

"Mr. Hill, I want you to find for me two of the finest blue white diamonds that money can buy, of a fairly important size. Similarly I want you to get me two superb Kashmir rubies and also two of the finest sapphires, all of about the same size. Then I want you to get me two fine Oriental pearl necklaces. and as soon as you have lined all of these things up for me to see, please telephone me and make another appointment to meet here, with the jewels. Then after we have arranged this I shall want you to get me some other things."

"I can assure you, Mr. Gary," Henry replied, "that I understand precisely what you have in mind and I shall get on the job at once, particularly as you want everything lined up as soon as possible."

A couple of weeks then passed, and my brother telephoned the hotel to tell Mr. Gary that he had all the jewels for him to see, and with which he told him he was sure that he would be delighted.

Mr. Gary then asked him to come round to the hotel right away, and as soon as he arrived Mr. Gary asked "his girls" to leave the room again.

As soon as they had gone he asked my brother to show him the gems that he had with him. My brother then laid out all of the gems on a side table so that Mr. Gary could see them.

With scarcely a glance he said, "They all look lovely, and just what I wanted you to find for me, and please call my office downtown and they will give you a check for them, and also I am sure that Mr. Leighton explained to you that he is not to receive any commission from you." Having settled this, Mr. Gary then changed the subject. "Do you know anything about comparative religions?" My brother replied that he had never studied the subject. "In that case, if you have the time I would like to talk to you about the subject, which is very dear to my heart."

My brother replied that he had all the time in the world and would be delighted to listen to what Mr. Gary had to tell him. Actually, he had not the slightest idea what the old gentleman wanted to talk to him about.

Mr. Gary then began to talk for about two hours about what he termed his life's study, without Henry uttering a single word. After Mr. Gary had finished he said, "Now I must thank you for a very enjoyable couple of hours that I have spent talking with you." Mr. Gary then told my brother about the two Oriental pearl necklaces that he wanted to get for his "girls," and Henry left.

Returning to our offices, my brother at once telephoned Mr. Javeri, an old Hindu friend and Oriental pearl merchant, and asked him to step up to the office, as he told him that he had a very special assignment to discuss with him.

Later that afternoon Mr. Javeri arrived and was told to find a pair of the finest pearl necklaces that money could buy for a very special client. Mr. Javeri then took from his valise several bunches of very fine Oriental pearls, all of about the size and quality that were called for, which he explained had just arrived from India for sale. He also explained that these bunches of pearls were not to be broken until after an offer had been submitted to India and accepted by the consignors. He told my brother that the moment the seals were broken the pearls were purchased. My brother told Mr. Javeri that he knew how these matters were handled and asked him to leave the bunches with him to show to our client, who he said would be most interested in this Oriental manner of trade.

Next morning Henry called and told Mr. Gary that he had the pearls for him to see and arranged to go round to the hotel right away. As soon as he arrived at Mr. Gary's suite he laid the two bunches of pearls on a table and explained to Mr. Gary that if he approved them an offer would have to be made before the seals were broken.

Mr. Gary then said, "The pearls look wonderful to me, and I am going to cut the seals. You can then make an offer, and whatever is acceptable I shall pay." As he said this he picked up a pair of scissors and cut the seals. He then said, "Now, Mr. Hill, please have these pearls strung as two identical necklaces and have suitable small diamond clasps made for each." Mr. Gary then told my brother that he was fascinated at the Oriental method of trade.

Actually, Mr. Gary had scarcely looked at the pearls but had said, "If you say that they are fine, then they are fine." He then again asked Henry whether he had the time to sit and have another chat about his favorite subject, and my brother replied that he would welcome it.

Next day Henry went downtown and received payment for the two pearl necklaces, which had in the meantime been offered for and which offer had been accepted by the Indian consignors.

Next morning Mr. Gary again called my brother. "Now I want you to duplicate the two pearl necklaces, exactly in cultured pearls, with precisely the same diamond clasps, so that the 'girls' can wear the copies without being aware of the fact and I can deposit the real ones together with the other gems in my safe deposit box. I am sure that they will never know the difference any more than will I."

The following week Mr. Gary again telephoned my brother and asked him to find some superb Chinese jade necklaces. However, these could not be found too quickly and before my brother could lay his hands on anything suitable Mr. Gary called and said that they had to return to the States and that he would have to leave the matter of the jades over for a subsequent visit. My brother then thanked him and after wishing him and the "girls" a happy voyage home said goodbye and hung up. After this we never again saw Mr. Gary, who presumably passed away shortly after his return to the States, and in fact from his conversation with my brother it appeared that he must have had some premonition that he did not have too long for this world.

Many years then passed and World War II in Europe had come and in due course gone, and by this time we were established in New York. One day we received a letter from London that had been mailed over to us for attention. This letter had been mailed by Mr. Gary's sister-in-law, a Mrs. Laramie, and in the letter she stated that she now wished to sell the necklace of Oriental pearls that Mr. Gary had given her, asking us whether we would handle the matter of the resale for her.

We at once wrote Mrs. Laramie and told her that we were now established in New York City and that if she would mail us the necklace we would be most happy to handle the matter for her.

At the moment of writing this letter to Mrs. Laramie we had completely forgotten all about the cultured pearl necklaces that we had prepared for the "girls" to wear. In due course the package arrived, and as soon as we opened it we saw that it contained the cultured pearl necklaces and at that moment we realized Mr. Gary's request about the duplicate necklaces. Mrs. Laramie had not sent us the Oriental pearls.

This then posed a predicament for us. How to tell the lady that she had sent us the cultured pearls? Whether or not she knew what Mr. Gary had done, we naturally did not know.

Nevertheless, we wrote her and explained that we were returning her the cultured pearl necklaces as at that time they were practically valueless. Upon receipt of our letter and the cultured pearls, Mrs. Laramie wrote us a most scathing letter in which she suggested that we had changed her real pearls for cultured pearls, retaining the real ones for ourselves.

We were now faced with a very serious problem. How were we going to ever convince the lady that we had done nothing wrong and that we had acted in good faith? We at once wrote our elder brother, Bertram, in London and explained to him our predicament and asked him whether he might have any ideas that he could suggest to us as to how to handle the situation.

As soon as he received our letter he was as perturbed as we were, and after checking through his files he found the original carbons of every one of the invoices that had been prepared for Mr. Gary, and among these carbons were those for the Oriental pearls and also of the cultured duplicates, with precise details of the number and weight of the pearls and also the details of the small diamond clasps. It was quite remarkable that Bertram still retained those carbons, as most of our papers had been turned over to the government during the war, when paper was needed for the war effort.

Bertram then mailed us these carbons, after having had them Xeroxed so that we could send Mrs. Laramie both the carbons for the real Oriental pearls and also the cultured ones.

We at once mailed these carbons to the lady, and as soon as she received them she wrote us a letter of the most abject apology.

Upon its receipt, we replied, chiding her, telling her how careful one has to be before making such serious allegations as she had done. As far as we were concerned this ended the matter.

It is perhaps interesting to speculate as to what had happened to the other wonderful gems that Mr. Gary had said he was going to deposit in a safe deposit vault without the "girls' " knowledge. It is within the bounds of possibility that they may still be there, safely locked away, without anybody having been aware of their existence. In today's markets they would certainly be worth a veritable king's ransom.

Chapter 13

Mr. Bowen and Fabergé, Georges Grillon and Purchase

It was at some time during the early thirties that we were introduced by a fellow jeweler in London to a Mr. Bowen who said that he would like to come to see us, as he had a proposal to make to us. He said that he was sure that his talk would be of great moment. We then arranged a mutually convenient meeting and as soon as Mr. Bowen had arrived he was shown into our private office.

Seated at my desk, he said, "Mr. Hill, you do not know me, but it was Jacques Hurwitz who suggested that you would be interested in what I have to say."

As soon as he said this I was most anxious to hear what he had to say.

"I am sure that you have heard about the oldtime international firm of jewelers, Karl Fabergé of Russia."

I replied that although I knew little about them, I knew that they had a shop on Bond Street.

He then continued, "I was the manager of that shop until after the Revolution, when of course we had to close our doors. With me at the shop was another man, named Bainbridge. Fortunately, I had the names of many of our customers and in this way I have been able to eke out a living, acting as a go-between for them. However, what I wanted to tell you was that when I left I took with me several pieces of their things, which I am now anxious to sell, and I think that if you were to put them in your window, they would sell very readily."

I then asked Mr. Bowen to show me what he had, and he took from his pocket two small enameled gold boxes, the sort of things that ladies carried for pills or cachous, also two small photo frames in gold, enamel, and hardstone, a small taper stick similarly of enameled gold, and also one other piece, which at this time I do not recall. The objects were to my mind really lovely, and I then arranged prices for each with him and told him that I would have the things put on display in one corner of our window and see what response we might get. Then taking the pieces from Mr. Bowen, I told our assistant to arrange the pieces in a corner of our display.

It must have been about midday that the items were placed in the window, and by closing time that same day all had been sold.

There was one gentleman in particular, a Mr. DuCann, a well-known attorney who later became a judge of the High Court, who was the buyer of four of the pieces. He told me that he had already amassed a small collection of the works of Fabergé, whom he considered one of the greatest master creators of jewels of his day. "I am sure," he continued, "that Fabergé's creations will in truth become the antiques of the future." How right he was.

Next morning I telephoned Mr. Bowen and told him that he could come to our shop and collect his check for all six pieces. Actually, I wanted to talk with him and learn more about the Fabergé operation in Russia prior to the 1917 Revolution. He then told me that Fabergé originally had shops in Saint Petersburg, now Leningrad, Odessa, Moscow, and Kiev. After closing these shops, the members of the Fabergé family all left Russia. The father, Karl, an Alsatian by birth, returned to Alsace, but died shortly afterward. One son went to Finland and another, Agathon, to Paris. Then there was a third son, but Mr. Bowen had no idea what happened to him. Mr. Bowen then told me that their business was conducted in a rather unique modus operandi. At each of the workshops they had a series of workmasters, as they called them, and these directed the operations of the craftsmen under them. There were some of these who excelled in superb enamels, others in hardstone carvings, and so on. These workmasters were permitted to place their initials on the pieces created under their control together with the Russian gold and/ or silver hallmarks, wherever these applied.

When the London shop was closed, virtually overnight, both he and Mr. Bainbridge were left high and dry. Thus the check that we handed him was, at the moment, a godsend. That evening, together with my two brothers, we discussed these very rapid sales and we decided that here was an opportunity for good business in an area that we had not previously known. The question then arose: "Where do we go to find more things?"

We decided to visit other jewelers in London and see what they might have available that we could buy, and although we were able to pick up a few pieces, we could not find enough for our purposes.

We then called and spoke with Mr. Bainbridge, and after we listened to what he had to say about the lovely creations that had been through his hands, he told us, "You know we made some fabulous creations for royalties all over the world and for many of the enormously wealthy potentates and Hindu maharajas, who were particularly attracted to important things of rock crystal."

I then asked him whether perhaps he himself had any pieces that we could buy from him, and he replied, "Regretfully, I have sold all of the things that I had taken for myself." He did say that the Rothschilds in London had been big buyers and that most of the objects that they had created for them were enameled with their racing colors of blue and yellow.

Mr. Bainbridge also described many of the wonderful objects that Mr. Henry Walters of Baltimore had bought from them in London and also from the shops in Russia, which are today in the Walter's Art Gallery, which he had established in his native Baltimore. This museum is today one of the showplaces of the east.

In the course of further conversation Bainbridge continued, "You know, after the Revolution many of the very wealthy Russians managed to escape to Paris, and it is there that you might be able to pick up some fine things."

We then realized that Paris must be a happy hunting ground for us, and the next weekend found my brother Henry and me in Paris, where in truth we were able to find some deliciously beautiful objects by Fabergé, and we returned to London our pockets loaded down with rare Fabergé objects of all sorts. Following our return we placed these objects on display in the same corner of our window and again, in very short order, all were sold. This being the case, we decided that we should be in Paris at least once a week and that either I or Henry should be there.

As the Faubourg Saint Honoré in Paris is the quarter where there are many dealers' establishments, we went to the Hotel Castiglione, similarly situated on this avenue, and arranged with the then manager, a Monsieur Montcomble, that suite 82 was to be reserved for our use for every weekend, from Friday to Sunday, unless we telephoned him that we would not be using it. This arrangement worked out exceedingly well for us, as we informed all of our dealer friends that whenever they acquired anything that they thought we should see they could leave a message for us at the hotel so that we could call in at their shops when we arrived. We thus continued our weekend visits for several years, until the outbreak of war in 1939 ended all of this. In those days many of the Paris taxi drivers were émigrés who had been grand dukes and princes in Russia, and one could usually tell them, as most wore their long fur coats that they had carried with them when they had escaped. Many of these persons were able to direct us to interesting situations where we were able to make some good buys, and they were always delighted to earn some extra commissions.

In those early days when one traveled to Paris by train, cross-channel boat, and then again train, the journey took some nine hours, but later with the advent of airplane travel this was shortened to about one hour. I still recall that on my first flight I had left London while my brother was speaking with a customer at our shop, and as soon as I arrived in Paris I telephoned him that I had arrived safely. He was astonished to hear my voice, as he was still talking with the same customer and I had actually been gone only about two hours.

As an aside, my mother loved marron glacés, and my first thought on arriving in Paris each Friday afternoon was a visit to the shop Marie to order some one of their specialties to pick up on Saturday and take home for Mother on Sunday. This soon became a regular routine for me.

After we had been making these weekly crossings for several months, we found that the world was descending on Paris. They were all on the chase for the creations of Karl Fabergé, and then we had to try to seek greener pastures. It was just at about this time that we had a very wealthy and highly valued client, the Belgian banker Baron Jean Cassel, the owner and director of the

Banque Cassel in Brussels, who after marrying his wife chang
his name to Baron Cassel Van Doorn, to incorporate her na
with his. This was, naturally, a little bit of snobbery.

The gentleman came over to London to see us and said that
he wished to buy for his baroness a necklace of the finest black
pearls that money could buy. For this project he told us that
money was no object, but "I want every pearl to be of the very
fine color known in the pearl trade as raven's wing black, that is
to say black with a tinge of green."

We told him that we would see whether such a thing was
obtainable anywhere in the market, but we soon found that nobody anywhere owned such a necklace and we would have to buy
pearls as they came into the market to accumulate a necklace for
him.

We were told to go right ahead and do what we had to do.
The central pearl was naturally to be the most important, and this
was to be approximately the size of a large green pea. After this
central feature, the other pearls were to graduate downward towards the back, where they were to be held by a diamond clasp
of suitable dimension.

Being thus commissioned, we contacted a Frenchman who
specialized in pearls and with particular emphasis on black ones
and who for this reason was continually traveling to Guatemala,
where such fine black pearls were to be found in the surrounding
waters. He was at that time the only person available to us who
handled such merchandise. We asked this gentleman to come up
to our offices to discuss the project that we had in hand; his name
was Georges Grillon. After we had told him what was required by
our client, he said that he understood perfectly, and as he was off
to Guatemala the following week, he would get us whatever he
found available that he thought would suit our purpose.

A few weeks then elapsed and Georges was again in to see
us. He had with him six important pearls that would be ideal for
our proposed necklace. Taking these from him, we at once
crossed to Brussels to show them to the baron, who when he saw
them was delighted and at once drew us a check in payment. At
this meeting he suggested that we buy a small necklace of black
pearls and then have these six fine ones placed in the center, after
which as we acquired further fine specimens we could gradually

discard the small ones. In this way the baroness could commence wearing her necklace.

Following this initial crossing to Guatemala, Georges was again proposing to return to see what the fishers might have found for him, but after a few weeks he returned empty-handed. However, he told us that the locals had promised to hold for him anything fine that they might find, until his next trip. Despite all these promises during the following two years, we were only able to obtain a few pearls that were suitable.

Now Georges, who had up to this time been making a living out of pearls, found that his source of income was rapidly drying up, and as by this time we had become very friendly with him, he told us that, in truth, he did not know where to turn for further business.

My brother then had a bright idea and, knowing that Georges lived in Paris, called and invited him to join us at dinner at Simpson's Restaurant in London's Strand. Over dinner my brother told Georges he would outline a plan for him that we thought would be very welcome.

Beyond this, Georges was a great gourmet and loved good eating, and the idea of a roast beef dinner at Simpson's was to him most appealing.

As soon as we were seated in our booth at the restaurant we asked Georges whether he had ever heard the name Fabergé mentioned anywhere. He replied that he had not. We then gave him a brief résumé of the operations of this firm in Old Russia and told him all about the wonderful creations that had been made in their ateliers.

As Georges lived in Paris, he might well be in a position to unearth some pieces that we could use. After explaining all about Fabergé's enamels and hardstone carvings as well as how to identify the markings that one could readily see on many of the pieces, we also told him that if he ever ran across a piece that he might not be sure about we could easily be over in Paris at a moment's notice.

Georges was not slow in the uptake and by the time dessert was being served had a very clear picture of the sort of things that we sought to buy. "I am leaving for Paris at noon tomorrow, and as soon as I get home I shall start looking around among some of the dealers that I know."

We told him that with a little bit of luck he could very well make a nice living for himself.

Next day Georges was on the telephone to my brother. "Why do you have to go to Paris to buy Fabergé's things? I am just at this moment in a gentleman's office, here in Hatton Garden, and I have seen two safes filled to overflowing with what look to me just like the things that we have been talking about by Fabergé, and what is more, you know the man who has them."

My brother then asked Georges who the man was.

He replied, "It is Mr. Nossovitsky, whom you always knew as Mr. Nosso. Through his brother-in-law, who is a commissar in Russia, he gets some very interesting leads."

Georges then put Mr. Nosso on the telephone, who told my brother that he had safes full of Fabergé available for offer and that they had to be sold very quickly.

My brother then said, "I have a dentist's appointment for this afternoon, but I shall be round to see you first thing tomorrow morning."

Mr. Nosso replied, "That may be alright, except that another dealer has already seen the collection and has made an offer which is presently under consideration and tomorrow may be too late."

My brother canceled his dentist's appointment and went right over. Within minutes Henry was in Mr. Nosso's office.

An hour or so then passed, and I received a call: "Come right over and bring the two suitcases that we have standing in the corner with you."

I at once took the suitcases and was on my way.

Arriving at Nosso's office, I saw all the objects that he had laid out on a long table and, after a moment's glance, saw that here was a most fabulous collection of some of the finest of Fabergé's creations. Without hesitation I said to Mr. Nosso, "If you will put back on the table the thing that you have put into your pocket I shall at once draw you a check for the amount that you have quoted Henry."

Mr. Nosso was quite startled by what I had said and at once proceeded to take out of his pocket a superb little enameled gold spyglass with a lovely Oriental pearl finial. "But how did you know that I had this in my pocket?" he asked. Actually, I had been making a joke, but he seemed to think that I had X-ray eyes.

The collection of things was so fabulous that it did not require more than a very quick glance to see that we were onto something very special. I at once wrote him our check, and packing the objects into the two suitcases, we took them back to our offices.

We had in truth unearthed a king's ransom in wonderful Fabergé creations; many of the pieces had obviously emanated from the palaces of the czars. In today's market what we had purchased would have enabled a person to retire and live very comfortably for life on the proceeds.

As soon as we had unpacked the cases we put several of the pieces into our window display. A couple of hours then passed, and Mr. DuCann, on his way to his club, came in and made a large purchase. He took all that we had placed in the window. Mr. DuCann was a great aesthete and lover of applied art in all of its various moods.

Next day, Georges, who had changed his plans to return to Paris, was up at our offices to collect his commission.

"Tell me, Georges," I said, "how did you come to those safes with all these Fabergé things in Nosso's office?"

With a laugh he replied, "You remember that I told you that I was leaving for Paris the next day when we had dinner together. Well, just before leaving for the airport I had a quick lunch with Nosso at a small restaurant, as he told me that he had some pearls that he wanted me to show in Paris and suggested that perhaps I would take a later plane."

He then continued, "After we had finished our quick lunch I needed to use the toilet, but as they did not have any such facility at this restaurant, he said, 'Come back with me to my office and use my toilet.' When we arrived at his offices Mr. Nosso directed me through two large offices to where his toilet was situated. On returning through the two rooms I said to Mr. Nosso, 'You are a pearl merchant, so what do you need so many offices for?'

" 'Come,' he said. 'I will show you.'

"Then going into the second of these two offices, he opened two large safes and showed me what they contained. 'These are all things by Fabergé,' he said, 'and I have to sell them.' He then explained that he had received them through the good offices of

72

his Russian commissar brother-in-law. It appears that shortly after the Revolution two firms of engineers, one British and the other American, had been called in by the Russians to do some work for them and after their assignment had been completed they quite naturally wanted to be paid. The Russians then explained that they were very short of foreign currency, but that they would pay them part in cash and part with this group of goods. The engineers were not too happy about this arrangement, but they had no alternative but to accept.

"Taking the objects with them, they left Russia, and on the advice of the commissar, Mr. Nosso's relation took the objects to him and left them for his handling on their behalf. They explained to Mr. Nosso that they wanted to have the goods disposed of as soon as possible and that they wanted to share the proceeds fifty/fifty with each other."

It was just at this juncture that Georges had to use the toilet and we were thus given the opportunity to buy what must of a certainty be the most important group of fine Fabergé ever to appear on the market. When we eventually got down to a thorough examination of what we had purchased we could scarcely believe our eyes. There were gold and enameled snuff boxes, innumerable small photo frames, for which Fabergé was so famous; there were spyglasses, taper sticks, Easter eggs, and objects of all types; everything was of gold, many inset with precious stones. Several of the pieces had obviously come from the imperial palaces, as they contained photographs of many members of the czarist families.

Thus had it not been for Georges' sudden call of nature we would never have been in touch with Mr. Nosso, who, although we knew him quite well, never associated us with anything other than pearls and other jewels. Today many of the objects from this collection are in the hands of the greatest collectors of Fabergé's creations and quite a few of the pieces are included in the collection of the Metropolitan Museum of New York, included in the bequest of the late Mr. Lansdell Christie, the great industrialist and lover of Fabergé.

Several weeks later Mr. Nosso called and said that he wanted to come over to see us to discuss a matter with us. We then arranged to see him at our offices next morning.

When he arrived he said, "Now that I know that you are interested in Russian things, if you would like to come to Russia with me, I will be happy to introduce my brother-in-law to you, and through his influences I am sure that you will be able to find some wonderful things. You will not be able to pay him any commissions on any introductions, but all that you must do is take with you a dozen silk shirts."

Henry and I told him that we would consider the matter and be in touch with him in a few days.

After he left, we discussed it among ourselves and decided that we would go with him, but we decided that we would wait a month, as Henry said that he wanted to learn a smattering of Russian before we left. We then called Mr. Nosso and arranged to go with him a few weeks later. My brother then found a tutor whose name was, of course, Mr. Popoff and proceeded to have some private lessons in Russian at our home. I did not join in these lessons but found that by passing back and forth through the room I was able to pick up some words at random.

In due time the few weeks that we had mentioned to Mr. Nosso had passed, and we called him and told him that we were then ready to go with him.

"Unfortunately, the Russians have just this week started a Five Year Plan, and this precludes all possibility of making any purchases at this time. But as soon as I hear that anything changes I shall be in touch with you." Apparently after this conversation nothing changed, and we never heard anything more from Mr. Nosso.

Chapter 14

Mrs. Dudley Ward and Fabergé Elephants

There are very many stories to be told about the various aspects of the wonderful genius Fabergé and his original creations. Some of these are quite amusing, and others are, to say the least, tinged with pathos.

Among perhaps his greatest achievements are the truly delicious little animal carvings and figurines that were created by his craftsmen in his ateliers, where they attempted to reproduce them as faithfully as was at all possible. The semiprecious stones that Fabergé used for his little animals were almost invariably chosen to convey as nearly as possible the true colors of the animal's pelts. Among the animals they carved were hippos, elephants, lions, tigers, cats, dogs, and ostriches and other members of the bird family. Some of the more amusing were his little monkeys, often depicted perched up on tree branches. The birds that he seemed to favor more than any other were the ostriches. In the case of his elephants he most often used the Russian gray stone known as *troitsk*, a color that almost precisely matches that of an actual elephant hide.

Among our many clients who collected these little elephants was the Honorable Mrs. Dudley Ward, who had been a great friend and confidante of Edward before he became King Edward VIII of England and before he married Mrs. Wally Simpson. It was Wally Simpson who always said, "Mrs. Ward was my husband's first love." Whenever Mrs. Ward found herself in our neighborhood she would invariably call in to inquire whether we had found any new elephants for her collection. She wanted none other than little elephants, and over the years that we knew her she had accumulated quite an impressive group of them in all shapes and sizes.

"Why do you only collect these little elephants?" I once asked her, and looking at me with a somewhat quizzical expression, she replied, "Because elephants never forget." Presumably there must have been something associated with the elephants that she never wanted to forget; it may have had some association with one or the other of the elephant hunts that King Edward had enjoyed on some of his Indian and African safaris.

Mrs. Ward must over the years have invested a small fortune in these lovely little objects, as she certainly by the time that I first knew her already owned several hundred.

It was shortly after we had moved to our much larger premises on Piccadilly, where we occupied one of the segments surrounding the front of the Piccadilly Hotel, that she came in to see us and to wish us success in our new venture, and also to inquire whether we found any more little elephants that she could buy. "Did we have anything?" Yes, we did, as only that morning we had purchased a model of exquisite beauty, the like of which we had never previously encountered.

This little fellow was carved not from the traditional *troitsk*, but out of a hardstone a most delicate shade of pink. As we had only just purchased this, it had been left standing on a side table preparatory to being entered into our stock; it had not as yet even been inventoried. The moment that she set her eyes on this she was all agog, and picking it up she said, "Of course he is mine," incidentally buying him before she had even been quoted a cost.

Then she said, all the while hugging it as though it were a baby, "As I am sure that I must have told you before, I have every one of my little friends named, and now we have to find a nice name for this new little animal.

"But what" she continued, "am I calling him?"

Now this little elephant had a particularly wide beam, and we were laughing about this when just at that moment my brother Henry passed through on his way out of the store, and looking at him from the rear she at once exclaimed, "That's it! We are going to call him Henry!" And that was that.

At this time we had another good friend, an American named Montgomery Evans, whose name he told us emanated from the fact that he was born in Montgomery, Alabama. He must have been quite wealthy, because he never seemed to have any particular work or occupation but spent a lot of his time in travel. He also claimed to be a direct descendant of President Wilson.

76

Montgomery loved Fabergé, and whenever he traveled he always took with him his little treasures, as he called them, packed in a special valise that he had especially ordered for the purpose. At the time that I knew him he must have been in his early thirties and unmarried. He explained that he could never bear to travel without his "companions," and indeed what he owned were some true little dream creations by the master.

Among these articles Montgomery had a small cigar box formed of sheets of green Russian jade, or nephrite as it is more correctly called, and all bound together with a narrow border of gold. It had a very imposing gold hinge at its back, and it had been, by an inscription on a gold plate set in its front panel, presented by Czar Nicholas to the "Bankers of Moscow." For this reason Montgomery had named it the Banker's Box.

On several occasions I tried to buy this unique gem from him, but I never succeeded. He did, however, promise me that if ever he did decide to part with it, I would have the first chance to buy it from him.

Evans was a terrible drunkard. In fact, I had never known another such as he. He seemed to thrive on Scotch whiskey, never a drop of anything else, and actually never seemed to eat anything.

After we had been together one day he told me that he was in the process of doing a book titled *Around the World with a Thirst*, and that he was leaving next day for Scotland, where he had arranged to visit at many Scotch distilleries and there to collect data for his volume, by interviewing some of the distillers.

At these distilleries there was, naturally, never any shortage of Scotch whiskey, as these companies were allowed to retain a certain proportion of their brews for publicity purposes, and upon which they were not required to pay any tax.

During these visits he later told me there was always a plentiful supply of the various whiskies, so that he could make complete comparisons after he left Scotland.

On this visit he had crossed to Ireland, as he felt that his work would not be complete without an analysis of the various Irish brands. He returned to London some six weeks after our meeting and at once telephoned me.

"Sidney, I would very much like you to join me at lunch here at the Ritz Hotel tomorrow, as I have a very special favor that I wish to ask of you."

Evans suggested the Ritz because whenever he was in London he had arranged with the barman there to receive and hold any mail that might arrive for him. Incidentally, he had a similar arrangement with the barman at the Ritz bar in Paris and also with the barman at the famed 21 Club in New York City.

I was not too happy about accepting this invitation, as I found it quite difficult to sit at the table and eat all the while watching Evans drinking his lunch. I promised, however, that I would meet him the next day at noon.

When I arrived there was Evans seated on a stool at the Ritz bar, drink in hand, and we soon went to the table he had reserved for us. As soon as I had ordered lunch he began to speak.

"Sidney, the great favor that I am going to ask of you is in fact really quite simple. I am quite positive that war is about to be declared at any time now, and I have been very fortunate indeed in getting myself a berth on the liner *Athenia*, which is set to leave for New York tomorrow. In the event that war should be declared while we are at sea, I want you to send me a cable to the boat reading: 'The cat's out of the bag.' "

I told him that I agreed with his thinking that we were going to be embroiled in war at any time, then, and I promised to accede to his request.

We then finished our lunch—that is to say, I finished eating and he drinking—and before we said good-bye to each other I again jokingly inquired as to when he was going to sell me the Banker's Box, but he said that he was still adamant and that he did not want to part with it. I then left him and returned to my office.

Next day he was off as scheduled.

After the *Athenia* had been at sea for about two days she was torpedoed. The war had begun and she was among the first the German raiders attacked.

The curtains had come down on the Europe as we had then known it.

Naturally, I did not need to send Evans any cables, as if he were still alive at the moment he certainly knew more about the war than did we. Now it is a well-established custom at sea that when a ship is sinking women and children are the first to be put into the lifeboats, and that is what happened in this instance. However, one of the sailors went through the cabins to see whether perhaps there might be any women or children in any of the bunks, and while doing this he saw Montgomery fast asleep in his bunk in a drunken stupor. The sailor decided that he could not leave him there to drown. As Evans was a man of slight stature, the sailor picked him up in his arms, with Evans' special valise attached to his wrist and locked there as with a pair of handcuffs, and bundled him into one of the lifeboats. Thus he was saved together with his little treasures.

Upon his landing in New York, his first port of call was the bar at the 21 club on West 52d Street to collect any mail that the barman might be holding for him. At the same time he handed over to the man the lifejacket that he had been wearing while on board.

After this visit they suspended this lifejacket over the bar together with the innumerable and fascinating collection of memorabilia for which the club is quite famous.

As soon as Evans had settled down in the city, he wrote to us in London to tell us of his experience at sea on the *Athenia*. "It is only fair to tell you," he wrote, "that it is only by a fluke that the Banker's Box is still unharmed, and if you still want it, then it is yours."

We immediately called him that we were mailing him a draft for the price that we had previously offered him and wrote that as I would be in New York shortly, I would collect the box from him upon my arrival.

Upon receipt of our draft, he wrote to thank us, and in the same letter he stated that he had suffered a very severe loss, as all of his manuscript had gone down with the boat, all being enclosed in a suitcase.

Thus the world lost what Evans considered to be one of the most valuable documents on the entire history of Scotch and Irish whiskey. This opinion was, of course, his alone.

The same gentleman, Henry Charles Bainbridge, who had been associated with Mr. Bowen in the running of the Fabergé shop was he who had originally sold the Banker's Box to Montgomery Evans.

Mr. Bainbridge came in to see us one morning and brought in with him another young man named Talbot De Vere Clifton, whom he said he wished to introduce to us as a buyer of Fabergé. Mr. Bainbridge said that he himself had nothing that he could offer to De Vere.

De Vere then told us that he had recently married an exquisitely beautiful girl and wished to buy her as many presents as he possibly could. He was a very wealthy young man and was the lord of the manor of a vast estate up in the north of England at a town named Saint Anne's. He said that he would be bringing the young lady in to see us next day, as he wanted to introduce her to us.

The next day De Vere was in again, but without his young bride, and he said that she did not come with him as she was not feeling too well, but he would bring her in at some future time. After he had gone, Mr. Bainbridge remained to talk with us and told us that De Vere had a very strong streak of irrationality in his makeup and for that reason the young lady always refused to go anywhere with him. He said that she had discovered this condition in her husband very soon after they were married and that she was, naturally, very upset by the matter.

After we had met De Vere on several subsequent occasions it did not take us very long to heartily agree with both the young lady and Mr. Bainbridge in regard to De Vere's mental state.

Several weeks then passed and one morning Mr. Bainbridge was in to see us.

"I am having lunch with De Vere at the Ritz tomorrow, and he has requested that I get from you a piece of Fabergé and have it packed in a little box, tied with string, and left unopened."

I asked Mr. Bainbridge what sort of piece of Fabergé he thought De Vere would like.

"Anything that you think might be pleasing to him." He then thought for a moment and continued, "I have to leave that entirely up to you."

I then went through our vitrines and selected a superb little paste pot carved from a solid block of the Russian fabricated red stone known as *pourpourine*. The little pot had a small hole in the top that held a tiny paste brush stemmed with sable hairs and with a fine Oriental pearl as a finial. The item was a dream in color and in the shape of a ripe tomato. As De Vere had asked us to do, we had the piece packed suitably and handed it to Mr. Bainbridge, who did not even inquire as to the cost. He said, "Whatever you charge must be left until later."

Next day after they had finished their lunch, Mr. Bainbridge again came in and reported that as soon as they were seated at their table at the Ritz, De Vere took the package from him and placed it in the center of the table, unopened, as he had requested.

They then began to eat, and De Vere said, "Please do not speak to me, as I hear the package talking to me and I do not wish to be disturbed."

As soon as they finished their meal, De Vere said, "Please send me your bill for this, and I shall at once mail you a check."

At this point neither De Vere nor Mr. Bainbridge had the slightest idea of the cost, nor, in fact, what was in the package.

Mr. Bainbridge then said, "Please mail De Vere your bill to Saint Anne's for as much as you wish; cost is no object."

The following week we received our check from De Vere. Mr. Bainbridge told us that De Vere was crossing to New York and that he would be visiting with our mutual friends the Hammer brothers: Armand, Harry, and Victor. In those days the Hammers had a very large establishment on Fifth Avenue and specialized in Fabergé and other Russian antiquities. Where they always held a most impressive collection of such works. Among their objects by Fabergé were several of the magnificent Imperial Easter eggs that Fabergé had created for the czar and other members of the Imperial Family and also for others in the royal circle.

A couple of weeks later Mr. Bainbridge told us that De Vere had acquired one of these Russian Easter eggs that he was going to bring back with him to London as a gift for his wife. He had informed Mr. Bainbridge that he always liked to bring home something nice whenever he traveled. Now if there was anything that De Vere enjoyed, it was a game of poker, and he wrote Mr. Bainbridge that he had met a gentleman at his hotel who had invited him to join in a "friendly game of poker" at his apartment. Mr. Bainbridge then went on to say that De Vere had written that he had accepted the "gentleman's" invitation with alacrity and that he had gone to the gentleman's apartment.

When he arrived he was greeted by a butler at the door and soon drinks were being served to a group of players who had already assembled. All, he wrote, was conducted with great propriety, and after a short while they sat down to play.

De Vere then commenced to win several important pots, and after a short while they said that they would like to raise the limit, to which De Vere agreed. All the while they were continuing to drink more and more, as a tray was being brought round continuously by the butler. At this point De Vere started to lose, and after a short while he had lost a very large amount. Then his "host" suggested that as it was getting rather late, they should play a last hand and then call it a day. De Vere then wrote out his check for his losses and returned to his hotel.

The next morning he was again in to see the Hammers at their shop and told them about his experiences of the previous evening.

Dr. Armand then told him that he had obviously been "taken" by a gang of card sharks, and he asked De Vere for the name and address of the "gentleman" who had invited him and also for the amount of the check that he had written.

Next day, by appointment, De Vere was again at the Hammers' shop, where the doctor awaited him with the money that he had lost. For this gentleman, Dr. Armand Hammer, as brilliant as he was in business, there was little that was impossible.

After this episode De Vere became entirely disenchanted with New York and, vowing never to set foot here again, returned to England. The moment that he landed he went straight up to Saint Anne's, and then as soon as he was home he handed a Fabergé Easter egg to his young wife. She took this from him and without a word placed it on a side table and left the room. She had scarcely given it a glance.

The mansion was an old one, as are so many English castle type homes, built of heavy stone. The walls of the rooms were of thick stone from floor to ceiling. Later that day De Vere and his bride had a violent quarrel. What the quarrel was about it is impossible to imagine. During the quarrel, noticing the Easter egg on the side table where she had placed it, she picked it up and threw it violently at De Vere's head.

As is quite usual in such circumstances, it missed his head and struck the stone wall, breaking up and falling to the floor in a thousand pieces. It was so broken that it was not even deemed repairable.

During his lifetime De Vere must have acquired quite a large collection of pieces by Fabergé, but what has happened to them is today unknown. It may be assumed that many pieces have suffered the fate of the Russian Easter egg.

I recall asking Mr. Bainbridge about this one day, but he had no ideas on the subject.

Chapter 15

Lady Brownlow and Confidential Message about Lord Brownlow's Leaving Bags in My Office

It was during the midthirties, when we were already installed in our new premises on Piccadilly, and with this move our business had increased enormously. We had a special shop front designed for us to be in keeping with the tradition of the Louis XVI style in France. In the front we had two windows, one of each side of a central doorway, and at each end we had pillars of green marble topped with golden finials.

Over the store we had another floor that was approached by a winding staircase in the rear, and across this entire front there was a very wide window that overlooked the street. This was an ideal spot to watch the various processions that passed on occasion, such as the famed Lord Mayor's Show, Royal Coronations, and such. Placing a row of chairs in this window afforded the equivalent of orchestra seats at the theater.

Being located, as we were, in the very heart of London's West End, we had an extensive international clientele, people coming in to see us from all parts of the globe—the United States, South America, India, and naturally, most nations in Europe, with the positive exception of the Soviet Union. It was indeed fortunate that I was able to converse in several foreign languages, particularly French, German, and Spanish, so that contact with our foreign callers was not too difficult. Actually, I was the only member on our staff who had this facility. And so it was that one morning in the early fall we were faced with a most interesting group of callers.

In our shop we had a series of small antique tables; some were of the Louis XVI period and some others of the English Regency. We were rather proud of these, as instead of having the traditional shop fittings and fixtures our interior seemed more like a large reception room than a shop. In all there were four of these tables spread harmoniously around the area. On many occasions some of our customers badgered us into selling them one or another of these tables, and this necessitated our continually being on the *qui vive* to find replacements.

On this particular day I was alone in the shop. Some of our staff were out at lunch and others out on other business when a French lady came in. She did not speak a word of English, and I seated her at one of the tables. Before she could even begin to tell me the reason for her visit, a very elegantly dressed Spanish gentleman came in, who similarly spoke no English, and I seated him at a second table.

Just as I was about to speak with the French lady, Marina, Duchess of Kent, entered, and she, being slightly lame, immediately seated herself at a third table. Seeing that I was alone and busy, she said that she was in no hurry to see me and would be happy to wait until I was able to attend to her. In any case she said that she was rather tired and would welcome the rest.

I then left her and went over to the French lady, and just as I was about to speak with her the door opened and a Hollywood producer entered, a man named Blumenthal. He could see that I was quite busy at the time and similarly said that he would wait for me.

I soon completed my business with the French lady, having sold her a very beautiful Louis XV gold and enameled snuff box from our collection, such boxes in those days forming a considerable part of our inventory. This sale did not take too much time, as the lady knew very well what she wanted. She told me that she already owned a considerable collection of these precious objects.

She was soon gone and then just as I began to approach the Spaniard, the door again opened and Lady Brownlow came in. Both Lord and Lady Brownlow were very well known in British royal circles, as His Lordship was at that time First Gentleman at the Court of King Edward VIII; actually this post lasted just about one year. Lady Brownlow, seeing Marina seated at one of the tables, went to the center of the shop and, in very theatrical fashion, gave her a low curtsy—this much to the interest of the Spanish gentleman. The producer, Blumenthal, did not seem to be in the slightest impressed.

I soon completed my business with the Spaniard and then went over to the duchess to see what I could do for her. She told me that she needed to find a nice gift for her husband, the Duke of Kent, and asked Lady Brownlow to assist her in her choice. After a short while Marina chose a small antique gold pillbox. Knowing the duke quite well, I knew that after receiving it he would put it into a drawer and forget all about it.

After I had completed my sale to the duchess, Lady Brownlow asked to speak with me confidentially and said she had a message from her husband, whom I knew well enough to call Perry; his name was Peregrine. The point of this confidential message was something that pertained to King Edward. Perry had asked her to find out from me whether it would be in order for him to leave his overnight bag in my office at any time, so that whenever he needed to cross to France he could do it incognito.

I told Lady Brownlow that I understood perfectly and that our offices were at his entire disposal at any time.

Lady Brownlow and the duchess then left, after Lady Brownlow told me that her chauffeur would be in later that same day to bring in Perry's overnight bag.

Later that afternoon the chauffeur did in fact arrive and I placed the bag in my private office.

I then spoke with Mr. Blumenthal, who it soon appeared was a man with plenty of talk but no real business for us, and he very soon left.

I then remained alone until various other members of our staff began to drift in and I went out to my club for what I considered a well-deserved lunch.

Chapter 16

Mrs. Levy and Her Battersea Enamel Collection

It was on a day in early April, during the early midthirties, that a very large open carriage arrived and stopped outside of our shop on Piccadilly. There were two men seated up front, one the driver and the other a footman, who immediately descended from his perch, dropped a small set of steps at the side of the carriage, and assisted a most elegantly gowned, very tall lady to step down.

She then entered our shop and, as I happened at that moment to be standing by the door, said to me, "I understand that you have some fine Battersea enamels from time to time, and I am interested in buying anything that you might have for my collection."

I replied that just at that moment we had nothing that we could offer her, but I promised to advise her of anything that came our way in the future.

She then gave me her telephone number and told me that she was the Honorable Mrs. Levy. She also gave me her address in Belgrave Square, in those days one of the most fashionable areas in London's West End.

The moment that I heard her name I knew that she was the heiress of the Shell Oil Company and also that her collection of Meissen porcelain was internationally renowned; I did not know that she was similarly a collector of fine Battersea enamels, although it was quite natural for a collector of such porcelains to collect Battersea, particularly because of the colorations in both. These Battersea enamels were named for the Battersea district of London, where a group of French Huguenots had established themselves during the eighteenth century, and it was here that they produced exquisite snuff boxes, cachou boxes, candlesticks, taper sticks, and many other small objects, all enameled in wonderful colors, primarily in pastel shades of apple green, pink, mauve, yellow, white, and blue. Many fine examples of these are today to be seen at London's Victoria and Albert Museum.

As soon as Mrs. Levy had left the establishment I made an entry in our special book about her interest and placed it aside.

It must have been about three weeks after this visit that my brother Bertram was approached one afternoon, while at his club, by another member, named Captain Emtage, who said to him, "Mr. Hill, I understand that your people have a business in Piccadilly where they deal in all types of antiques, and I wonder whether they might be interested in handling a very fine collection of Battersea enamels that I own and which I must sell as quickly as possible, as I am in very urgent need of cash."

My brother told him that he would speak with us and give him an answer, even later that same day.

Telephoning us immediately, Bertram asked me what I knew about Battersea enamels, as he himself had no idea what they were. I at once told him about the visit that we had received from Mrs. Levy and to tell the captain to bring his collection in for us to see, because if the pieces were in fact as fine as he suggested they were, business could be done in short order.

After hanging up the phone, Bertram at once contacted the captain, who was at that moment waiting for him in the club, and told him that we were very interested in seeing the collection. The captain then suggested that he would come to the shop the next morning and bring the collection with him.

Next morning when I arrived at the shop, there was the captain waiting for me with a large suitcase. He told me that he had spoken with my brother, who told him of our possible interest. We then entered the shop, and as soon as we were there the captain opened his case and began to place his pieces of Battersea enamel on our table. As he did this I saw some of the most exciting pieces that I had ever seen, one more beautiful than the other. In the collection there were several large snuff boxes, which are as rare as the proverbial hen's teeth.

I told the captain that I was sure that we could place most if not all of the pieces quickly, if he would leave them with us. As I now recall there were about fifty items in the collection. We then went through the collection piece by piece and established individual prices for each. He said that he would be satisfied if we were only able to sell a few pieces, as he needed ready cash as soon as possible.

The moment that he left, and as soon as I had gone through the group piece by piece, I segregated them into color groups and then telephoned Mrs. Levy and told her about the collection of Battersea that had just come in. She said that she was quite excited at what I had told her and that she would be in early next morning, exacting a promise from me that I would not show the collection to anyone else until she had the first sight. I assured her that I would not let anyone know that I even had the collection until after her viewing.

I was confident that if she liked what we had to show her she would want to acquire most if not all of the pieces, and I was happy, because the captain had made such a point of his requirement of immediate cash and as he seemed to be a very nice person, I wanted to help him as much as I could

Next morning, quite early, and as she had promised, Mrs. Levy was again at our shop in her carriage. I showed her the pieces all laid out on our table. She was quite overwhelmed, as the collector I knew she had to be. With scarcely a glance she at once selected about half of the group, including the best specimens and of course the very large snuff boxes, which she said that she did not even know existed. She then asked me the cost of her selection and at once wrote her check.

She then said, "Would you please have my selection packaged so that I can get my man to put them in my carriage?" She then added, "Whenever I make any additions to my collection I cannot wait until I get into my library to 'play' with them."

As she requested, I had our man make the package up, and her footman put the package in the carriage and she left. Before she went she told me that she intended to furnish one of her rooms with the Battersea and that she had already ordered a series of special cabinets that were to line her walls, each of the cabinets reserved for a single color, each fitted with concealed lighting so that the beauty of the objects would be appreciated to the fullest. She then just as she was leaving said, "As soon as the cabinets are in situ I shall invite you to visit me and see what I have done."

Next morning she was again in the shop and asked to be shown the balance of the group that she had passed over, adding,

"I have returned as I want to be sure that I did not miss anything yesterday."

We then again had the pieces placed on the table for her study and she then went through them again.

"The reason that I did not buy these other pieces was because they are all in tones of sepia or gray and I prefer pieces of higher color. However, I am going to take them all and I shall have two extra cabinets made to contain them." Saying this, she then wrote out her check for the total. She again requested that the items be packaged so that she could take them home with her.

While waiting she remarked she would like to tell me why she was so interested in these objects, and I replied that I would like to know very much indeed. She then recounted the following story.

"As a very young man my father was quite poor and commenced to make a living by collecting the colorful shells that abound at the seaside. These he set into small objects that he sold to tourists as 'presents' from Brighton or Eastbourne or any of the other English seaside resorts.

"After he had been doing this for some years, he was invited by some of his Dutch friends to join in with them in an oil venture." At that time the oil business was in its infancy.

"He did join with them, and after he had become part of the company, they suggested that they should have a name. My father then suggested, 'Why not call it the Shell Oil Company?' They all followed his thinking, and of course today this name is respected throughout the world."

The moment that her package was ready, Mrs. Levy again thanked me for having given her the opportunity with this collection, and after asking me to promise to call her if any other pieces of similar nature came our way, she left.

As soon as she was out of the door I called the captain and told him that all of his pieces had been sold and that he could come round and collect his check whenever he wanted to. He was overjoyed and it seemed to me that he was round at the shop before I had finished speaking with him: "Mr. Hill, you have just about saved my life with the money." I then suspected that he may have been in the hands of some loan sharks.

After this about a month passed and I received a telephone call from Mrs. Levy inviting me to her home to see the collection that she told me was now in her "Battersea room."

I thanked her and told her that I would be round the next day.

When I arrived I was ushered into an anteroom and told by the butler that the lady would be down to greet me in a few minutes. While waiting I was able to see some of her Meissen porcelains, similarly displayed in another room, and I must say that what I saw was of the finest quality imaginable. I could see at once her reason for collecting fine Battersea. After the space of about ten minutes Mrs. Levy came down and invited me into her "Battersea room."

This was a large room, the elongated walls of which were in an oval, surrounded with the series of cabinets that she had ordered, and incidentally, these cabinets were themselves in the nature of works of art. In each of the cabinets she had placed her specimens. There was a "green" cabinet, a "blue" cabinet, a "mauve" cabinet, a "pink" cabinet, and so forth, each of them fitted with concealed lighting, and the effect in the room, which was darkened, was quite breathtaking. This was one visit that after all these years I always recall with great pleasure.

It was a short time after I had visited with Mrs. Levy that her husband passed away, and she later remarried another gentleman and became Mrs. Basil Ionides. Today her collections are always referred to under this new name.

Several years then passed and I never again was able to make Mrs. Ionides any more offers. The war had come and gone and I was in London together with my wife, Leona, and after having told her about the wonderful Levy/Ionides collection of Battersea, I told her that we should go to the Victoria and Albert Museum to see it, as Mrs. Levy had at one time suggested that she would be leaving the collection to this museum and after this passage of time she had of a certainty passed away. However, at the museum I could get no information about her collection of Battersea and I had to presume that perhaps during the terrible bombardment of London the collection may have been destroyed.

Later, while I was speaking with another dealer friend of mine, he told me that the entire Ionides collections were dispersed at auctions during the early sixties and that the speciments were spread over many collections and that some of the pieces were, in fact, in the Victoria and Albert Museum.

Despite my inquiries, I could not discover whether the museum had itself acquired any of the specimens by purchase or, in fact, by gift by a donor. It was quite distressing to learn that she had not left the entire somewhat fabulous group to the museum as planned, but I was gratified that at least the pieces were not casualties of the war.

Our first transaction with Captain Emtage having been so satisfactory for him, he came in to see me again.

"I have decided that I have to go to work, and I propose going to commence trading in the jewel markets. I know that I can do an excellent job because my friends all over the world will buy from me."

He then continued, "Would you be prepared to help me get started?"

I told him that we would be most happy to assist him in any way that we could.

He then said, "As a matter of fact, I just have a gentleman who has commissioned me to find a nice gold cigarette box for him, and if you can lend me one I can let you have the cash in a few days."

I gave him a nice gold case, and he left.

A week then passed and I did not see the captain. One week turned into two weeks and then two into three, so I telephoned him and asked for the return of the case or the cash and he replied, "I cannot get the case back from my client, and I have no money to pay you for it."

I remonstrated with him.

"Listen, once in conversation with me you said that you could only be swindled once by any one person. Now I am swindling you, and what are you going to do about it?"

I was so taken aback by his effrontery that all that I could do was laugh.

He then continued talking about his Battersea collection, as he quite obviously wished to change the subject as quickly as possible.

"When I made my collection, I studied the subject of Battersea in great depth and found that the subjects on the enamels were drawn after the great eighteenth-century triumvirate of painters—Boucher, Fragonard, and Watteau."

I told him that I knew this quite well. I also knew that he had kept the conversation going so that I would let the matter of the cigarette box drop, which I did.

After this the captain must have fallen to a very low financial ebb, and a few weeks later I hailed a taxi and saw that he was the driver. Without turning his head, but seeing me in his rear mirror, he said, "As far as you are concerned I am a taxi driver who does not know you, nor do you know me."

When I left his cab I gave him an enormous tip, probably the largest that he had ever received or was ever likely to get at any time in the future.

Chapter 17

The Skeffington-Smythe Story

At their auction sales of jewels at Christies' of London there are always masses of jewels of all types and periods being offered for sale. Thus it happened that on one occasion while viewing the items to be included in a forthcoming sale we saw what we considered to be an absolute must for us. It was to our mind a certainty that were we to place this as a central feature in our window display it would create quite a sensation. As it is always interesting to discover the origin or at least the names of the previous owners of such a piece, we endeavored to do this, but in this we were unsuccessful. We decided that we would buy this piece at any cost. Actually, it is almost impossible to place any specific valuation on such a jewel.

We were present on the day of the auction, and within an hour the piece was ours. It was the type of jewel that can be termed either a necklace or a sautoir. Shortly after the end of the auction we collected the jewel at the desk and returned with it to our offices. Once there we contacted our jeweler to take it away and clean it up. It was quite dirty and had not, in all probability, been touched in many a year.

Our man returned with the piece after about three days, and at this point it was an absolute knockout as far as we were concerned.

We at once placed it as a central feature in our window, where it displayed its magnificence to the full. We knew from experience that it would not be too long before we had some callers in to view it. It was a true connoisseur's jewel.

As we expected, about two days later we received a caller who came in to see it. This was on one of those very foggy days in November when we never expected to receive anyone.

This caller was a young gentleman. Quite tall, he must have been about six feet in height, immaculately dressed, his shoes shined to a brilliance that bespoke the hands of an old-fashioned gentleman's gentleman. The man wore a traditional bowler hat and carried an umbrella that appeared to have a handle by Fabergé. He looked like a millionaire, and later we were to discover that he was just that. He asked our assistant whether he might see the sautoir out of the window and in his hands.

"I saw it in your window yesterday when passing during the afternoon, but I was in a great hurry and could not stop in.

"However, I dreamt about it all night, so as you can see, I came in as early as I could today, fog or no fog.

"In fact," he continued, "I was afraid that I might lose it if I hesitated."

My assistant took the jewel from the window and handed it to him and then invited him to take a seat at one of our tables.

As soon as he was seated and had it in his hands he commenced to fondle it lovingly, as though it were a baby. At this point the assistant came into my office and asked me to come out and see the gentleman and discuss the jewel with him.

I told him that in our opinion the sautoir must have been created to a special order, and possibly for someone who owned the rather remarkable set of emeralds.

After we had been chatting for some little time the gentleman inquired the cost. He did this quite casually, as though this were a matter of little consequence to him.

He then said after I had told him the price, "I would like to buy the piece from you, and I would like you to keep it for me until tomorrow, when I shall give you a definite answer." I told him that we would be happy to do this for him.

He then told me that his name was Terence Skeffington-Smythe and that he lived in his own townhouse on Belgrave Square. Then saying good-bye he rose and left.

The following morning when reading the *Times*, I noticed that a young man of his name had seen a man robbing a jeweler's shop on one of the side streets off Pall Mall and had brought him down with a rugby tackle. This accounted for the young man's athletic appearance. Later that day, and as promised, he again came in and told me that he had decided that he would buy the necklace. I then asked him about the report in the press and he laughed. "As far as I was concerned, it was a lot of fun, as I played rugby at school when I was on the school team."

He then said, "If you don't mind, would you continue to hold the necklace for me for a couple of days until I receive my allowance, when I shall bring you the cash to pay for it."

I replied that this was in order and as far as we were concerned the necklace was his.

A couple of days passed and the gentleman entered and handed me a thick wad of bills; this was for an enormous amount of money. I did not find out until later why he did not pay us by check, which would have been more normal for so large an amount.

We then began to talk about things in general, and he told me that he had always loved and admired beautiful jewels and that he loved to handle them. Then almost as an afterthought he said, "Isn't it a damned nuisance? I have lost one of my pearl evening dress studs, and I suppose that I shall have the nuisance of telling my insurance company about it."

I then asked him what sort of pearl stud it was, and he replied, "Just a largish pearl."

I replied that if he gave me the name of his insurance company we could handle the matter of the loss on his behalf.

"If you would do that for me it would be wonderful," was his reply.

He then gave me the necessary information, and as soon as he had gone we telephoned the insurance company and arranged to have them draw a check and mail it to him in our care, so that we could settle the matter of the claim for him.

The following week we received the check from the company, and then I telephoned him and asked him to stop by and collect it.

Next day he came in and when I handed the check to him he said, "Oh, dear, now what do I have to do with this?"

I was of course quite taken aback at this reply. "You should deposit it at your bank."

He then replied, "But I have never done anything like this before and have never been near a bank. Every two weeks a young man comes to my home and brings my allowance in cash, and that is how I paid you the other day. I have never had any occasion to visit the bank or make deposits there."

I then asked this rather strange character what sort of work or profession he followed and he replied, "Oh, I do not do anything, nor have I ever done anything."

"Don't you have anyone looking after your affairs for you?" I asked, and he replied, "No, I don't, and perhaps you might be willing to act for me in all matters?"

I must say that I was quite stunned at his reply as, after all, I had only known him for a couple of weeks and I had only one transaction with him, and in any case we had not become more associated with him than as a jeweler and his customer. Nevertheless, I agreed. "Yes," I said, "if you wish me to act for you, I shall be happy to do so, but only in conjunction with my attorney."

"Whatever you arrange will be fine with me," was his reply.

While he was still at my desk I telephoned my attorney and arranged to be at his office next morning with the gentleman who wished me to act as a trustee for him. The attorney said that in principle he understood precisely what would be required.

Next morning, as we had arranged, we met at the attorney's office and I introduced Terry to him. By this time I was already calling him by the name of Terry.

The attorney then placed some papers before him, which he asked Terry to sign, and which Terry did, without so much as a glance at what he was signing.

In effect, Terry had handed over to me everything that he owned, including his townhouse, and I was to arrange everything on his behalf without any questions. He passed over to me the right to all of his money, and I was to be the only person who could write checks in his name. This was quite a responsibility, as he owned many hundreds of thousands of pounds sterling.

The next day he was in again to see me and to thank me for what I had done for him.

"You have no idea," he said, "how relieved I am that you are going to look after my affairs for me. It is too wonderful of you to go to all this trouble on my behalf."

Later that afternoon the attorney called me. "That was the most extraordinary matter that I have ever been called upon to arrange." He then continued, "I have been going through the

97

matters that Terry has put into your hands, and it is certainly in the area of several millions' worth of securities."

I then discussed with the attorney what he considered our remuneration should be for the work that would be entailed. He then replied, "Let this stand for the time being until we see how much work is required. And in any case I would need several weeks to ponder the matter."

Later that same day the attorney called me back and suggested that I make Terry an underwriter at Lloyd's of London. I told him that I considered that this would be excellent and at least it would give him something to think about.

At this point I was in the position, had I wished to do so, that I could write myself a check for whatever salary I wanted to collect from him.

Later that same week Terry was again in to see me and, after again thanking me for what I had done for him, said, "I am thinking of getting married, and I would like to bring the young lady in question in to introduce her to you." As he spoke he showed me a very magnificent diamond tiara interspersed with sapphires.

"I would like to have you make a copy of this in paste jewels, so that after our marriage my wife can wear it at court functions and she will never know the difference and I will not have to pay any more insurance on it." He then added, "I would like you to accept this original one as payment for the copy."

He then proceeded to buy several other pieces of jewelry that he wanted to give to his fiancée and I drew myself a check in payment. By this time I had been inscribed at the bank and could draw against his funds at will. Terry then told me that he was closely related to a lady whose name was Countess of Something—I do not at this time recall her name precisely. He also told me that his forebears were probably represented in every rank of the Peerage and Baronetage.

From that day on I began receiving mail on his behalf, as he had gotten his secretary to write to all and sundry that in future his address would be in my care. The mail that then began to arrive consisted of letters from all sorts of titled gentry, lords, ladies, duchesses, knights, earls, etc., etc. As he had said he would do, Terry then brought the young lady in to see me, and she told me that although she was born in England she was half Dutch and half Indonesian, an exotic combination that frequently accounts for great beauty. She was an exquisite beauty. Terry then showed her the emerald sautoir that I had been holding for him in our vault and told her that this was to be her wedding gift. She was naturally thrilled and delighted and told me so.

After this, Terry seemed to make a regular stop at our shop every day. On one of these visits Terry said that he had decided to have a very quiet wedding, as otherwise, he said, "I would have to invite half of the House of Lords, and I don't want to be bothered." He then continued, "I shall be in to see you again very soon about our honeymoon plans."

Then a couple of days later he was in again and said, "We have arranged to go on a trip round the world, and I would like you to arrange all matters with your travel agent."

He then continued talking: "I would want you to book three roundtrip tickets for me, as I will be taking another young gentleman with us. I think that we should make our first port of call at Shanghai."

I thought that this was a very strange request, but it was his affair and not mine.

He then said that he would be in again very soon, as he wanted to buy several other pieces of jewelry for his fiancée.

When eventually they did arrive to see me they had with them the young man who was to accompany them on their trip. He was quite unmistakably a homosexual, and after they left I discovered he had dropped several small rouge pads on the floor, the sort of thing one might expect to find in a lady's handbag.

By this time I had concluded that Terry was gay, although in the thirties such thoughts were not so uppermost in people's minds as they are today. Who the young man was I could not make out, nor did I know whether he was being included in the party as a boyfriend for Terry or for the new wife to be.

After this I was deluged with letters and all sorts of bills that I had to pay on Terry's behalf. The bills came from coutourières, tailors, milliners, and bootmakers and also for some repairs to his house.

Then his butler called to tell me that he was having trouble with the roof on the house and also that the toilets were not flushing too well and he wanted me to instruct some contractors to do the necessary repairs. In retrospect I concluded that the butler had arranged to get a share of whatever the contractor charged. Despite this, I called the butler and told him to have the work put in hand and to have the bill mailed to me for payment.

A few days later I received all the tickets for the round-the-world trip and I called Terry and told him that all was ready for him to collect and that I had them in my hands for him.

Next day all three were in again, collected the tickets, and, saying good-bye, left.

After they had gone I continued receiving innumerable letters for Terry, all of a very personal nature, and as arranged with Terry, I opened all mail and sent on to him all those letters that he might enjoy seeing; others were deposited in my wastebasket.

Most were from people in high society and addressed to, "My darling Terry" or "My dear Terry," and there were some addressed to "My Darlingest Terry." Those that were to be forwarded I mailed to Shanghai marked "To await arrival."

It must have been about a month after they had departed that returning one day from lunch, I noticed a newsboy carrying a placard. Now I had never bought any midday newspapers, as basically they were mostly concerned with the horse races that did not interest me. But on this occasion the placard took my eye, as it read: "Young Englishman found dead in a Shanghai opium den." Of course I had no reason to suppose that this had anything to do with Terry, except that I knew that about that time Terry must have arrived in Shanghai, but I bought the paper.

Sure enough, it stated in a short report that a young Englishman named Terrence Skeffington-Smythe had been found dead in an opium den in Shanghai. Whether he had died of an overdose I had no way of knowing. Whether he had been murdered for the money that he had with him I could not say.

After all, I felt that Terry would have had his pockets stacked with cash. As far as I now recall this was before the days when travelers carried traveler's checks; they usually had letters of credit, and I was sure that if Terry had anything of this nature I would have been asked to arrange it for him.

Immediately I had several things that I had to do. First, before they left I had arranged a life insurance policy on Terry in the sum of ten thousand pounds. In those days this was quite a large sum, and I had to call the insurers and advise them of the loss and tell them that they would have to pay out the ten thousand pounds. This was a most unpleasant thing for me to do.

However, I made this call, and later that same afternoon I received a call from the managing director of the insurance company, who said that he wished to speak with me personally. When I was on the line he said, "I know, Mr. Hill, how unpalatable it must have been for you to tell us of this loss, and the only way that you can repay us is to bring us another policy." He then continued, "Our public relations people will make very good use of this claim, and this will probably be worth much more than the ten thousand pounds."

I then realized that with Terry's death my responsibility ceased, and I had not at that time received a single penny for my work on his behalf; neither had my attorney. I could not get it into my mind that Terry had died from any overdose of dope, and I concluded that he must have been murdered. I then discussed the matter with a friend of mine, a detective at Scotland Yard.

"If you take my advice you will do nothing about the matter, as you will get nowhere fast with the Shanghai police," he told me.

After hearing this, I decided to forget all about the matter. From that day on I never heard a word from the wife nor the young man that they had taken with them. However, I knew that she must have inherited all of Terry's fortune.

Thus the matter must now forever remain somewhat of a mystery.

Chapter 18

Lord Vestey's Cruise—West Africa and Rail Tickets to the Ashanti Mines

It was some time after our father had passed away that my family decided that it would be better for us to return to the London of our birth and leave the house that we had been occupying in the suburbs. At that time an apartment house in the Regent's Park district of London was in process of construction. This house was being acclaimed to be as fine as anything of its type that had ever been built in London or, in fact, anywhere in England. It was stated to be the prototype of the finest in New York City. Together with my sister, two brothers, and our mother, I went to view it. After walking over innumerable girders and planks of wood that had been laid down purposely, we all decided that this was where we wanted to live. The location was ideal and the layout seemed perfect.

We immediately signed a lease.

This apartment house stood in its own grounds, with a garden in the rear, and was situated at Hanover Gate in London's northwest district. It was actually on the fringe of Regent's Park.

Behind this house stood the very large mansion that had been erected for Barbara Hutton, which as far as I can recall she never occupied for even one night. Later she presented the house to America for use as the home for the ambassador. Fortunately, it was left undamaged by the wartime bombing.

It was some six months after we had signed our lease that we were able to take up our tenancy. After residing in the house for several months, we began to get on to a friendly basis with several of the other tenants, and among these there were some of England's famous.

One was Sir Thomas Beecham, the famed conductor whom I used to meet on occasion either descending or ascending in the elevator, and who would invariably be waving his arms as though conducting a symphony concert.

Besides Sir Thomas there was the family of the Honorable Leonard Vestey and his wife, Marjorie, with whom I became on a very friendly basis, and as the house stood in its own garden we would often meet there to stroll around after dinner.

Leonard and Marjorie, whom by this time I called Lenny and Margie, frequently invited me into their apartment to chat. In the course of conversation Lenny told me something of his family background. He was a son of Lord Vestey, an enormously wealthy man who owned vast cattle ranches in the Argentine and who shipped the beef back to England in his own fleet of ships, the Blue Star Line. When the beef arrived in England it was at once transhipped for sale at retail at the thousands of butcher shops that he owned and which were spread far and wide throughout England. During the winter months when no beef was shipped, Lord Vestey had his flagship, the *Arandora Star*, transformed into an all first-class cruise liner.

It was one winter a few weeks before Christmas that Lenny told me that his father had promised him and Marjorie a cruise round West Africa as a Christmas gift and he had at the same time told him that he could include in his gift two of his friends. What a wonderful surprise it was for me when both Lenny and Marjorie invited me to join them as one of their guests; the other was to be his niece, whom they called Jimmy.

I must say that when I received this invitation I was quite taken aback. The prospect of such a cruise was just too fabulous. I could not believe my ears, and I accepted with alacrity.

Lenny then outlined the projected itinerary. We were to leave from Southampton and cruise down the South Atlantic to the west coast of Africa, where our first port of call was to be British Gambia. After leaving there we were to continue farther south as far as the then Gold Coast, today's Ghana, and after leaving there we were to return north, calling at Las Palmas and the Canary Islands.

The cruise was quite superb, particularly as the weather was excellent, and as I was traveling with the owner's son, we were greeted on all sides by high government officials at every port at which we docked. While in Gambia we were met by the British colonial agent, who invited us to be his guests at the British Club, and we all accepted with pleasure.

This British Club stood in a clearing in the jungle. It was a square wood-paneled room set up on high stilts and approached by a series of steep wooden steps, much like a giant child's tree-house.

We were invited to climb these stairs, and actually we were not sorry to get away from the ground, as we saw a very ugly group of carrion birds lined up beside a sluggish stream in which lay several crocodiles.

In the club we were received by several stewards, all in starched whites, standing at attention and looking like soldiers, which they probably were. We were then escorted to a large wood table and invited to be seated while one of the stewards inquired what we would like to drink, we all asked for Planter's Punch with the exception of Lenny, who was a teetotaler.

While the barman was preparing our drinks we saw what looked like an enormous bug swooping around the room. It appeared to be about the size of a small pussycat. Now none of us were heroes and we did not care for this bug one little bit.

I then called one of the stewards over to our table and asked him about this flying bug. "Tell me," I said, "are these flying things dangerous?"

He at once replied, "Oh, yes, sir, they are very dangerous indeed, but if you don't interfere with them they will not interfere with you."

We were, none of us, happy with this reply and all found that we were not at the moment very thirsty. Calling over our host, we told him that we had another very important meeting that we had to attend on the boat, and saying our good-byes, we very hurriedly left.

Putting the matter very bluntly, all four of us were quite petrified with fear.

After leaving Gambia, we cruised for some forty-eight hours until we tied up at Takoradi, the Gold Coast port. Here again we were greeted by the colonial governor general, who asked us whether we could care to go upcountry and visit the famed Ashanti Gold Mines.

Lenny looked over at me. "Knowing of your interest in gold, would you like to visit these mines?"

I naturally was delighted at the prospect, and we all agreed in unison to go. The following morning we were called for and escorted to the hut that served as a railroad station. This hut was set in a small forest clearing, and it was here that we were to buy our tickets for the local train that went up to the mines. After a short while we saw the train, a sort of Toonerville Trolley that had been sitting outside the hut awaiting our arrival. As we approached the ticket window we saw some twenty natives waiting in line to get their tickets, each naked except for a very dirty loincloth. Each carried a long spearlike object with which they worked in the mines.

I thought that we would get in line to get our tickets, but no. The agent, dressed in his Bermuda shorts and open-neck shirt and carrying a short cane under his arm, went over to the line of natives and switched them across their legs with it, whereupon they all cowered away and we were allowed to pass through to receive our tickets.

This horrified me and I could not wait until we boarded the train to speak to Lenny about it.

When I told him how disgusted I was with what I had seen he replied, "Oh, yes, I know just what you mean, but we have to keep the natives in their place; otherwise they might get too high-handed."

From my childhood I had been brought up at school to learn that in the British Empire the powers that be looked upon the natives, in all of the farflung colonies of the empire, as children who had to be protected. This was not, then, my idea of protection. In a flash I suddenly became entirely disillusioned, and it was just at that moment that the thought of possible immigration to the United States as an eventual possibility entered my mind.

It is today most interesting to reflect that past events do so frequently cast their shadows before them and perhaps do foretell the future. Today the great British Empire as it was in those days is but a memory, the natives having taken their rightful place in most of the nations of the world.

After we had visited the mines, while strolling through some of the native villages we saw many of the natives seated cross-legged outside their wood huts offering to sell us all sorts of little wood statuettes and figurines. Today this so-called tourist junk, to which I have always had an aversion, is being keenly sought by collectors of African art. At this same time I could have bought anything for pennies.

After leaving the Gold Coast, we started on our homeward journey and stopped off at the Canary Islands and several other places. I so enjoyed Las Palmas that I made up my mind that one of these days I would return and enjoy its beauty.

Many years have now elapsed, and together with my wife, Leona, I have returned to the various places. But with the rush of tourists with their ships and the loads of airplane travelers they have all lost their allure and charm.

There is thus so much truth in the saying that you cannot go back.

Shortly after the outbreak of war, the British authorities had rounded up most of the Italian maîtres d'hôtel throughout England (as a group they numbered some six hundred persons) and sent them off on the *Arandora Star* for internment in Canada. When the crowded ship was halfway across the Atlantic, it was attacked by German U-boats and sank with all hands, including the captain, who had been my very good friend during our cruise. He went down with his ship, in the true tradition of the British navy. Thus the *Arandora Star* was among one of the first casualties of the war.

Chapter 19

Visit to Lord Brownlow's Home

Besides being a very good customer of ours, Lord Peregrine Brownlow was a valued and intimate friend. He loved coming into our establishment and could talk with us for hours on end about art and antiquity. He was a connoisseur and collector of fine antiques and objets d'art, and whenever we purchased anything especially intriguing we would call him and he would then come in to see it; this sort of thing was ever his great joy, as he always told us.

One day during one of our chats, in the course of conversation, Perry, as we called him, told us all about the "Museum Room" up at his House Belton in the country. When I mentioned that my brother and I would love to see this room, Perry invited us to spend a weekend with him. Naturally we both accepted immediately. It was then arranged that we would drive up one Friday afternoon, spend the night at the house, and then return to London about midday on Saturday.

In due course we arrived at the mansion, and mansion it was in truth. It stood in a park situated about a mile from the front gates of his estate. What we saw was a truly magnificent edifice in purest Queen Anne style. Upon arrival, at the front door, we were greeted by two footmen, each attired in the Brownlow livery. One of these men took our bags and conducted us up a very long and wide staircase to the first floor. (Here in America it would be called the second floor.) We then entered a room that had been allocated for our use.

This bedroom was very large, covering what might be the area of an entire medium-sized New York apartment. As soon as we were settled in, the footman asked us to follow him, as he wished to show us where the bathroom was located. Otherwise, he said with a smile, we would never find it.

As it transpired, this was quite true, as the bathroom was a long way along a corridor that was lined with doors on both sides and all along its length. Without being shown, it would have been a sort of Chinese puzzle to find it, especially during the night. This bathroom was most unusual in that its walls were lined with a series of antique oil paintings and portraits, all of the seventeenth and eighteenth centuries.

In truth, this bathroom was in itself a museum in miniature, but here one could sit enthroned at the far end and study the paintings one after the other. After this visit to the bathroom we were again conducted back to our room and invited to freshen up after our drive from London.

The footman then informed us that he would leave us and return in about an hour to conduct us to His Lordship's living quarters downstairs. In due course, the footman returned and led us to a very large and most beautifully appointed living room, where Perry awaited us and where he introduced us to his sister and brother-in-law, Mr. and Mrs. Huth. Both were elegantly attired.

We then sat and chatted and had a drink together and Perry announced that after dinner he would have the pleasure of giving us a tour of the house and also of the "Museum Room."

After we had spent the better part of an hour or so over our drinks, we were again invited to go upstairs to dress for dinner. When we arrived at the bedroom we found that our dress clothes had been pressed for us by the valet and our cuff buttons were already in our shirts, so that we were ready to go.

After dressing we returned downstairs, where another footman was waiting to lead us into a magnificent dining room, where a central table had been laid for five with some of the renowned Brownlow silver. This family silver, all of the King Charles period, is very well known in art circles throughout the world. While dining, and the dinner was truly Lucullan, Perry told us something of the heirloom silver, saying that after dinner we would first visit the "Museum Room" and then go down to the silver vault and see all of his antique silver arrayed on a series of shelves round the small room.

The dinner was served on the Brownlow silver plates and platters, which, as Perry explained, had been in use by his predecessors of years gone by. Perry explained that all of this silver had been acquired by his ancestors during the periods of King Charles and Queen Anne. Nothing had been added since.

On finishing our repast we retired to an adjoining room, where over cognac and cigars Perry continued the fascinating history of his family. He told about his father, the late Sir Lionel Cust, for many years the private secretary to Queen Victoria.

After we had spent about an hour in this room Perry then suggested that we join him and go to the "Museum Room." In truth it was a museum in miniature and was the raison d'être of our visit. The walls on all sides were covered with memorabilia, and so were the tables that surrounded the entire room, all filled to overflowing with objects of antiquarian interest.

On one wall I noted a gold-handled sword hanging from a peg. I asked Perry whether there might be any particular history attached to this, and he replied, "But most definitely. This was the sword that was used by Her Majesty Queen Victoria when she raised a gentleman to the rank of Knight, and when at such ceremony the gentleman would kneel facing the queen, who would tap him on the shoulder using this sword and say, 'Rise, Sir——' and after which ceremony he would be entitled to use the title of 'Sir' and his wife that of 'Lady' in front of their names."

As I recall, one of the most interesting objects that we saw was a typewriter that Perry told us was the first such made in England, and which had been presented to the Queen. It was of highly colored mother of pearl and papier-mâché and could only be used by someone standing. It obviously had never been used.

In one of the showcase vitrines there was a series of gold and jeweled medals and orders of chivalry that had, over the years, been presented to members of his family by royalty and potentates from all over the world. Actually, there was so much in this "Museum Room" that it was quite impossible to absorb it all. Hanging on the walls beside the memorabilia there were paintings of all types and periods, each of some antiquarian interest.

After leaving this room, we went down to the silver vault. This was a long, narrow room all lined with green baize, and despite the lateness of the hour, a footman, wearing a green baize apron, stood polishing the silver that we had used at dinner. Perry informed us that it was this footman's job to check every piece of silver each evening to be sure that there was nothing missing. He also had to return each piece to its special allotted space on the shelves. This checking was done down to the merest salt spoon.

Shortly after this visit the Huths said good-bye and left, and we then said our goodnights and similarly left to go to bed.

When we arrived at the bedroom we found that our pajamas and slippers had been laid out for us. Our shoes had been shined to a brilliance that they had never previously achieved, and which they were never likely to achieve again.

After a most restful night, we arose next morning and went downstairs to the breakfast room, and while walking down the stairs, we saw at the foot a seventeenth-century sedan chair and noticed that it had been broken, as it stood leaning to one side, one of the legs having been snapped across its middle.

In the breakfast room Perry was seated at the table, his hair all tousled, wearing a very old and very dilapidated dressing gown. As we entered he invited us to join him. On a very, wide long sideboard that extended almost the entire width of the room there was every conceivable type of food for breakfast. There were the traditional English kippers, a must in most English homes, and there were scrambled eggs, kidneys, cereals, a variety of jams and preserves, breads, and naturally tea and coffee.

It seemed that there was sufficient to feed an entire regiment of soldiers. Everything had been placed on hot plates and was ready for eating.

In order to make some conversation with Perry, I asked him about the broken sedan chair that we had seen in the hall, and with a laugh he explained. "One weekend we had a rather large party here and among our guests was the young Lord Sele and Seale, having imbibed too much—he had been drinking all evening and had become quite drunk—had fallen down the stairs. Landing on top of this family sedan chair, he broke one of its legs." Perry then continued to reminisce. "In my opinion, it was a miracle that he did not break his bloody head."

I then asked why he had not had it repaired, and he replied that just at that moment he could not afford the cost of any such work.

This last remark was entirely unbelievable, as there was evidence of enormous wealth on all sides.

After finishing our breakfast and having thanked Perry for his great kindness and hospitality, we rose to leave and found that the footmen were standing at the main door with our bags already packed for us. These were the same footmen who had received us upon arrival. They asked for some remuneration for our stay at the house, at the same time informing us that if we did not "come through sufficiently" we would never again be included on their invitation lists.

We then handed them a handsome tip, and they explained that in conjunction with the other members of the household staff they always arranged large parties and that His Lordship had nothing whatever to say in regard to these. They continued to tell us that Perry never interfered with their list of guests. They then went on to explain that by arranging these large parties and by being the recipients of substantial remuneration from the guests they were able to get their wages.

While going through one of the sitting rooms the previous evening with Perry I noticed what appeared to be a superb Rembrandt oil portrait of a man, and despite the fact that it was hanging on a wall, I could see that it was clearly signed and dated at the center right. I asked Perry the history of this magnificent work of art, and he explained that after the death of his father, Sir Lionel Cust, the estate was involved in enormous inheritance taxes, and so finding himself with plenty of valuable antiques, he decided to sell some of them at auction to raise the necessary cash, again stating that at that particular moment he had been very short of funds. Thus he had sent a large consignment of all manner of objects to Christie's for inclusion in suitable auctions and among these goods he had included this painting. The portrait was at the time very dirty, as it had certainly not been touched since its painting, and in all probability any signature or date would have been obscured by time; there must have been several layers of grime on its surface. In the catalog it was recorded as "Attributed to Rembrandt" and a reserve figure of one hundred pounds had been placed on it.

Now old paintings attributed to Rembrandt are frequently offered at auctions, and as such they are not too well studied by the attending dealers. The painting was offered and remained unsold.

"Now a few days after the sale," said Perry, "I went over to Christie's to collect this unsold painting, and while it was being wrapped up for me by the porter I thought to myself that I could see no reason why it should not be a genuine Rembrandt, as I knew nothing had been added to the family treasures over these many years. So taking it away with me, I went over the road to see a firm of painting restorers whom I knew and left it with them for cleaning and restoration.

"They told me," he continued, "that the work would not take too long, and I arranged to pick it up myself in a couple of weeks."

He then went on speaking. "When eventually I returned to pick up my painting I was handed the portrait as you see it now, and at the same time the restorer stated that it was as fine an original Rembrandt oil as he had ever seen in his lifetime."

I do not know whether or not this Rembrandt is still in the Brownlow family at Belton, but if it is, in today's market it is certainly worth a small fortune. Original paintings by the great master Rembrandt van Rijn are today virtually unbuyable, and whenever such a one does come into the market it is most keenly sought by collectors and museums from all parts of the world.

Chapter 20

Country Auction and Cabinet Filled with Antiques

In our never ending search for fine antiquities it was one of our weekly chores to check through the out-of-town newspapers to see what auction sales might be reported in the press. At some of these country house sales there were often items of great interest for one or another reason. Many of these country houses contained from time to time objects of the greatest rarity.

One day we read that there was slated an auction sale to be held at a house up in the Midlands, and the announcement must have contained some mention of an interesting object to impel my brother and me to be present. On the day of the auction we left town quite early in the morning so that we could have an opportunity to view the lot before the hour announced for the sale to commence.

Upon arrival, we saw that there was a small collection of soi-disant antique jewels, but in the group we decided that there was nothing that could in the least be of interest to us. However, on going through several cabinets surrounding the walls we saw in one of them a very beautiful little Louis XV gold snuff box, causing us to feel it would pay us to stay and endeavor to buy it, so that in any case our trip would not have been a total loss.

This little box lay in a cabinet intermingled with all sorts of other items. All these other pieces we simply ignored; it was the box that was a real delight. We had the attendant open this cabinet and take the box out so that we could examine it, and when we had it in our hands we saw that it had been made by one of the leading French goldsmiths of the period. It was of gold bordered with enamel, and the top and bottom were inlaid with small pieces of striated agate. It was, in truth, a little dream, and we knew that we had to buy it at any cost.

The auction commenced precisely at two o'clock in the afternoon, and we had to stand around while a continuity of bits of old china, some chairs, and other odd pieces were disposed of.

113

After a couple of hours the lot containing the little box was offered for sale, and as it was so small an item, the auctioneer did not even bother to have it taken from the cabinet.

Fortunately for us, there were few buyers in the room for anything of this nature, and so it was knocked down to us for the sum of four pounds. This was, as far as we were concerned, a proverbial song.

We then had to wait around until all of the other items were disposed of before we could pay for and collect our little box.

When eventually we did go to collect it, we found that we had purchased not only the little box, but all of the other items that were in the cabinet. To say the least we were astonished, particularly when we found that our purchase also included about a dozen large porcelain vases of all types that stood around the base of the cabinet.

We then packed all of the pieces—there were some twenty in all—into a small carton, and as we found that we could only accommodate about four of the vases, we had to leave the others at the house.

Next morning when we arrived at our offices we unpacked the carton and found that the pieces that we had simply ignored were all of considerable antique interest. In this group there was an early nineteenth-century French perfume flacon of pure platinum; there was an iron casket inlaid with damascened gold of the seventeenth century and probably produced in Persia or some other place in the Near East. In addition to these two items there was a pair of wrought iron candelabra of miniature size that we still to this day retain on the mantelshelf of our cottage in Connecticut.

Beyond these special items there were other pieces of more or less minor appeal, the details of which I do not recall.

Now it happened that Lord Brownlow, the gentleman at whose house in the country we had spent the night, who was a regular caller, came in to see us and to have his weekly chat with us. And he arrived just as we were opening our carton. We told him all about our adventure of the preceding day, and he was most fascinated to see what we had in the carton. Seeing the little Louis XV snuff box, he took it in his hands and also asked whether he could buy some of the other items.

I told him that he could have anything that he wanted, except for several items that I wanted to keep for myself. Lord Brownlow was so good a friend that he was permitted to open our safes himself and take out anything. If there might be any item that he wanted to buy, all that he needed to do was hand to our assistant the little price tag that was on everything.

Just as he was leaving he said, "I would dearly love to buy the little gold box for myself, but I know that it is worth a lot of money and as I am at this moment in somewhat of a financial bind I will not even ask the price that you are asking for it."

At this time Lord Brownlow had been appointed First Gentleman at Court, and he was an old buddy of the king. It was because of this old friendship that the king had appointed him to this most exalted position at court. At this time the king was almost in semi-residence in Paris and in the company of Mrs. Wallace Simpson, and Perry had been asked by the king to act as his go-between between himself and Mr. Stanley Baldwin, the then prime minister.

So close, in fact, were we to Perry Brownlow that he began to leave his overnight bag in our offices so that he could travel between London and Paris incognito, as I mentioned previously. Perry was virtually crossing back and forth to Paris almost weekly at this time, and after one of these crossings he returned to see us one Monday morning. "I told Eddy all about the lovely little gold box that you showed me the other day, and he has asked me to select a small gold box that he can give to Mrs. Simpson as a present."

We then went through our trays of gold boxes and found one that Perry said he thought would be ideal, and he said that "Eddy" did not want to spend too much at this time.

Perry then said to me, "You know when Eddy asked me about getting a gift for Mrs. Simpson I thought that I was going to get you an order to create a complete set of Crown Jewels."

The following weekend Perry was again off to Paris, taking with him the little gold box that he had selected and which he wished to show to the king. The following Monday morning Perry was back and came in to see us. "Eddy loved the little gold box we selected and wants you to put a small diamond crown on the center of the lid before he gives it to Wally Simpson."

Now at this moment, nobody, including the king himself, knew whether Wally Simpson would be accepted by the Royal Family or not. It was at that time also positive that they were to be married. Was she going to be queen of England, and if not, would she be accepted as a royal duchess, or if not, what? If she were to become queen of England, she could use a Royal Crown. Otherwise, what would be the appropriate crown for her status?

Every degree of the Peerage or Baronetage has its distinctive crown or coronet, and as we did not wish to make any mistakes, we discussed the question with Perry, who himself knew all about the various crowns and coronets. It was then arranged that he would ask the king during the next visit to Paris.

Next weekend Perry was again off to Paris, and when he saw the king he spoke to him of our predicament and asked him for his opinion, to which he received the following reply: "How the bloody hell do you think that I know?" Eddy stated that this was the best laugh he had had in years, and said, "Tell Hill to call Mr. Cartier and ask him to send him a sheet of paper that he is making for Wally so that he can use the same crown as they are putting on her stationery." As soon as Perry had given me the king's instructions, I telephoned Mr. Cartier and told him what the king had requested.

Mr. Cartier responded to my request with a loud guffaw of laughter.

"What's so funny?" I said, and he replied, "I will tell you what is so funny. We have designed a bastard crown, and I shall send you a sheet of the paper so that you can copy the crown on your box. You will then be able to see for yourselves what we have invented."

Next day we received the sheet of stationery and at once set our man to work on making the crown in diamonds to be set on the top of the little box. In a couple of weeks the box was ready for delivery and Perry took it with him over to Paris.

Upon his return a few days later Perry told me that when the king saw what we had done he was delighted and also said that he knew that Wally would similarly be delighted. He then sent back the following message for me: "Tell Hill that I am delighted with what he has done for us." We were later told that when the

116

king gave the box to Wally Simpson she stated, "I shall never move without this box in my handbag."

Many years have now passed since the event, and one day my wife, Leona, was at her hairdresser's in New York, Roger Vergnes, whose wife had been Wally Simpson's private secretary for a short while in Paris while Roger had been her hairdresser. Leona took a small gold box out of her handbag that I had given her to hold some little cachous, and when she saw this, Mrs. Vergnes said, "You know, Mrs. Hill, your little box is just like the one that the Duchess of Windsor always carries in her handbag, and she always refers to it as her favorite gift from the king."

This was not at all surprising, as both of these little boxes emanated from the same womb.

It was shortly after the time that the king had given the small box to Wally Simpson, and just after the opening of the London season, on one of those beautiful days when one would have preferred to be out on the golf course rather than in an office at work when we received a telephone call from Buckingham Palace.

It was from Queen Mary's private secretary, who said to me, "Mr. Hill, I am calling you at the request of Her Majesty to tell you that she wishes to call at your shop tomorrow at one o'clock to view your collection of antiques."

I replied that we would be honored to receive Her Majesty as she suggested.

Now what was quite exciting about this call was the fact that the queen was coming round to see us herself at our shop, something she had never previously done. Whenever we had any business dealings with the queen I had always been received by her in her private quarters at Buckingham Palace. Not only had the queen never set foot in our shop, she never seemed to visit anyone else in our vicinity. Situated as we were in the heart of Piccadilly and quite near Piccadilly Circus, an area much frequented by hookers, it was universally accepted that this was the reason she always kept away from this part of town.

Next day promptly at one o'clock, a large open Royal Coach stopped outside of our door. There were two footmen in Royal Livery on the coach, one in back and the other seated up front next to the driver. One footman then stepped down from his perch and lowered a small row of steps at the side of the coach, whereupon the Queen alighted, followed by Mary, Princess Royal, and two ladies-in-waiting.

As this was now the heart of the London season and the weather was really beautiful, the street was crowded with pedestrians. As soon as the public saw the Royal Coach, all traffic stopped, and in about five minutes Piccadilly was jammed with cars, taxis, and people, right from Piccadilly Circus at one end to the Ritz Hotel at the other. Everything had stopped moving. There were people actually standing on top of taxis to see what was going on.

As is customary, I received the Queen at the door and welcomed her to our establishment. "Would you kindly step upstairs with me, ma'am?"

She then followed me to the rear of the shop, and we all went up to our large upstairs gallery.

As soon as we were there the Queen said to me, "Mr. Hill, I have never previously been here to see you at your shop, but now both Mary and I would love to see all the lovely things that I know you have."

As soon as she said this I asked one of our assistants to bring out some trays of "things" from our safes and lay them on a side table.

As soon as they were in situ the Queen began to examine each and every piece quite slowly, all the while asking me all sorts of questions about some of the pieces. It seemed to me that she was doing this in slow motion.

She then continued looking at all the objets d'art for about two hours, during which time she asked Mary to come and look at this or that piece. It was obvious that she had no intention of making any purchases at this time, as she had not as yet even inquired the cost of any item.

There were trays with all sorts of antique gold boxes, Renaissance jewels in gold and enamel, rare horological specimens, small Fabergé objects, and many other things of a similar nature.

She then walked over to the front window and, looking out at the crowds assembled on the sidewalk, said, "Mr. Hill, isn't it a shame that whenever the public sees my coach all the streets jam up and become virtually impassable?" All that I could do was agree with her.

Then returning to a table, she picked up a superb eighteenth-century English snuff box made up of two enormous facetted topazes and, turning to Princess Mary, said, "Mary, do you remember the gold box with the topaz top and bottom that I gave some years ago to your dear papa as a present?"

And Mary replied, "Yes, Mama, I remember it quite clearly."

It was now approaching about three o'clock, and the Queen again turned to Mary. "Don't you think that it is high time that we went home, Mary?"

Apparently the princess agreed with her, and after they had thanked me for my courtesy to them, we all went downstairs and they left.

As the party emerged into the street the public began to cheer them and this cheer soon turned to a roar. Now from our experience we knew that it was almost unheard of for the Queen to remain at anybody's shop for more than an hour at most, and we could not understand why she had selected this particular day to visit us. It was quite soon after she left us that we were to discover the reason behind this visit. It was later that afternoon that King Edward VIII made his historic and famous speech over the radio announcing that he was abdicating the throne for "the woman I love" in favor of his brother. It became quite obvious to us why the Queen had visited our shop on that particular day and why she had spent so much time with us. There were always more people on Piccadilly than perhaps on any other street in London, and she wished as many people as possible to see her. Of a certainty she knew that Edward was about to make his radio speech later that day and wished the public to know: "The king is dead. Long live the king."

Chapter 21

Javeri and His Pearls

There are jewel merchants and there are jewel merchants, but such a rara avis as a Hindu gentleman named Javeri must inevitably stand head and shoulders above all others. Javeri, whose name, incidentally, means "jeweler," was a member of the little known Hindu sect of Jain, whose members are renowned for their utter piety and adherence to their faith. This faith precludes them from eating anything from which life can grow, and thus their eating costs are reduced to a minimum.

Javeri was a London-based pearl merchant's go-between and a man who in the normal course of his business carried with him enormous shipments of Oriental pearls that were consigned to him for sale by pearl merchants in his native India. These pearls were always sent in bundles, and it was Javeri who graded them on the owner's behalf. As a man he was loved and honored for his great honesty across several continents and especially in the capitals of Europe. It was customary for him to receive these original consignments of pearls in bunches always tied together as "original bunches" as they were called, and it was these bunches that he offered to possible buyers. It was always understood by buyers that as soon as the cord of any bunch was cut, the pearls became the property of the buyer who had cut it. This was a somewhat curious way in which to conduct business, but it was the way that the Hindu owners operated.

The merchants in India would never place any price on any bunch of pearls. But Javeri would submit the bunches to his prospective customers, who would then make him their offers, which he would submit to his principals in India. These merchants then would either accept or refuse the offers. If the offers were refused, Javeri would then endeavor to get the buyers to increase their bids, until eventually a price was established that was acceptable to the owners.

Of a certainty, all of such bunches of Oriental pearls were of great value. At any time Javeri might have in his possession, even carrying on his person, many thousands of pounds' worth of unsold pearls. These consignments were in fact of so great a value that Javeri had a specially constructed valise that he carried with him at all times held handcuffed to his right wrist, much in the same manner as diplomatic messengers carry their pouches of documents whenever they traveled.

As in those days Hatton Garden was the center of the London jewel trade, it was along this narrow thoroughfare that Javeri was to be found. Here the sidewalks were usually crowded with jewel merchants, who were frequently seen clustered together, actually conducting their business of buying and selling right in the street.

And so it was that on one afternoon in spring when the street was perhaps more crowded than usual, Javeri was making his way to meet an important client with whom he had an appointment to show some of these bunches of pearls that had that week arrived from India. Suddenly he was attacked by three men, one of whom threw pepper into his eyes while the others attempted to snatch his valise.

The valise was at the time filled with a particularly valuable group of pearls, but as this was fastened to his wrist, the thieves found that they could not get it away from him.

The thieves, finding that the crowds were beginning to approach Javeri, who had begun to scream in pain, started to run away, leaving the almost blinded Javeri lying on the sidewalk.

Many of the jewelers who were there and saw what had happened knew Javeri very well and at once hailed a taxi and drove him to the hospital, the valise still attached to his wrist. The moment that they arrived at the hospital, Javeri was taken into the emergency room, where the doctors did all in their power to save his eyesight and to alleviate his agonizing pain.

From that moment on Javeri lay in the hospital with the doctors doing all in their power to help him. After he had lain in the hospital for some time he was discharged, but with only partial vision in one eye, the other having been completely blinded. As far as Javeri was concerned, this was bad enough for him, as his eyes were his most precious possession, but for him there was something else that had occurred while he had been in the hospital and was of vital interest to him.

The Japanese had begun to flood the markets internationally with their so-called "Japanese cultured pearls," which was having the immediate effect of curtailing the desire of any of the merchants to even attempt to buy any pearls. The Oriental pearl market had entirely dried up, almost overnight. Nobody would buy pearls at any price. Thus poor Javeri found himself in a frightful bind. Not alone was he almost blind, but he had with him several hundred thousands of pounds' worth of pearls, at that moment almost quite valueless. He felt that he was duty bound to pay the owners for their consignments. Despite the protestations from these gentlemen in India that he was not under any circumstances to worry himself about paying them, he felt that he was obligated for every last cent.

Javeri then made up his mind that given time he would repay the owners every penny for the value of their pearls, even if it were to take his entire lifetime. Being a Jain, he knew that he could survive on scarcely nothing, and together with his wife, also of the same sect, he decided that they would save together every penny possible and place any money into a special account at their bank until such time as they would have saved enough to commence paying the owners in India for their indebtedness.

It had been spring when Javeri had been attacked, and by the time that he had been released from the hospital fall had commenced and with it the colder weather. My father, meeting Javeri on the street one afternoon when it was particularly cold, saw that he was coatless and, seeing him shivering and without any protection and knowing of his great financial problems, went over to him and said, "Look here, Javeri, I have two overcoats, one of which is hanging in my closet at home doing nothing, and I must insist that you come back with me to my home and accept it from me. If you refuse you will be insulting me, and in any case I will not take no for an answer."

Javeri then thanked him and said that he would be pleased and honored to accept my father's kind offer and, returning with him to our house, took the coat away with him.

Every merchant throughout the jewel trade then began to ponder ways and means in which they could assist Javeri. All were asking themselves what they could do to help him without it appearing that they were giving him any charity.

It so happened that just at this time my father had purchased a very fine parcel of jewels from an old estate and, calling Javeri to come up to his office, said to him, "Javeri, I have just purchased this lot of fine jewels that I am sure that you can sell, and I want you to take them on consignment at our cost and keep whatever profit that you make for yourself." He did not tell Javeri that the cost he had mentioned was actually half of what he had paid for the lot.

Javeri looked the jewels over and said, "This looks like a beautiful group that I can sell very well indeed, and I must thank you for this opportunity."

With this he left, taking the jewels with him, and a few days later he returned to tell Father that he had sold the entire collection and that he had done very well with it financially. At this time my father was not the only merchant who wanted to and did help Javeri.

After this, several years passed and Javeri, having continued to save every penny that he could lay his hands on and having vowed that he would repay the owners of the pearls in India what he felt he owed them, commenced to make the repayments and eventually repaid them down to the last penny. It is interesting to know that during all these years the Hindu merchants had not once asked Javeri for a single penny.

Chapter 22

Baron Jean Cassel

Among our international clientele we had many men and women who were perhaps as curious and unusual as many of the objects that we handled. One such person was a Belgian banker named Baron Jean Cassel, who owned the bank of that name in Brussels. It was here at the bank that we had arranged to assemble the necklace of fine black pearls for him whose commission had ended up in our acquisition of a great collection of Fabergé.

However, finding himself in Brussels with his wife, the baroness, and two daughters, and with the ominous threat of invasion by the German army quite obvious on his horizons, he decided that he had to do all in his power to get himself and family away from Belgium and, he hoped, to the safety of America.

He later told us that despite the fact that they were Catholics, his father had originally been Jewish before he had converted and he was convinced that the Nazis would, because of this, make life unbearable for them, even with the possibility of incarceration in a concentration camp. Knowing that we were at that time well established in America, he cabled us at length and asked us to do all in our power to arrange passage of any sort so that they could cross. In his cable he said that they would require accommodation for himself, the baroness, their two girls, his secretary, and their two borzoi dogs. We knew from previous conversations with him that this secretary was most necessary for him. In the cable he requested that he wanted us to work on the matter for him with all possible speed and that cost was of no consequence. He added that he had plenty of dollars in the bank vaults that was the property of his depositors, which he wished to secure from the Nazis on their behalf.

Using some little influence, we were able to arrange suitable accommodations for them all on a Portuguese liner that would be leaving from Lisbon, and we cabled him to this effect. But we explained that he himself would have to arrange some way to leave Belgium. As he was an enormously wealthy man, we knew that he would be able by dint of some considerable bribery in the right places to obtain the necessary exit papers, and very shortly after our cable he again cabled us that they would be able to leave and be on their way to Lisbon in time to make the boat.

As Portugal was a neutral country, they had no problems the moment that they crossed the border, and this did not take them long to achieve.

We had arranged the best possible berths for them on the ship; he had paid handsomely for the privilege.

Upon their arrival at the port of New York, after a quiet and uneventful crossing, my brother Henry went down to meet them, and he told the baron that he had arranged a large suite for them all at the New Weston Hotel on Madison Avenue, where they could also keep their two borzoi dogs.

Upon arrival in New York, the baron said that as long as they were safely here in the city he did not care where they stayed.

As soon as the party had disembarked at the port, the baron, who carried with him an attaché case, asked my brother to hold it for him until they were actually installed at the hotel, which Henry did.

As they had brought with them an enormous amount of luggage, it took them quite some time to get through Customs. So much luggage did they have, in fact, that they required three taxis to take it all. They had not been installed at the hotel for very long before the baron went out and bought himself a small radio so that he could listen to the news, which he then did from morning to night after his arrival. After they had been at the hotel for a few days, the baron called and asked my brother whether he could introduce him to a good bank. He wished to open an account over here.

My brother then told him that we had very satisfactory arrangements with the Manufacturer's Hanover Trust Bank, which bank we had dealt with for very many years, and that he would be happy to introduce him to the manager, a Mr. McGrath.

The baron then said that he would consider this, and after a couple of days he again telephoned.

"Last night while I was listening to the news on my radio I heard an advertisement from the bank offering to make small personal loans of one hundred dollars each, and as a banker I was quite astonished at this. First," he said, "I feel that any such advertising is infra dig, and second, I asked myself how an account could be safe in such a bank."

Despite this, he said that he would like to meet with Mr. McGrath and open his account with him, and it was then arranged that my brother would meet the baron and that they would go to the bank together.

Upon their arrival at the bank and after meeting with Mr. McGrath, he asked that they all go into a private room, and as soon as they were seated in there the baron opened the attaché case that he had asked my brother to hold for him. Inside McGrath saw that it was jammed to the top with American currency, which the Baron wished to use as an initial deposit. The baron then asked McGrath to count the bills, and when he saw all of this money he looked as though he were prepared to faint. It is doubtful whether McGrath had ever previously seen so much cash brought in at any one time. However, he did count the money, and it amounted to $3 million. He then opened the account, and the banker thanked the baron and told him that his confidence would be respected. They then returned together to our offices. The baron then explained that this cash was all that he had in the vault in Brussels before they left. The baron then returned to his hotel.

Next morning he again telephoned us and told us that he had tossed and turned all night and that he had not slept a wink, worrying about the safety of his money at the bank. In fact, he said that he could not wait until morning to call us.

"How can my money be safe at such a bank?"

We repeated that we were positive that his money was perfectly safe and at that time perhaps even safer than if it were in the Bank of England.

Still he was not satisfied and again stated that actually the money belonged to depositors at his bank in Brussels. Now he continued, "I know that you have good relations at Lloyd's of London, and I want you to cable your brother Bertram in London and ask him to check with them and find out how much they

126

would charge to insure my account. Remember that this is all the money that I have available at this moment and I cannot afford to take the slightest risk."

We knew that this request was a silly one, but nevertheless we cabled London and asked our brother to contact Lloyd's and get a premium quote from them.

Later that same day we received a reply cable from our brother Bertram reading: "Who is insane, you or he?" We then cabled in reply and said that in our opinion the baron was quite insane, but this is what he wanted.

Next day we received word from Bertram that Lloyd's of London had quoted one thousand pounds as an annual premium. We at once telephoned the baron and told him of this quotation, which he accepted, and he asked us to remit the money immediately, which we did on his behalf.

A couple of weeks then passed and we received a letter from Bertram to say that he had spoken with the underwriters at Lloyd's, who told him that this premium of one thousand pounds was the "sweetest" money that they had ever earned. The baron then again told us of his problem with this cash that he had taken from his bank vault before leaving Brussels. He had been advised that some of the depositors in Belgium were demanding that he return their money, which they said they needed to live on, but by that time the Nazis had already overrun the country and he had no way that he could turn any funds over to them. He then heard through the grapevine that the depositors were very angry with him, but there was nothing that he could do except hold onto the money as securely as possible on their behalf.

The baron, however, did try to make some efforts to return some of the funds, but without avail.

He then came up to our offices, as he had another idea that he wanted to explore with us, as he wanted the money to work rather than allowing it to lie dormant at the bank. He knew as did we that there were wonderful objects in all areas of art and antiquity being offered at auction in New York every week and suggested that we buy whatever we felt would be desirable for his account, utilizing these funds from the bank for this purpose. We were to hold everything that we purchased aside until the end of the war, when we could resell everything at a good profit, which we could then split fifty/fifty. In the meanwhile we would not charge him any commission for our work.

Henry and I then discussed this matter from all angles and concluded that this was an excellent idea and decided that we would go along with him. We then arranged to meet and sealed a contract as we would have done in Europe—with a handshake.

Unfortunately for us, as it later transpired, we did not have a legal contract drawn up.

The moment we had agreed on this procedure we commenced making purchases. The baron had been named as the actual purchaser and would be required to pay the then city sales tax of 5 percent on everything. During all of these negotiations, the baron's wife always sat in on our conversations, but never opened her mouth to utter a single word. It was for this reason that he always referred to her as "the Sphinx." She always just sat and smiled.

Now we had a problem—the baron was entirely allergic to the payment of any tax. Sales tax or otherwise, in his opinion, he said, any such tax was an insult. He then found out that if he had all of these purchases shipped out of the city to an adjoining state, the tax would not be chargeable to him.

Bearing this in mind, he at once sought the advice of a realtor and bought a home in New Jersey just over the George Washington Bridge and from that moment on there were almost daily shipments going across the bridge with his purchases.

The fact that the cost of such shipping was probably far in excess of anything that he might have been required to pay in tax was something that he did not even consider.

After we had been buying on his behalf for several months, we saw at the auction what was without doubt the most beautiful Louis XV table that had ever come to light. Together with the baron we decided that it should be bought at any price.

On the day of the auction there was considerable opposition to our bids, but despite this we were the last bidders and the table was knocked down to us. At the time this purchase created a record for any such piece of French furniture of the Louis period. Next day it was similarly on its way to New Jersey.

We were then later to discover that the underbidder had been Mr. Blumenthal, who wanted to buy the table for the Metropolitan Museum of Art.

From that time on we found the baron becoming more and more morose and difficult as the days went by. Besides the enormous sums that we were spending on his behalf for our joint venture, he was playing the New York Stock Market and making some enormous profits. While making these large profits he seemed to be having a satanic delight in making life difficult for the stockbrokers with whom he was working. For instance, the brokers closed their offices at four o'clock each afternoon, but the baron would frequently arrange to meet them there at around five o'clock. The brokers, knowing that they were making a lot of money working with him, were always willing to wait after hours for his arrival. However, he never arrived on time but would invariably turn up at around midnight without so much as a "sorry."

We similarly were having many problems with him, until one morning after a particularly unpleasant contretemps with him, and having somewhat of an explosive temper, I called him over the telephone a "lousy bastard." This latter remark quite naturally astonished him and fell on very unhappy ears. Nobody had apparently ever spoken to him in such terms, although there were many people with whom he was doing business who would have wished to do so.

This incident suspended all operations between us, and incidentally, the entire operation was becoming more and more onerous as the days went by; despite this, our handshake contract still held firm and intact.

After this we did not hear another word from him but found that he had changed his name to Baron Cassel Van Doorn, incorporating his wife's name in conjunction with his own. This was, as far as he was concerned, a sort of glamorization, Doorn having been the place where the ex-kaiser, Wilhelm had been interned after the First World War.

Shortly thereafter we heard that the Baron had passed away, and this was approximately at the same time as hostilities had ended and the war was over. The baroness, knowing full well of our contract and without our knowledge, closed the house in New Jersey and quietly had everything shipped over to Paris, where we later discovered she had sold everything at auction and that she had made an enormous profit on all that we had bought. Of a certainty we were entitled to 50 percent of the profits but heard nothing from the lady. Foolishly, perhaps, we decided to allow the matter to slide.

Then reading the *Connoisseur Magazine* one day we read that the Louis table had been sold and had achieved the sum of sixty thousand dollars, four times the price that we had paid for it originally. It had been acquired by the Wrightsmans, great connoisseurs that they were, and as benefactors of the Metropolitan Museum of Art they had presented it there where it now resides in all its splendor. I must confess that although I am most gratified when I see the table at the museum, I do get some pangs, as certainly the baroness owed us half of the money that she received as profit on all of the purchases made for the baron. As an afterthought I can only say that in retrospect I am heartily sorry that we ever assisted the baron to come over to the United States and feel that we should have allowed him to remain in Brussels and face the Nazi music.

Chapter 23

Ragnar Halle and His Norwegian Silver

The repatriation of ethnic antiquities had always been a very interesting part of our normal operation in London. We discovered and placed Swedish antiquities back in Sweden, French to France, Norwegian back to Norway, American back to America, and so on and so forth.

Obviously there always had to be some catalyst that made a collector decide whether he wished to contain his collecting in the various fields of sculpture, silverware, paintings, or what you will. And so it was that a gentleman named Ragnar Halle, a native and resident of Bergen, Norway, decided that he wished to collect antique Norwegian silver of the eighteenth and early nineteenth centuries. As he told me, it was his ultimate goal to have the finest and greatest accumulation of the rarest and best specimens to be found anywhere in his native country. Mr. Halle was a tall, thin gentleman, always superbly dressed, and as he was a very wealthy shipowner, controlling a vast fleet of ships under his own flag, he was well able to satisfy his desire whenever the opportunity came his way. Despite this fact, he always held that this fleet of ships was his bread and butter. His silver collection became his love, and over the many years that we knew him, we were able to assist him by finding many superb specimens for his collection.

Mr. Halle was a very frequent visitor to London, and whenever there he never failed to visit with us at our shop on Piccadilly. He often said to me that he had important business to do in London, but that primarily he wanted to see what he could buy, although whenever we found an object that we knew he would want to add to his collection he was never quite satisfied that perhaps we might be holding something out for another collector of similar antiquities. Beyond this he always held that he was able to acquire things in London that he never even saw in Norway.

It was towards the end of the nineteen-thirties and shortly before the outbreak of war that in discussing his collection with me one day he said, "You know, Mr. Hill, there is one object that I would dearly love to find, perhaps even more than anything else, and that is a *brudderkrone*."

Not knowing what a *brudderkrone* might be, I asked him to tell me what such an object was and he explained, "A *brudderkrone* is a sort of crown that was worn by a bride at her marriage and which was always handed down from mother to daughter. As these *brudderkrone* were invariably made of silver, they remained in the hands of the very wealthy and thus very rarely were to be seen on the market and only were they possibly buyable when such a family had died out and there were no descendants who could possibly use such an item." Mr. Halle then went on to tell me that these items were quite distinctive. They had hangings, known as leaves, suspended round the base of the crown, these leaves being engraved with the names and life and death dates of the various couples. These dates were always engraved after the death of the wearer. Thus, although the silver was not hall-marked, the dating was quite simple. Mr. Halle then explained that these *brudderkrone* are so distinctive that it would be almost impossible to make a mistake. In fact, once seen they cannot be mistaken.

I told Mr. Halle that any time such an item came my way I would surely buy it for him, but I had never so far even seen one. Thanking me, he left; then after the door had closed, he again came and asked me to join him for lunch, as he thought that perhaps he might be able to fill me in on the subject of these crowns over a leisurely meal. I thanked him and we both left for a lunch together down in the Piccadilly Hotel where my shop was located.

After lunch he again said good-bye and left.

As we were approaching the end of spring and the weather was really delightful, together with my family I decided that we would drive down to the south Coast for a breath of fresh sea air, and then after spending most of a Sunday at Brighton, we began our drive back to London.

Now, fortunately for me, the road back was crowded and as we passed through some of the small towns we were often held up by traffic jams in the very narrow roads. While so halted in one of these towns we had to wait for quite some time, and this happened to be outside the shop of an antique dealer whom we did not know, but looking from the car into his window, there I saw what was obviously a *brudderkrone*, and from what Mr. Halle had told me I knew that I could not be in any way mistaken.

Fortunately for me, I have a habit of never traveling anywhere without a pen or pencil and notepad in my pocket. So as soon as I saw this object I at once jotted down the name and address of the dealer so that I could call him first thing on Monday morning. As the shop was closed on Sunday I knew that I could not possibly lose the purchase.

The first thing that I did on arrival at the shop on Monday was telephone the dealer and ask him the price of the crown. When he told me, I asked him to mail it down to me at once and said that my check would be in the mail to him immediately. He promised to do this, and in short order the *brudderkrone* was in my hands. When I saw it I decided that not only was it a genuine article, but a very interesting specimen at that, with all its dated leaves attached and in excellent state of repair. The item dated back to the early part of the eighteenth century.

My first reaction was to telephone Mr. Halle and tell him the news of what I had found for him, but for some reason, and one that I could not at that moment fathom, I could not get through, so I sent him a telegram. The moment that he received my wire he at once cabled back asking that I mail him the *brudderkrone* at once. He said in his wire that he could not wait until it was in his hands and in his collection.

As soon as we received his cable we had our man package the object and take it to the local post office. He was soon back with the package to say that the post office was as from that day not accepting any more mail for Norway, as only that morning the country had been invaded by the Germans. We were in somewhat of a quandary. Certainly Mr. Halle wanted the *brudderkrone* in Norway, invasion or not, but there was no way that we could arrange to get it to him. We then decided to put it aside and hold it for him until the end of the war, as although we were unable to contact him, he would know that we would hold the object for him.

We made up our minds that after the cessation of hostilities if he were still living he would be able to buy it or not, but that he would have the privilege. Since shortly after this we were preparing a very large shipment of antiquities to send to New York, we thought to include this *brudderkrone* so that it could be held over there for safe custody.

As soon as the shipment arrived in New York we placed the *brudderkrone* in one of our safes and almost forgot all about it.

In the meantime, during the war years such items were becoming more and more valuable. But we decided that as Mr. Halle had committed himself to the purchase, it belonged to him until he could tell us that he did not want it.

One day, quite soon after the end of the war, we received a letter from our brother Bertram in London, enclosing a letter to New York, as he had no idea what Mr. Halle was writing about nor for his part did he know what a *brudderkrone* was.

The moment we had the letter in our hands we wrote Mr. Halle and told him that we had the *brudderkrone* safe and sound here in New York and we also wrote him that we could easily airmail it over to him, as soon as we heard from him that he wanted us to do this.

We then received a following letter from Mr. Halle to say that he was overjoyed to hear from us and that "his" *brudderkrone* was safe, but he asked us to hold it in New York, as he intended coming over very shortly himself, when he would come to see us and pick it up. He also wrote: "When I see you I shall have a story to tell you that I am sure that you will find most interesting."

Later that same month Mr. Halle arrived together with his wife and both came up to see us. He looked quite well, although very, very thin, and his face betrayed signs of intense suffering.

As soon as he was at my desk I took the *brudderkrone* out of the safe and handed it to him. He picked it up in his hands and began to stroke it lovingly, as though it were a small child.

Then suddenly he burst into uncontrollable tears. When his crying subsided he excused himself and then told me the following story.

"Shortly after I received your telegram about the *brudderkrone*, Norway was overrun by the Nazis and I was picked up by the German military together with a number of my fellow shipowners. We were all placed under arrest and were taken to an old farmhouse where we were pushed up into the attic. Here the ceiling was very low, and as we Norwegians are inclined to be rather tall, it was, to say the least, somewhat uncomfortable. At no time could we stand up straight to stretch. We were forced to sit or lie on the floor, which was covered with filthy, stinking straw. It was then here that I remained during the entire period of the war years. During this period whenever one or other of the Nazis were slain by members of the underground, one of our number was taken out and shot in the grounds outside. We could not see what was going on but could always hear the shots being fired.

"Actually, we were being held as hostages. As far as I was concerned they never took me out, because I suppose that as one of the principal shipowners I would be useful to them after they won the war, which at that time they felt positive they were going to do. Anyhow, I survived that frightful ordeal, but more interesting is the role that this *brudderkrone* played during all these years.

"Every night as I settled down to sleep I found myself picturing my silver collection as I had left it in my cabinets, but in my mind's eye I was ever rearranging the pieces, always with this *brudderkrone* as a centerpiece.

"Thus during the war I must have mentally rearranged my collection some hundreds of times, and I am sure that only by doing this in my dreams was I able to retain my sanity."

All the while he spoke he continued to stroke his *brudderkrone* and asked me how much he had to pay me for it. I told him that it had been sold to him originally at a set figure and that the same figure pertained at this time. He said that he was delighted and we then shook hands and Mr. and Mrs. Halle left with obvious great pleasure on their faces. As he left he said again, "Don't forget to let me know of anything that might turn up here in the States that you think might enhance my collection. I know that there are many Norwegians over here in the States, and any one of them might have a piece for me." As they left he hugged the *brudderkrone* as though he were afraid that he might lose his treasure.

Some six months or so after he had gone we acquired a rather lovely eighteenth-century Norwegian beaker that we knew would fit happily into his collection. We had it photographed in several positions and mailed the prints to Mr. Halle together with details of the hallmarkings and our description. We were somewhat surprised that we received no reply to this letter. Presuming that perhaps he was traveling, we mailed him a duplicate of the letter, but similarly we received no response, and that being the case, we placed the piece on offer elsewhere and forgot the matter.

It was some years later, actually 1953, that returning to New York from Cairo, where I had been attending the King Farouk auction sales, that I found myself seated on the plane next to a young gentleman. I got into conversation with him, as one usually does in such circumstances, and he inquired as to where I lived and I then asked him where he lived.

He replied, "I live in Bergen, where I am a shipowner."

I then inquired whether by chance he was acquainted with a gentleman named Mr. Ragnar Halle, and he replied, "But certainly I knew him very well indeed and I also know many of his friends and his family, as the families were always together at each other's houses."

He then continued talking: "As a matter of fact, my father was together with Mr. Halle in the terrible farmhouse in which they were imprisoned during the war years, but you will not be hearing from Mr. Halle anymore, as he passed away quite some time ago." He also said that he was quite positive that Mr. Halle's early death was the result of the awful conditions through which he had passed during the war. He also added, "Similarly my father passed away after spending those terrible years in what he always alluded to as those stinking hellholes."

Some few years after my meeting with this young gentleman my brother Henry, while on holiday in Bergen, decided to telephone and see whether perhaps some member of the Halle family might still be in residence and if so whether he could see the Halle collection in situ. It was Mr. Halle's son who answered the telephone, and he said that he would be delighted to welcome Henry at his home, where the collection was still housed. He told my brother that the house was quite close, and when Henry arrived he was received most cordially by the young gentleman, who said, "I am delighted that you thought to visit us, as my father always spoke of you with the greatest regard." The young man then explained that he would neither add nor sell any single piece, but that after his death it would all be going to their local museum, as this is what his father had always stated was his intention. It may well be that by this time the collection may already be housed at the Bergen Museum, but if it is not already there, it is surely slated to go there at some time in the future.

Chapter 24

Schiaparelli and Mrs. Millicent Balcom

Both in business and also socially, Madame Elsa Schiaparelli, the renowned couturière of the twenties, was a dear friend of ours. Elsa had a superb shop and atelier in Paris on the Place Vendome, and although she has now passed away, the firm still operates at the same location.

As a friend she was always endeavoring to introduce to us as many of her wealthiest and best clients as she could, and she numbered many of the great and famous from all over the world, with perhaps special emphasis on those from the States.

Among those ladies from America was the exceedingly beautiful heiress, Mrs. Ronald Balcom. This was her name at the time at which this story takes place, because in the course of the several years in which we did business with the lady she was continually changing husbands and consequently names. Millicent Balcom loved to collect exotic jewels and wished to make an important collection of such objects for herself in this area; there was nothing that we ever showed or offered to the lady that was too outré for her tastes.

Thus it was that during the early thirties Elsa came over to see us in London and told us of Millicent's wishes. She also told us that Millicent loved to wear such exotica with the fabulous gowns that she always acquired from Elsa at her Paris fashion shows. She told me that we would be hearing directly from the lady very shortly, as she was most desirous of working on her collection without any delay.

I particularly recall this visit from Elsa, because to this day I remember the fascinatingly beautiful outfit she wore. Elsa was quite short in stature and very neatly trim in size so that whatever she wore looked elegant and charming on her. The outfit to which I refer was a startling red coat with a black caracul hat tilted to one side. The coat was certainly the shocking pink that Madame

Schiaparelli later made so famous and which is today a household word in the fashion industry.

As she stated that we would, we did hear from Millicent, who telephoned us from somewhere in the Tyrol to tell me about her desire to form what she stated to be "the greatest collection of antique and exotic jewels." I then promised that I would let her know about anything special in this area that came our way.

It was then arranged with her that anything that came in that category was to be communicated first to Elsa Schiaparelli in Paris, as she told me that Elsa would always know where she might be at any given time.

Millicent was an outstanding beauty, and before her marriage to Ronald Balcom she was Millicent Rogers, daughter of the fabulously wealthy Colonel Rogers of Standard Oil fame and from whom she inherited many millions of dollars. For some curious reason we were never able to fathom, she would never allow herself to be seen by me or any other member of our establishment. We were never able to make any contact with her face to face. However, we know of her great beauty both from what Elsa told us and from the innumerable pictures that were always appearing in the press.

In the many years that we were in contact with Millicent she was so often divorced that we had some difficulty in keeping up with her various names in our filing system; this was, naturally, before the advent of the computer.

From the moment that she telephoned us from the Tyrol, we were almost in weekly touch with her, and over a short period we were able to find a fascinating group of jewels for her collection. Some were of the period of the Italian Renaissance; many in the manner of the great Cellini. We supplied her with quite a few superb pieces of the Victorian period, many by the great Giuliano of that period. It was during this very long Victorian period that some of the most exquisite pieces of exotic jewels were created, quite a few that emanated from the workshops of French and Italian craftsmen.

When Millicent was in the Tyrol, and this was quite frequently, she always spent most of her time at Kitzbuhl, where we were frequently in touch with her on the telephone. Whenever we offered Millicent anything her communications were short and to the point and mostly by telegram if she happened to be home in the States, by cable. We would invariably send Elsa a full description of any exotic jewel. If Elsa approved the item she would pass the information on to Millicent, who would always advise us by cable or telegram: "Will take." As far as Millicent was concerned, if Schiap, as we called her, said that the item was something for her, she was always satisfied to buy unseen.

It occurred that on one occasion we had a very special jewel of the Renaissance period that we could not satisfactorily explain, either in writing or by telephone, so I called Schiaparelli, who at the time was in paris, and told her about it. I also told her that it had to be seen. She told me that as she was at that time preparing for one of her fashion shows, she could not possibly come to London to see it. I told her that I could easily come over to Paris to show it to her, and we made a mutually convenient appointment at her Place Vendome atelier.

When I arrived in Paris and as soon as I checked in at my hotel I telephoned Elsa and she told me that at that moment Millicent was actually at the Plaza Athenée Hotel in Paris and that she would certainly be at her fashion show. She also said that after showing the jewel to her I could call Millicent at her hotel and see her myself. Now I thought that for the first time I would be able to meet the lady face to face.

Later that same day I showed Elsa the jewel and she at once approved it and called Millicent at her hotel and told her that I would be coming over to show it to her next morning.

When I arrived at her suite I was greeted by Fagan, who was her confidential maid. Fagan took the jewel from me through a side door into an adjoining room to show it to Millicent.

As soon as Millicent had it in her hands she began to shout questions about it to me over the transom, and I shouted my answers back to her in similar manner.

After several of these back and forth shoutings she said, "Will take," and the transaction was completed and all that we needed to do was mail her our bill, when in due course we would receive her check in payment. So even at this time I never got to see the lady in the flesh.

Some months then passed and we were able to make her quite a few offers through the hands of Schiaparelli, most of which we sold her. Then one day we acquired a superb jewel that could be worn as a belt or as a long necklace in the form of a flexible snake, each portion linked to the next and the entire body of which was covered with what are known as "old mine diamonds." (Such "old mine stones" were so named because they were among the first to come from the South African diamond mines.) The jewel was about a yard in length. The head of the snake was about two inches in length and had two tiny rubies in its eyes. This diamond-headed snake was certainly of the early Queen Victoria period and certainly a creation by a jeweler in London.

The moment that I had it in my hands I telephoned Elsa in Paris and told her about it. She said that she was all excited about it and wanted to see it at once, but that as she was again preparing another fashion show she could not possibly leave Paris. I again arranged to see her at the Place Vendome and we made an appointment for the following day.

Next day I crossed to Paris and went straight to see her at her atelier, and when I arrived the receptionist told me that Madame was upstairs in her private suite and was waiting to see me. I was directed upstairs and when I arrived at the top of the staircase I was confronted by a sight such as I had never previously encountered.

As they were preparing for the fashion show that Elsa had mentioned, the room was filled with a bevy of beautiful models all parading around the room, most of them if not actually in the nude, then almost so, wearing the briefest of underthings, and certainly most of them were topless. This was something that I had never previously seen, but I had to act in a most blasé manner, as though this were a normalcy for me. Actually, this was the first time that I had ever been upstairs at the atelier.

After a short while Elsa emerged from her private office and greeted me and invited me to her sanctum sanctorium, where I at once showed her the diamond snake. When she saw it she was astounded by its exotic beauty. She declared that it would be better worn as a belt than as a necklace and fell madly in love with it. "I wish that I could afford to buy this for myself, I love it so, but I know full well that Millicent will want it so I will not even try to buy it from you. However, in the most unlikely event that she does not want to take it then one way or another it is going to be mine."

We then arranged together a rather long telegram and sent it to Millicent. And within hours I received a telegram from her with the usual terse clause: "Will take." Today, as I believe this snake jewel is in the possession of Millicent's family, she having now passed away, it is frequently mentioned in press society columns. In these columns it is reported as "Italian Renaissance," which it certainly is not; it is also ofttimes reported as by the great Fabergé, which again it is certainly not. To this day I have never yet seen it correctly reported as "early Victorian period."

During the many years that we were in touch with Millicent we sold her a very important collection of exotica and some jewels that virtually beggar description. I do not know what has happened to the collection now that it is so many years since she has passed from the scene, but if the family still retains it then they have quite a fortune in their hands.

It was just at the time that war had been declared in England, and when I knew that Millicent was in New York I cabled her to say that I was crossing to the States and I asked her to withhold her payment to us that was at the time owing, as I cabled that I would collect from her in New York.

At that moment she was indebted to us for a considerable sum of money. She, however, was smarter than I was, and because the pound had fallen in value she at once cabled her remittance to us in London, completely ignoring my request. She was of course entitled to do this, as the debt to us was in pounds, and in so doing she made a handsome profit for herself. She was not Colonel Rogers's daughter for nothing.

Chapter 25

The Maharani's Belt

One morning we received a telephone call from the private secretary to a Hindu maharaja, just arrived from India who had taken up residence at the old Carlton Hotel on London's Haymarket, where he had reserved an entire floor for himself and his staff. (This famous hotel no longer exists.) The secretary then asked me to come over to the hotel to discuss a project, and we arranged a mutually convenient appointment for the following day.

Upon arrival at the hotel, I went up to the floor, and there all along the side of the corridor were Hindus, some seated and some lying. I then saw the secretary beckoning me into one of the far rooms, and as soon as I was there he introduced himself to me. We then sat for a short while and discussed the weather, this being a normalcy in England. The secretary then told me that the maharaja wished to have something quite special and this was a commission that had to be handled with extreme care.

After speaking to him for some little time, I suggested that perhaps it might be best if our manager, Mr. Christie, handled this assignment for the maharaja, as I explained that he was much more accustomed to handling matters with Hindus than I.

The secretary thought that this was an excellent idea and one that His Highness would heartily approve. I at once telephoned to our shop and asked Christie to come right over so that I could introduce him to the secretary, and as the shop was just around the corner from the hotel this presented no problem.

It took almost no time at all for Christie to arrive, and as soon as the three of us were together the secretary explained that the maharaja wished to have made a "solid eighteen-karat gold belt of heavy gold that the maharani would be able to wear round her waist." He said, "The belt is to be two inches in width and a quarter of an inch in thickness, and it is to be pierced with a very special design that is a secret." He then asked that we swear that we would not mention this commission or the design of the belt to anybody, and we, of course, agreed to this. We then asked for the length that was required and said that we needed to measure the maharani's waist.

Here we were at somewhat of an impasse, because the lady was in strictest purdah.

I then suggested that as Christie was quite elderly he could take her measurements, but the secretary said that only the maharaja himself would be able to do this. Anything else, the secretary said, was quite out of the question.

Being rather intrigued by this whole matter, I inquired the meaning of the special design, as the secretary had handed me a rough drawing of what was required, and he replied, "This I cannot tell you, as the design is quite secret and belongs to the maharaja's sect." The secretary then said, "The maharaja will himself take the measurement of the lady's waist, and I shall telephone you tomorrow morning." He then continued, saying that as soon as we had the measurement we could put the matter in the hands of our craftsmen.

We then told him that we would be happy to prepare an estimate of the cost as soon as we had the measurement, and he replied that this would be quite unnecessary, as His Highness had implicit faith in us.

Next morning, and as arranged, the secretary telephoned to say that the maharaja had taken the measurement of the length of the belt. When we heard this we were quite astonished and had to presume that there had to be some mistake; the length mentioned was about six feet. When we queried this dimension the secretary explained that the maharaja had made no mistake, because the lady was enormously fat and for that reason never left her chair. In fact, he explained that she had a chair especially made for her and that this chair was always transported with them when they traveled.

We then put the making of the belt in hand, and it did not take us too long for the work to be completed. When the belt was ready for delivery it was so heavy that we could scarcely lift it, and Christie then said that he felt that perhaps he might be allowed to try it round the lady's waist, she being in purdah or not. After all, he said, "I am quite elderly and could not possibly do the lady any harm." Christie then telephoned the secretary and told him that the belt was ready for delivery and that he proposed bringing it over himself later that same day and the secretary arranged to wait in for his arrival.

When Christie arrived with the belt at the hotel room, he was asked to take a seat while the secretary took the belt into another adjoining room to show it to the maharaja, who would then try it on the maharani himself.

After about half an hour had elapsed, the maharaja came in, introduced himself to Christie and said, "It has turned out better than I could have expected." He then continued, "Everything about the belt is perfect even to the line of the special secret motif," and he asked Christie to congratulate our firm on our efforts in his behalf. The maharaja then asked his secretary to draw us a check for our bill, which Christie had handed to him, and it was paid at once without any bargaining. This latter aspect of the transaction was almost unheard of when dealing with Hindus.

It is quite positive that when the maharani had the belt round her waist she could never move from her chair, as she was entirely imprisoned in it. We then decided that perhaps as Hindus love gold so much, this was a sort of hedge against inflation, as the belt was so very heavy and the value of the gold was very high indeed. In today's market it would certainly be worth a very large sum, because of the enormous increase in the value of gold bullion.

Chapter 26

Coutt's Bank—Box of Things

It was on one of those well-known days in mid-November when the London atmosphere was heavy with fog and the sky was leaden and overcast. All was most unpleasing both to sight and smell, to such an extent that we were on the point of deciding whether or not to close our establishment for the day and allow our employees to go home when just at this point our door opened and in walked a very well-known and old client of our shop. He was a tall and handsome gentleman in his middle forties, with always a very pleasant smile on his face, and as soon as he entered he said, "I have a request to make of you. I have just been bequeathed a 'box of things' which is at present down in the vault of Coutt's Bank in the Strand. I haven't the slightest idea what the box contains, but as one of my ancestors was in some way associated with London Bridge, there may well be some interesting memorabilia in it. I would like you to ask Andrews whether he would be willing to go to the bank and collect the box for me and bring it back to the shop, so that we can open it together."

I told him that I was sure that Andrews would be delighted to do this for him and all that would be required would be a letter of authority instructing the bank to hand the box over to him.

The gentleman at once sat at my desk and wrote such a letter, which he handed to me.

I then arranged that Andrews would go down next morning, after which I said that I would call him and tell him that we had the box. As the gentleman was about to leave, he said, "I have a curious feeling that the box must contain some very interesting items; from what I have heard my ancestor had something to do with the rebuilding of the old London Bridge."

As soon as he was out of the door I called Andrews into my office and arranged with him to go down to the bank next morning and, armed with the letter, get the box and bring it back to the shop.

Next morning just as Andrews was at the point of leaving for the bank, I said to him, "You know, Andrews, I think that I would like to go down with you, as I think that the vault at the bank may be quite an interesting place to see."

And so we left together and hailed a taxi and drove to the bank. En route, by dint of a little bribery, I arranged that the taxi would wait for us outside the bank and bring us back with whatever we collected. If the box was large and valuable we did not wish to have to stand on the sidewalk fighting to get another taxi.

Upon entering the bank we were greeted by an elderly gentleman wearing an old-fashioned cutaway, to whom we handed the letter of authority.

The gentleman then opened and read the letter, and while he did this I saw that the tellers were all dressed in similar cutaways and that on a long counter that extended from one side of the bank to the other there stood antique pewter snuff boxes and also large pewter inkwells with quill pens stuck in each. Whether or not these were simply for decoration I did not discover.

However, as soon as he had finished reading the letter he telephoned downstairs and asked us to proceed down, where he said that the custodian would be awaiting us. Before we had gone down the stairs the gentleman stated that the box would be handed over to us without any delay.

When we arrived downstairs we were both astonished to see the interior of the vault. It was, in fact, a very long, rather narrow room that must certainly have extended across and under the roadway. On both sides there were long shelves that reached from one end of the room to the other, all laden with rows upon rows of so-called boxes or plate chests, as they might be more correctly termed. These chests, lined up as they were, looked almost like a regiment of soldiers on parade, standing to attention. I mentioned this to the custodian, who laughed and said that he thought this was a great joke.

The custodian then said, "If you will just excuse me for a few minutes I shall get your box down for you." It took the man just a few moments to locate the box, and he set it down on the floor in front of us, remarking, "The box is now yours."

Most of these chests were of solid oak, and many of them had strips of beaten copper binding them; most had side handles for ease in carrying. The box that we collected was no exception. We then signed for the receipt of the box, and although it was quite heavy, we managed to carry it upstairs and into the waiting taxi. It was a good thing that I had gone with Andrews, as else he would not have been able to manage alone.

As we put the box into the taxi I noticed that there was a very dirty handwritten label hanging from one of the handles, but in the taxi I could not read what it said so I had to wait until we were back at the shop before I could try to read it.

When I could eventually read the label, I saw it stated that the box had been deposited at the bank during the early part of 1740. While in conversation with the custodian at the bank I had asked him how it was that they managed to have so many of these plate chests on the shelves, and he replied quite simply, "Oh, when the boys went off to fight Napoleon many of these chests were deposited here for safekeeping and they will not be taken out until somebody comes to collect them, just as you are doing today, except that yours was left here much before the Napoleonic period." He then continued talking, as though in an afterthought. "I am afraid that many of those boys must have fallen in action, and so many of them may never be claimed."

As soon as we had the box safely back at the shop I telephoned the gentleman and asked him to come over with the key, which he had already received from the solicitor for the estate. He stated that he would be down first thing the next morning, as he could not wait to see what he had received.

As the interior of the bank vault was very dry, the key turned quite easily when put into the lock, and as soon as it was open we saw that it was filled with all sorts of objects, all packed in tissue paper. The first thing that we took from the box was a superb silver inkstand, still in its original wrapping as it had been delivered by the silversmith; it was quite untarnished when unwrapped, so new-looking that it might have been a piece just delivered from Tiffany's. The date of the hallmarking was 1740, the year that had been written on the old label; it was obvious that it had never even been used for a single day. It was of the very rare type known as "Ambassadorial." As soon as the gentleman saw this he said that he was sure that the Victoria and Albert

Museum would like to have it for their superb collection of antique English silver and asked us to make the presentation on his behalf. When eventually I did show it to the curator at the museum he said they would be delighted to accept it; it is surely on display in the museum to this day.

The next item that we took out was an antique coffeepot, and this piece was engraved all over its belly with the dimensions of the old London Bridge, together with a sketch of the bridge, and there was also mention of the work that the gentleman's ancestor had been associated with.

As soon as he saw this he said, "This is something that I shall take home with me, because we really do need a coffeepot and can certainly use this one."

Then there was a very fine old gold watch with its traditional double case that was usual during the eighteenth century, and this he said he would enjoy carrying in his waistcoat pocket, despite its bulk.

Then we found several tankards, all of silver and naturally all dated prior to 1740, together with a few pieces of jewelry, which he said that we could buy from him if we wished to do so.

Did we wish to buy anything? Of course we did.

Just as we were about to close the chest we saw some more tissue paper at the bottom, and when I lifted this up I found a superb pair of George II silver candlesticks, similarly looking like new, and these the gentleman also said he wanted to take home with him. He told me that he did not want the oak chest, which he said we could retain; this was a beautiful example of the old cabinetmakers' art. It was one with beaten copper strips, and I took it home with me. Today it still occupies an honored spot in our Connecticut cottage, where it is being used as a small coffee table.

As an afterthought, it is interesting to speculate on the possible value of the contents of all those other chests, not alone those that I saw at Coutt's Bank, but at other banks that must be spread around England. The total value must be colossal if what we saw in "our" chest is anything to judge by. As far as I know, everything will remain where it is unless one of these days the laws in England are changed. If the law were changed there would be a wealth of untold proportion that would certainly come to light. Possibly the value could cover the national debt. Here in the States after seven years any such valuables become the property of the Treasury Department, but as far as I know there is no such provision in England.

Chapter 27

André Simon's Food and Wine Society

It was a gentleman named André Simon whose name was renowned as that of one of the great connoisseurs of wines and who was one of the world's great gourmets. He was one of the financial organizers of the Food and Wine Society, which is today a worldwide organization. It was he who introduced us to the society at its inception back toward the end of the thirties. André Simon was a dear friend of one of our connections and was instrumental in our joining as charter members. The basic concept of the society was to attempt to improve the quality of the wines and foods offered at the restaurants in England. It was Simon's thinking that though London possessed some of the finest restaurants in the world, if you knew where to find them, the moment you stepped outside the city limits the food served in most places was terrible, with the certain exception of roast beef. It was arranged that the society would hold four banquets each year, all to be at the Ritz Hotel on London's Piccadilly. At each of these banquets there were to be ten tables, no more, no less, and at each there were to be ten diners. Each of these tables was to have five waiters assigned to them so that each of the waiters could serve at the same moment, one to his left and the other to his right. Although I recall with clarity being present at the first of these banquets, which was called the "Savoyard," I do not remember the menu, although I do recall that the wines and food all honored the Savoy District of France.

However, the second of these banquets that I attended I do recall with greater clarity. This was the "Muscovite," and being so intensely interested in the arts of old Russia, I could not readily forget it. At this dinner the wines and foods of old Russia were served, and the chef who officiated at its preparation had been the principal chef to Czar Nicholas in the old pre-revolutionary days. It was at this function that Lord Louis Mountbatten, later brought down by assassins, who was father of the prince consort, husband of Queen Elizabeth II, had acted as host.

As the guests sat at the table, each in his own mind attempted to forecast what might be on the menu. Most considered that caviar served with vodka would be the first course, but this was not the case. The dinner was served as it would have been in the old days at the Czar's table, and as such we commenced with blinis and curaçao liqueur.

Unfortunately, this was the last of the banquets, as very shortly after this the war started and all such functions naturally ceased.

Among the guests that we invited were Lord and Lady Brentford. His Lordship known affectionately to his friends as "Tubby," for very obvious reasons, was the son of Sir Joynson Hicks, at that time home secretary and a very important personage in British political circles.

It was with very good reason that we had invited the Brentfords to be our guests as at this particular time. Lady Brentford had made it her main objective in life to assist, through her father-in-law, as many people as she possibly could in escaping from the horrors prevailing in Nazi Germany and Austria.

We were in the process of endeavoring to obtain a permit for a young friend of ours whom we had known as an employee of the very old and highly respected firm of Schwartz and Steiner, jewelers of Vienna, and as a Jew he wanted to escape as quickly as possible. He had written us a most heartrending letter stating that he could not bear to live under the frightful conditions and atmosphere that prevailed at that time in his native Vienna, and upon receipt of his letter we had discussed this young man's situation with Lady Brentford. Later at the dinner she had told us that she was just on the point of finalizing the arrangements for getting a visa for him to enter England. But she said that this would still have to take a little time, as there was much red tape that had to be cut.

Then about two months after this conversation at the dinner, she telephoned to say that all papers necessary were in her hands and that we could tell the young man that he could leave Austria and enter England without any difficulty.

No sooner did we have this information from her that we tried to make contact with the young man in Vienna, but all of our letters and subsequent telegrams were returned to us marked "Undeliverable." We could only presume, with much sadness, that he had already been arrested by the Nazis and surely imprisoned by them, if he had not perhaps already been liquidated, but there was nothing further that we could do. We felt that we had unavoidably failed him.

Chapter 28

A Collection of Miniatures

Often circumstances that occur in people's lives are surely stranger than fiction, and I am sure that antiquarians and art dealers are no exception in this regard.

Among the many and varied aspects of art that we handled was that of the miniature portrait. Such miniature portraits were very prominent during the eighteenth century in Europe, and naturally to a minor extent over here in America, as they preceded the daguerrotype and later the photograph. Of a certainty, the countries in Europe most concerned with this art were England, France, Germany, and also, but to a lesser extent, Austria and Russia.

England was certainly the most prolific. During this period there were several miniature portraitists in America who were most competent in their art, and probably the greatest of the era was Charles Willson Peale, father of the dynasty of the Peale family of artists who somewhat humorously, to our minds, named some members of their progeny Rubens Peale, Rembrandt Peale, and Titian Peale.

Although we handled such miniatures, we never considered ourselves the greatest experts in this particular field. Despite this aspect, the names of such English greats as Copley, Engleheart, Smart, and Shelley come readily to mind.

And so it was that one morning we received a telephone call from a Spaniard who said that he had just arrived in London, having escaped the frightfulness of the Spanish Civil War just at that time in progress, stating, "I have brought over with me my very important collection of miniatures that I have accumulated over the past many years and which, of necessity I have now to sell, and as quickly as possible." The man said that he had only just arrived from his native Barcelona and that it was a real miracle that he had managed to flee with all of his collection and that

154

conditions in Spain were frightful. He continued to speak of the terrible things that were happening in Spain so that I became very sorry for him and told him that I would do all in my power to assist him.

He then continued to say, "I am an architect by profession, and now that I am here in London, I must raise cash so that I can live in England until I can set myself up in my profession over here, when I can once again perhaps start over collecting miniatures, as the selling of my collection at this time is going to be a dreadful wrench."

I then asked him how he knew of our firm, as I did not recall having any particular clients in Barcelona, and he replied, "Many of my friends in Madrid have spoken to me so many times of the high situation held by your firm in London, that you are the people that I want to deal with."

I then suggested to him that he bring us the collection so that we could know better what we were talking about, after which if the miniatures were as he said they were, cash would be forthcoming immediately.

While we were still on the telephone I asked him to enumerate the names of some of the artists involved, and he then gave me a list of some of the greatest names in the entire field of English miniature art. I then suggested to him that he bring his miniatures round to us the following morning so that I could go through the collection and advise him of their value for immediate cash sale, and it was then arranged that we meet at our gallery next morning at nine o'clock. I told him that although this was a little early for us, as we usually commenced at around nine-thirty, nevertheless I would be there to meet him.

Next morning at nine he was waiting for me on the doorstep with two valises in his hands, and as soon as I opened up he commenced to lay his specimens out side by side on one of our tables. As he did this I saw about fifty of the greatest examples that I had ever laid eyes on.

He then reiterated that his entire life had been wrapped up in this collection and, in fact, he had never married so that he could have all of his income used for the purchase of fine specimens. He stated that he had had considerable difficulty in getting the collection through the Spanish Customs and only done it by considerable bribery of the officials on the Franco–Spanish border.

We then discussed the values and I explained to him that although we handled such specimens, we were not the greatest experts, but that since we wished to do the best for him in his present circumstances I would like to show the entire collection to a friend of ours that same day so that I could get him the best offer for cash by the morning. I also told him that while the miniatures were in our possession they would be covered by our insurance at Lloyd's of London and that he would have to leave them with us.

He did not appear to be too pleased with my suggestion, but with the prospect of cash on the barrelhead next morning he agreed. I offered to give him a receipt for the collection, but he replied that this would not be necessary, as he knew that we were entirely reliable.

The moment that he had gone I telephoned to speak to my friend, and expert, a gentleman named Arthur Tite, but his secretary told me that Arthur was away and out of the country and that he would be gone for several months. But she said, "Why not discuss the collection with Mr. Adhemar, whom I know you know quite well and with whom, in any case, Arthur would consult about your collection?" She then considered for a few moments and said, "If anything, Adhemar is a much greater expert than Arthur." She also stated that she knew that Adehemar was at that moment in London, as she had spoken with him only that morning upon his return from Paris.

As she had said I should, I at once telephoned to Mr. Adhemar and told him about the collection that we had for offer and which had been left with us by a Spaniard. I then recounted to him our entire conversation of that morning and also mentioned the names of some of the sitters and artists involved in the collection, and to my surprise, he said, "I am positive that I know every one of these miniatures, and as far as I know they are the property of a Spanish collector who is now in Paris and with whom I spent yesterday afternoon." He then continued, "I do not even need to come round to see the collection, as from what you have been telling me I know every miniature very well indeed." He then said, "As soon as you hang up I am going to telephone my

156

Spanish client in Paris and tell him your story and see whether he knows anything about the matter of the suggested sale, and fortunately, the gentleman rarely leaves his hotel suite in Paris, so I am sure to get him right away."

It was no more than half an hour after my conversation with Mr. Adhemar that he was again on the telephone to me. "I have just spoken with my client in Paris, who has told me that the architect is attempting to steal his collection. He then went on to tell me the following: 'I know this architect very well indeed and asked him whether he would be able to get my two daughters out of Barcelona, as he knew many of the people on the frontier. He said that he could, but that this would require a lot of money, and he suggested that I write a letter addressed to my daughters telling them to hand over to him all of the collection and any other pieces of jewelry that they might have in the house. Armed with this he knew that he would be able to smuggle the two girls safely out of Spain and into Paris. And when he had the letter he would return at once to Barcelona.' It now appears that the architect did in fact return immediately to Spain and went to the house and showed the two daughters their father's letter and without a moment's hesitancy they handed over the collection, together with several important pieces of jewelry. Obviously, the architect had not the slightest intention of even trying to get the girls out of Spain, but had brought the collection to London to sell for himself.

The gentleman said, 'The architect is a thief.' " Mr. Adhemar then stated that with my permission he was going at once to contact Scotland Yard and see what could be done, and of course I at once gave him permission to go right ahead.

Later that same afternoon a detective arrived at our shop from Scotland Yard and we discussed the entire matter.

"I shall be round at the shop tomorrow morning with an associate and we shall then act as your assistants and as soon as the Spaniard arrives you will greet him and introduce us to him and tell him that we wished to negotiate the purchase with him."

Next morning when the Spaniard arrived at about ten o'clock, he was in a very jovial mood. After all, he felt that he would return to his hotel laden down with cash, and he seemed to be delighted to see "his" collection all laid out nearby on the table, and as he looked at the miniatures, he said, "Don't they look lovely?"

At this point I introduced the two "experts" who I said would take over and arrange matters with him directly.

The detectives then proceeded to ask him some questions about "his" collection, to which he gave them obviously lying responses, and after they had heard a sufficient tissue of lies, they told him that they were detectives from Scotland Yard and that he was under arrest. The man was so taken aback by what he heard that he began to flounder and try to make some apologies, but all to no avail. The detectives at once hailed a passing taxicab and took him away to the police station, where he was duly booked and charged with attempted theft. It did not take too long for the Spaniard to appear on trial at the Old Bailey, where he was charged. The trial was a very short one, as the evidence against the man was so positive and conclusive. I was required to give evidence of what had occurred and to appear in court, which I did. The judge then admonished the Spaniard for his most dastardly attempt to steal the miniatures and also for not having had the slightest intention of even trying to bring the two daughters safely out of Spain, where at that moment they were in the greatest danger. The judge then sentenced the man to quite a long term in prison and also told him that he would be safer there at that moment than if he were to try to get home to Barcelona.

As soon as the judge had concluded sentencing the man he told Mr. Adhemar that he had his authority to collect the collection from us and return it to the gentleman in Paris.

Mr. Adhemar then came to see me that same afternoon and later in the day crossed to Paris, taking the collection with him.

Next day he returned and came in to see me and said that the gentleman wished to thank me for saving his collection of miniatures for him. We later heard again from Mr. Adhemar that the gentleman in Paris had somehow managed to get his girls safely out of Spain and that they were then together with their father in Paris.

Fact is thus stranger than fiction at times.

Chapter 29

American Silver—Faneuil Hall Candlesticks

Despite the fact that our business was located in London, we were entirely international and had clients with whom we were constantly in touch from overseas and particularly collectors from America. With so many American collectors of antique silver, we found that we were always discussing the subject with them and always with particular reference to antique silver made in America and by American silversmiths. Following up on these conversations, I decided to investigate the possibility of finding such silver in England.

My first objective was to buy as many books as I could find on the subject, but I was soon to discover that any such material was almost impossible either to find or to buy, at any price. I found that there had been one small volume on the subject of American colonial silversmiths and their marks compiled by a London antique silver dealer named Ensko. But when I asked him where I could get a copy of his book, he told me that it had been out of print for quite some time and was unobtainable anywhere. He did, however, offer most kindly to lend me his own copy, which I at once took and had Xeroxed. As far as I know, this book is still today accepted as the basic authority on antique American silver, although today there are many volumes that have been written by experts on various aspects of the subject.

It was after much investigation on my part and in conversation with American dealers and collectors that, unlike their English prototypes, such silver was almost invariably marked with the initials of the makers only, and in some instances together with facsimiles of English hallmarks. It did not take me long to discover many such pieces with apparently "false" hallmarks. Being armed with such information as I was able to obtain, I found that going through the things being offered at London auction houses, the English dealers were, at the time, simply ignoring many such pieces that were not fully hallmarked with English markings. The silver made in colonial America was almost invariably copied from their English prototypes, and I found that in short order I was able, quietly, to pick up quite a few items, many pieces of which were indeed quite fine.

Actually, in a short while I had accumulated quite a collection of early eighteenth-century pieces and also quite a few of the nineteenth century by American silversmiths. Each of my purchases at the time had cost me a mere pittance.

One day while going through a collection of silver I saw a pair of cast silver candlesticks that looked exactly like their English eighteenth-century originals, but when examined I saw that they were each marked underneath with only the maker's initials. However, I decided to buy them, although at this time I had not as yet seen the Ensko book.

After their purchase I just placed them in my showcase marked "Origin - unknown." At the time I did not realize that they could be American colonial pieces.

While they were in the showcase many dealers saw them, thinking that they were English, but the moment that they had them in their hands, not finding any English hallmarks on them, they returned them, entirely uninterested in their purchase.

Later, when I did get hold of the Ensko book, I was able to trace the maker of these candlesticks and discovered that the initials "N M" on each were the marking of Nathaniel Morse.

The more that I looked at these sticks, I noted that each was engraved with some sort of coat-of-arms.

On further study I saw that these "arms" included thirteen stars, and because of this I felt that in some way the stars might have some association with the thirteen original colonies.

I asked several of my American friends if they might have any idea what these "arms" might represent, but no one apparently had the slightest idea.

One day an English dealer with whom we did considerable business, was in to see me. Knowing that I had been quietly buying up as many pieces by American makers as I could find, he told me that he had an American dealer over who wanted to buy some pieces of American silver.

As I had been basically making these purchases for my own personal collection, I told him that I was not particularly interested in selling any of my specimens, but despite this he asked to see what I might have in my collection, and in the course of conversation I showed him this pair of cast candlesticks. He similarly said that he did not know the meaning of the coat-of-arms with the thirteen stars. At the time I had no reason to disbelieve him, but today I feel that he did know. He then told me that he thought that his American client would perhaps buy these candlesticks and I then told him that I was not particularly interested in selling them out of my collection, but at his insistence I agreed to let him have them. He then asked me how much I wanted for the pair and I told him that they had cost me almost nothing but that I would be willing to split with him fifty-fifty anything that he could sell them for.

In retrospect I am now quite positive he knew what he was looking at. Next day he called and told me that he had sold the candlesticks to his American buyer for one thousand dollars so that, splitting this sum down the middle, I would receive five hundred dollars, which satisfied me. Today I am quite sure that he sold them for much more than the thousand dollars, but this is the sort of untruth that is more or less accepted as legitimate in the antique trade. As these candlesticks were in my personal collection, I had every piece photographed so that I could enter them into a special book with all details together with the photographs for my personal records.

The years then passed and we were established in New York for quite some time when, studying an auction catalog that had arrived in the mail from the Parke-Bernet Galleries, as they were called in those days, glancing through the pages I saw an entire sheet with one of these candlesticks photographed in color. The notation beneath, which I at the time of their purchase had not been able to discover, stated that they were from Faneuil Hall, the "Home of Liberty." To say the least, I was astonished. I then knew that they must be very valuable.

I could not wait until the day set for the auction to see how much they might bring.

When eventually the day of the sale arrived I was in the audience and heard the auctioneer announce that these were "perhaps the greatest examples of historic American silverware ever to come to light." Actually, he said that he did not recall ever previously having been privileged to offer so great a rarity for sale.

The bidding then commenced and proceeded at a fast and furious pace, and in due course they were knocked down for the then enormous sum of fifteen thousand dollars each.

Certainly this pair of candlesticks is today in the collection of some private collector of colonial American silverware, or in fact, they may well be in some museum. At this time I do not know where they are, but maybe one of these days I shall discover the owner and perhaps be able to supply him with some background history of my original purchase.

Since this auction I have often pondered whether or not my dealer friend knew at the time that they had emanated from Faneuil Hall. If he did, I do not blame him for not telling me. Such happenings do frequently occur in the handling of antiquities in all areas, and it is perhaps this aspect that does add its modicum of fascination to the world of art and antiquity.

Chapter 30

The Sammel Collection for South Africa

In an establishment such as ours, we could never know from moment to moment what or who would come in once our doors opened. And so it was that one very desultory day in the early summer of 1939 a gentleman came in to see us. He told me that he had just the day before arrived in London from South Africa and that a friend of his over there had given him our name as people with whom he might be able to do business.

I inquired his name and he told me that he was a Mr. Sammel and that he would be staying in London for a couple of months before returning to his home.

His concept, he told me, was to establish a museum in South Africa that the native blacks could perhaps visit without hindrance and that in so doing they might be able to improve their knowledge of the world around them. I asked him in what way he intended to do this, and laughingly he said, "I am searching for what you would certainly call white elephants; naturally I don't mean live ones." He then continued, "Over the past several years I have been acquiring very important and large pieces in crystal, glass, porcelain, hard stone—in fact, anything of quality in these various areas that had visual beauty and was of heroic size. Nothing is too large for my concept."

"Where do you keep these things that you have already acquired?" I asked him, and he told me that he had a large warehouse down in the city, filled to the rafters with objects that he had already purchased, during the past several years that he had been collecting. He then began to explain why he was doing all this. "Over the past many years and in fact since I was a small boy who had been brought to South Africa by my parents, I have made a lot of money. We left Russia to escape the pogroms that were at the time running in full spate, and even as a small child I felt that I should try and do something for the natives. In fact,

163

I want in some small measure to repay South Africa for what it has given me.

"The idea of a museum was uppermost in my mind, and I thought perhaps, in my ignorance, the natives would only understand objects of large size, rather than anything in the nature of minutiae. None of them, or at least very few, had ever had any schooling and the thought of period or antiquity entirely escaped them."

While he was explaining all this to me, I did not entirely agree with him that only large sizes would appeal to the natives, but I let this thought pass. I could not see why oil paintings would not be of interest to them, but I kept my own counsel. It was not for me to tell him how to spend his own money.

At the time we had nothing in our collection that could possibly be of any interest to him, with the possible exception of an enormous pair of Victorian silver candelabra, but after looking at these for a few moments he remarked that he did not think that they would be important enough for his conceptual idea.

"As a matter of fact, what I love beyond anything else is jade, and any very large piece carved in this stone is something that I would always buy; at the moment I already have many such pieces."

I told him that from my experience, large heroic-sized pieces of Chinese jade of good color were very, very rare indeed, and he said that he knew this, but also he had discovered that there are very few buyers for any such and that this had always been his good fortune. Beyond this, very large pieces of carved agates of varied colors were also very much in his mind.

"One of these days when everything is established, I will want you to be my guest in South Africa where the museum is to be erected. I have already selected the site in my hometown of Johannesburg. It is to be known as the Sammel Museum of Fine Arts."

I promised that I would hold anything that came our way and give him a call so that he could perhaps pass by and look at it.

During the following week there was nothing offered us that I could call him about, but he, being anxious to buy things, came in again to see us.

We then chatted a little and it seemed to me that he was very lonely and wanted to have somebody with whom he could talk.

"When we came over, my father arrived without the proverbial penny in his pockets, and so by dint of doing any odd jobs that were available he managed to feed my mother and me; there was, however, no money for me to go to school. Thus by the time I was fourteen I decided that I would try to do some business and help out at home. I was a businessman at this very young age.

"While growing up it always pleased me to watch the natives at their various occupations, and it seemed to me that they were devoid of many of the implements that would have eased their toil. They did not have many of the tools that might be today considered a normalcy.

"I then conceived the idea that I would buy leathers from the local hunters, and instead of paying them in cash, which in any case I did not have, I would pay them eventually with any such merchandise that I could buy in England, where I felt sure that I could sell the leathers. Naturally, when I started I had to convince the hunters of my sincerity so that I could buy from them on credit, and for some reason that I cannot at this time explain, many of them trusted me.

"After getting a large quantity of leathers from these men, I needed money to buy me transport on one of the liners that plied across to England, and I suppose my idea seemed a good one, as one man in particular took a liking to me and lent me the necessary cash. Maybe I was a very convincing talker, or maybe I just looked honest.

"Eventually he was to discover that his trust in me had not been misplaced. I repaid him with interest."

Next week we were offered a piece that I felt positive he would like, and I called him on the telephone; when he heard my voice he seemed to be quite excited and told me that he would be right round.

The item was not for him.

"Then, Mr. Sammel," I said, "why don't I, together with my brother, come down to see you at the warehouse, look over the many items that you already have, and then perhaps we will have a much better idea of what you are seeking?" As they say, a picture is worth a thousand words, but the actual objects even more.

"That's a great idea, and I don't know why I did not tell you to do this the first time that I came in to see you."

We then made an appointment to meet him at his warehouse the next morning. Upon our arrival we were amazed by what we saw. There were shelves all round the very vast area that he occupied, and they were crammed with the most fascinating objects of enormous dimensions—some were indeed beautiful; others were to our eyes of extreme ugliness.

Looking carefully through these objects, particularly those of Chinese jade, many of animalistic form, and which he said were his favorites, I saw there were lions, tigers, elephants, giraffes, and panthers, which he said the natives would immediately recognize. Almost unseen behind a large object was hidden a small jade hippopotamus that without a question must have emanated from the ateliers of Carl Fabergé.

"That piece is quite out of character among all your wonderful pieces!" my brother exclaimed. "Could we buy it from you perhaps?"

"Why not?" he replied. "I agree that it is quite lost among my other things."

"How much will you take for it?" we asked, and he countered with, "How much will you give me for it?"

My brother and I then went into a huddle and made him our offer. Mr. Sammel listened carefully to what we said and replied, "I will take double of your offer."

Without a moment's hesitation we accepted his suggestion, and on the spot we wrote out a check, lest he refused to honor his acceptance, and we did not wish to give him time to change his mind.

After we had paid him for it, we took it away back to our offices with us. It was actually an exquisite piece by the master and one very similar to another such that had been made for King Edward VII, which is now illustrated in the book on Fabergé by Bainbridge.

The following week he was again round, but this time he came to say good-bye, as he was returning home, saying that he felt that he should be back in South Africa and that he thought that he had left his business alone for too long a time. On this last visit he had with him his "secretary," who remained seated in

166

his car when he entered. The young man "secretary" was quite handsome, with flowing blond hair that he wore in somewhat Byronic fashion, and this was very many years before it became fashionable for young men to sport long hair.

When we saw this young man we realized why Mr. Sammel had informed us that he had never married; he was surely a homosexual. Not that this made any difference to us; that was his business and his alone.

We then told him that one of our clients was going to bring something in to us the next day that might well be something for him, and it was arranged that he would be in to see us the next morning to view the object. Next morning when he arrived he was carrying a newspaper in his hand, but it was upside down, and as he held it he pointed out a headline as though he were reading it. "See what it says? We are going to be involved in a terrible war with the Nazis at any moment, and when it does happen the bombing is going to be something awful." He then went out to his car and we realized that he could not read and had the young man read to him, and having a very retentive memory, he was able to repeat what he had been told. Apparently, he never went anywhere without this young man at his side, who apparently read the newspaper headlines to him every morning.

Next morning Mr. Sammel was again in to see the piece that we had mentioned to him. And in very short order he purchased it; it was a largish piece of colorful carved agate, possibly of Chinese origin.

He then for the first time asked the young man to come into the shop to write us a check, which he himself signed on Mr. Sammel's behalf. We then were sure that he could neither read nor could he write. After all, he had informed us originally he had never been to school.

He then said good-bye and told us that he would write us well in advance of his next visit, but then jokingly he remarked, "Now everything must depend on the outcome of any war."

There was never to be another visit, because while he was on the high seas the war and the bombing began. As his warehouse was located right in the heart of the city of London, it was one of the first places to be destroyed, and with the bombing certainly every one of his pieces must have gone to dust.

After the passage of several years we received a letter from Mr. Sammel's "secretary," who was at that time in South Africa, to tell us that his boss, as he called him, had passed away soon after he heard from London that his warehouse had been gutted and that all had been lost. He wrote: "I am sure that Mr. Sammel died of a broken heart on hearing this news." As Mr. Sammel had never married and as the young man had been with him in Johannesburg, the chances are that he inherited a small fortune or perhaps even a large one. One thing is certain—Mr. Sammel's museum never materialized, and upon thinking over his concept that the blacks would never understand what we term *fine art*, I am today quite positive that they would.

Chapter 31

Fabergé Hippo and Mary Clapp

After we had purchased the wonderful little Fabergé hippopotamus in Russian jade or jadeite, as it would more correctly be termed, from Mr. Sammel, we decided to advertise it in one of our forthcoming *Connoisseur* advertisements. This magazine, being at the time perhaps the world's greatest journal for art and antiques, had subscribers spread all over the world. Thus a few weeks after our advertisement appeared we received a letter from a lady living in Seattle, Washington, Mrs. Norton Clapp, or Mary, as we later began to call her. In her letter she wrote that she had seen our advertisement about the little hippopotamus and asked whether we could perhaps let her have some further particulars about its history, and then, as a sort of afterthought, she inquired the cost.

We replied to her quoting her the price and telling her that as far as we knew, Fabergé had only created two such little models and that each of them was about five inches in overall length, and also as far as it was our understanding, the other was in the collection of the Royal Family and it had been especially modeled for King Edward VII, who had used it with its gold mouthpiece as a cigar lighter.

The moment that Mary Clapp received our letter she cabled us to say that she was crossing to London and would be arriving in about two weeks, and she also inquired whether we would hold the piece aside for her to see as soon as she arrived.

In this cable she referred to the hippopotamus as her "little gem." We then sent her a cable in reply saying that we were withdrawing the object from sale and that we would hold it for her to see upon her arrival.

As she had cabled, she duly arrived in about two weeks, and the moment that she had checked into her hotel she came in to see us.

Setting eyes on the little hippo, she said that she had fallen in love with it, but that actually it was much more beautiful than the advertisement had suggested, and she immediately wrote us her check in payment. Not only did she fall in love with her "little gem," but we soon became fast friends, especially as she told us that she was all alone in London, where she had absolutely nobody that she could even talk with. That same evening she was our guest at dinner and in the course of conversation happened to mention that she had never witnessed a boxing match and that she had read in the morning paper that there was to be such a fight later that same week.

We told her that we would endeavor to buy seats for this and invited her to be our guest, in the event that we were able to get them. It happened that this was to be the now famous Tommy Farr fight, and by dint of much back door influence we were able to buy three seats in the front row.

As soon as we had these tickets we telephoned her and told her that we would pick her up in good time for the bout. In due course we were seated, and shortly after that the bout began. She was all agog with excitement, especially as the stadium was jammed to the rafters, everybody waiting for the bout to begin.

Then just as the referees were making their little speeches to the two contestants, I bent down to put my hat under my seat; by the time I was up again the bout had already been in progress for several seconds and the fight was over by a knockout.

So much for Mary's first boxing bout in London.

We then remained seated for a short while, because there was another bout due to commence, but after we had watched this for a short while we all became rather bored and decided to leave and go somewhere for supper.

After this evening spent with Mary we had several further dinners together until she told us that she was leaving London and going to Paris for a couple of weeks and then she said that she had decided to leave for home, directly from Le Havre. She did say that the moment that she was in Seattle she would write us and tell us what she had been doing and seeing in France, and also saying that she did not wish so delightful a friendship to end.

A few weeks later, true to her promise, we received a long letter from her, and from that time onward we were in continual correspondence with her. Some little while later I wrote her and told her of my impending marriage and that after the ceremony and a short honeymoon I would be crossing to New York with my bride. As soon as Mary received my letter she sent us a beautiful wedding gift and wrote that the moment we were settled in New York we were to write and tell her where we were staying, so that she could come east to be with us.

Then following upon our arrival in New York I wrote her and gave her my news, and upon receipt of this letter she telephoned me from Seattle to say that she would be arriving in a few days and that as the World's Fair was just then at its height we were to be her guests there. She said she would not accept a "no" for an answer and also wrote that she had already made a reservation for dinner at the Spanish Pavilion so that we could again be together.

As soon as she was in the city she called to say that she would be coming to pick us up at our hotel in her limousine together with her friend, a Mr. Cini. When she did arrive at our hotel she handed my wife, or now should I write my ex-wife, a most beautiful yellow orchid, the likes of which neither of us had ever previously seen, and insisted that she wear it for that evening.

Dinner at the Spanish Pavilion was fabulous, and after eating and walking about the fair we were all rather tired and decided to call it a day and we returned to our respective hotels.

As soon as we were in our room at the hotel, my ex-wife said, "Isn't it a pity that such beauty as this yellow orchid has to die so soon?"

I replied that I did not think that it had to, and finding an old jar in our room, I filled it with rubbing alcohol and then placed the flower inside. I then sealed the top with candle grease. Believe it or not, this worked out beautifully for the several months that we were still at the hotel, and then when we moved into a more permanent apartment we took the jar with us, where it remained looking as fresh as ever until we were divorced some ten years later, when I suppose I must have thrown it out.

Following upon this wonderful evening at the fair, Mary again insisted that we be her guests the following evening at the old Stork Club, where she told me that her friend Mr. Cini had made reservations for the four of us. Now it so happened that Mary was the daughter of the bishop of Oakland, California, but she was inclined to be quite buxom and a little on the blousy side and, for a matter of fact, somewhat Semitic-looking. As we arrived at the door of the club the doorman gave Mary the once-over and said that they had no reservation for our party. Mr. Cini argued with the man, but to no avail. We were not admitted. Later I discovered that the club was notoriously anti-Semitic. Next day Mary called to say that she had had a violent quarrel with Mr. Cini and that she had found for herself another beau with whom she had fallen madly in love.

She said that she had to come over to our hotel to tell us all about this new beau, an Australian, and then she told us that she was going to Sydney in Australia to be with him. The fact that she had a husband and three daughters at home in Seattle did not affect her one little bit. She also announced that as soon as she returned to Seattle she was going to arrange for a divorce and that she would marry the Australian.

She then left with him and wrote that on her way home from Australia she would stop off in New York to visit with us and that she would have her little hippo with her, as, she explained, she never traveled without him.

She also wrote us that as she knew that my brother Henry similarly loved the little hippo she was going to bequeath it to him in a new will that she was going to prepare.

It could not have been more than a few weeks after she had written us this letter about the hippo that there was a report in the press that a lady named Mary Clapp and her three daughters had been involved in a terrible motoring accident and that all four of them had been killed. Upon reading this report of the tragedy we wrote Mary's husband offering him our sincerest condolences, and also in this letter we referred to Mary's letter to us about the bequest of the hippo. Upon receipt of our letter her husband, Norton, replied that he would dearly love to honor Mary's wish about the hippo, but he wrote that he had searched high and low for it all over their house, but he had been unable to find any trace of it anywhere.

Many years had now passed, and in a recent advertisement of an auction we saw a full-page color picture of the little hippopotamus, where it stated that it had been consigned for sale by an Australian. It then became clear to us that as Mary had written us that she always carried the little hippo with her wherever she traveled, she must have had it out in Australia with her and that, forgetting about her promise, had left it in the hands of the Australian. We then searched high and low for Mary's letter but could not find it anywhere.

Had we been able to locate the letter we knew that Christie's, the auctioneers, would have withdrawn the object from their sale. But without this letter the auction proceeded and the hippo was sold for an enormous sum of money.

Chapter 32

Maniac Sultan of Malay State

It was at some time during the thirties that the London press was being filled on a virtually daily basis with wild stories of a man whom they described as "some sort of maniac" who was apparently rushing headlong through the crowded London streets in a very high-powered supercharged automobile and that at the same time he was completely ignoring everybody and everything in his path.

According to these press reports he was apparently entirely protected by diplomatic immunity, and for that reason the police were quite helpless in their efforts to restrain him and possible mayhem on the streets. How he managed to proceed without killing anybody is even to this day, as I think back, a miracle.

At the time while reading these reports it never entered our minds that we would ever meet up with him. The thought was that such things always happen to the other person. After all, London is one of the largest cities in the world.

And so it happened that on one glorious morning in spring our door opened and just at that moment I was standing near the entrance. A man entered who seemed to me to be of enormous stature, both in girth and in height; he was certainly well over six feet tall, and as for his dress, he was as flashy as anybody could possibly be. He sported a bright canary yellow waistcoat, the palest of pale blue trousers, and a snowy white blazer; he wore no hat on his head, which was covered with a thick mop of snowy white hair that stood out against his light brown skin. He was quite obviously Oriental, but I could not make out from whence he came.

I did notice that he carried in his right hand a walking cane of very thick wood. It was most unusual, as though it might have been an entire limb of some tree, surmounted by an enormous and surely very heavy bulbous gold knob engraved on its top with a very large crown. Seeing this, I had to presume that he was a notable of some sort, but I had no way of determining who he might be.

At the moment it never occurred to me that here was the so-called maniac that the press had been writing about.

Then, speaking with him, I asked him what I could do for him, and he replied with a very loud guffaw of laughter that reverberated throughout our entire establishment.

Looking around me, I noticed that our entire staff was standing at the rear all aghast at this apparition. Then in order to make some conversation with him I inquired his name, but instead of replying he took a large pocket wallet out and extracted a postage stamp from it and handed it to me.

Looking at the stamp, I noticed that it had a value of one cent, and beneath this figure was the man's name.

"This is my visiting card," he said. "I am the Sultan of one of the Malay states," and as he mentioned his name I then recalled that he was the man that the press had been writing about.

Despite these reports, coming into the shop I had to presume that perhaps he wanted to buy something, possibly a gift for somebody. After all, what is the purpose of a shop?

I then inquired whether there was anything special that we could show him, but in reply he roared with laughter. "Don't ask me any questions like that; you find out for yourself what I want."

Had it been raining I might have presumed that perhaps he wanted to get in out of the rain, but the day was beautiful and the sky was quite cloudless. Then not knowing quite how to handle the man, I thanked him for the stamp. "I would like to thank Your Highness for the stamp that you have given me." To which he replied:

"I did not give you the stamp. I only wanted to show it to you, and now I want it back."

Remember, the value of the stamp was only one cent. I at once handed it back to him, taking the entire matter as some sort of ridiculous joke.

Then placing the stamp very carefully back into his wallet, all the while laughing, "His Highness" without another word turned and left.

175

The moment that he was out of the door I called our manager, Mr. Christie, and the entire staff over to me. "That was the maniac that the press has been writing about; he is the Sultan of one of the Malay states. Because of his maniacal rides through the streets with his automobile I never want to see him again, and if he ever comes into the shop again I don't want to be called from my office."

It was some few weeks after this incident that a very wealthy gentleman who we knew lived in one of the Malay states came in to see us.

I then said to this gentleman, "Have you perhaps ever run across the Sultan in Malaya?" and he replied, "Certainly. I know him very well indeed. He is enormously wealthy and could at some time or other be a very good customer, but only if you can take him." He then continued, "The Sultan is quite mad; he has a weekly custom of going into one of the many bars in Singapore, always on a Saturday night, when such places are invariably crowded with sailors off the many international ships that are always lying tied up there, as Singapore is a very large port. When he enters, the barmen, who know him, at once take cover under the counters, as laughingly he draws a revolver from his pocket and begins to fire at the rows of liquor bottles that line the bar, breaking as many bottles as he possibly can. When he has finished with the bottles he proceeds to break up as many chairs and tables as lie in his path and then having finished with these shenanigans politely says, 'Excuse,' and leaves.

"Why he does this nobody could ever fathom, but invariably on the day following he always sends his secretary to the bar to find out how much he owed the patron for the damage he had done, and after being informed of the amount the secretary would return the same day with a check in full settlement.

"In Malaya it appears that the patrons of the bars appreciate what he does, as they certainly make a handsome profit by exaggerating the amount of their losses."

When our customer had left I said to the staff, "Despite the fact that the Sultan is enormously wealthy, I do not like people who carry guns, especially when they have diplomatic immunity, and I hope that we never see him again. Also, I don't think that he is very funny, although funny he may be."

A few weeks then passed peaceably, until one morning the press again began reporting that the Sultan was back in town, and the following morning he was again in our shop and, after saying good morning to one of our assistants who greeted him at the door, proceeded to walk leisurely all around the place, peering into all of the showcases that lined the walls, but without uttering a single word. He never asked about anything or even inquired the cost of any particular item. Seeing him do this, Christie came onto the scene and began to follow him around so that he would be available to answer any question that the Sultan might ask, but he never said anything, and not a word was spoken by either of them.

After he had been in the shop for maybe an hour or so, he again left without a word. All of us were happy to see him leave.

All the time that he had been in the shop I had been watching him through a special mirror that we had had fitted into the door of my office in the rear. It was the sort of mirror that one could look through quite clearly from behind and which from the front looked just like any ordinary mirror.

I was looking at him very closely, as I thought that perhaps he might have a gun in his pocket and that he might possibly think that he was at home in one of the Singapore bars on a Saturday night. Had he started shooting I really do not know what I might have done, except call the police.

When I saw him leave I was very relieved. The week following, the Sultan again came into the shop and this time he said to the assistant, "Today I have to see your boss."

The poor assistant was afraid to tell me that the Sultan wanted to see me, and on the other hand, he was similarly afraid to ignore the request. So saying to the Sultan that he would call me, he asked him to sit and wait a few moments.

He then came into my office. "The maniac Sultan is here again, and this time he says that he wants to speak with you."

I was not too happy when I heard this, but nevertheless, I came out to greet him.

"I have just come in to see you because I am returning home to Malaya tomorrow and I wanted to say good-bye, and also I wanted to present you with the stamp that I asked you to return

177

to me some months ago. I want you to have some memento of my very pleasant meeting with you."

He then handed me the stamp, for which I thanked him, and he left.

After this last visit I am happy to relate that he never again came to London or at least never came to see us, and as he must have been quite elderly at the time we had to presume that he had gone the way of all flesh. Certainly the populace of London was not unhappy never again to see him in town.

Chapter 33

Hurcomb's Auction House

For several centuries past, London and Paris have always been considered the two primary centers for art and antiquity; today New York City appears to a great extent to be taking over, particularly as the two leading auction houses are today Christie's and Sotheby's, both of London and now established in America.

For this reason many great collections in both of these fields seem to be veering toward New York for sale at auction.

Nevertheless, London does still have, as it always has had, many smaller auction rooms. One such, which for very good reason no longer exists, is worth describing.

The auction house to which I refer was called Hurcomb's and was named for its owner-founder. At the auctions that he held fairly frequently, Mr. Hurcomb was always himself the auctioneer; he never allowed anyone else to take his place on the rostrum. Were he ever unable for any reason whatsoever to conduct an announced and scheduled auction then that sale would be postponed.

In his person Mr. Hurcomb was invariably dressed in severely sober fashion, in dark, somewhat priestlike attire that made him look the epitome of piety. He always wore a very quiet tie round his collar. Putting the matter quite bluntly, in his business operation he could be considered a sort of Sweeney Todd, Demon Barber of Fleet Street.

Every week and without fail, he would himself write a very long letter to the *London Times*, which although it was an advertisement was so written by him that to the uninformed had to appear as news.

In these columns he would always write such items as "Mrs. Jones of Manchester recently sent us a very fine Persian rug that she said she wished to sell at auction, and in her letter she stated that she felt that it should realize about fifty pounds. But when I put it up for sale it brought five thousand, and naturally when she received my check she wrote me to say that she was overjoyed at the result." Or he would write something like this: "A gentleman wrote us one day from Scotland to say that he had inherited from an old aunt an antique diamond stomacher which he wrote he could not possibly use. He reported that it had been appraised locally at about one hundred pounds and asked whether we would offer it for sale on his behalf if he shipped it down to me.

"On this occasion I at once wrote him that we would be most happy to offer the piece for him and that I hoped that he would be entirely satisfied with the result. Upon receipt of my letter he at once sent us the jewel, and a couple of weeks later I included it in one of my jewel sales, when it realized ten thousand pounds, and I was able to mail him my check for this amount, less my nominal commission. When the gentleman received my check he wrote that he was quite bowled over by what I had done for him and that he was going to ship me a further consignment of things that he wanted me to dispose of."

The above two letters are but a sampling of the columns that Hurcomb wrote week in and week out. And they were quite lengthy columns. In each of these columns he would always end by stating they were willing to accept any fine antique silver, whether English or Continental, porcelains, statuary, furnishings, either antique or modern, rugs and carpets of all types and of all periods, and any other items that might have any antiquarian interest. Beyond this he would emphasize that there was always a very good demand by collectors for ancient Greek and Roman coins and that such were fetching enormous sums, in the event that anybody wished to consign any such items to him for sale.

After each of these letters appeared in print he would invariably receive many important shipments of all manner of objects. People, it is well known, are very gullible when reading the printed word. All believed implicitly whatever he had written. What he wrote was so cleverly worded that the public could only think of him as some sort of preacher reading the Gospel to them.

On occasion instead of shipping many of their things to him by mail or truck, many clients would themselves come to see Mr. Hurcomb, always by appointment, to discuss their valuables with him in his private office. On such occasions he would be attired in a semi-clerical-looking garb.

Whenever he would accumulate a sufficiency of any particular type of goods, he would arrange for a special announcement to be printed in the press that on such and such a date he would be holding an auction of very fine jewels, or what you will, and buyers would flock in from far and wide to view them.

Especially was this the case when one day he announced a special auction of a fine collection of jewels from an old estate. Now whenever he held any particular auction he would always arrange with a coterie of dealer friends that he would "knock" down very valuable items as quickly as he could to one or another of his friends, always pretending that he had not seen anybody else overbidding. Of course there were many arguments, which he invariably ignored, proceeding with the following lot.

Then, after any such auctions, Hurcomb would meet with this coterie of dealers in a back room that they always reserved at a local pub and they would then reauction each of the items that he had knocked down very cheaply. Then they would all share in the additional profits; in so doing they made for themselves a very handsome profit. If after any such auction on receipt of a check with which the consignor was not satisfied and which would invariably be much less than he had expected, he would write that he was going to write to the police about the matter. Hurcomb would always reply that he was extremely sorry at the disappointment results, but that the auction had been held on a very bad day.

Now there was one jewel dealer who was renowned far and wide for his honesty, who had always been a thorn in Hurcomb's side. So much so was this the case that on many occasions Hurcomb had attempted to lure him into his special group of unscrupulous dealers, but never with any success. And at Hurcomb's jewel sales, whenever this dealer would put in a bid for any item, it would always be knocked down to one of Hurcomb's own friends, and this dealer's bid would be overlooked.

Now it happened that one day Hurcomb had collected together a very fine group of very desirable jewels from an old and wealthy estate, and he announced that this estate would be offered at auction on a specific day at eleven o'clock in the morning. In

181.

his advertisement he wrote that this was one of the finest collections that he had ever been able to offer for sale. Aware that this honest dealer would be sure to be present, he decided that he had to find some way to prevent him from attending. Knowing from previous experience that this dealer always carried a large sum of cash in his pockets whenever he attended any auction sale, so that he could take away with him any purchases that he might make without any problem, Hurcomb waited until ten o'clock on the morning of his auction and telephoned the local police to tell them that if they went to this dealer's home they would be able to pick him up, as he was about to meet with some jewel thieves and buy from them some jewels that they had with them from a recent burglary. He also told the police that they would find a vast amount of cash in the pocket of the "fence," as he called him. When they asked him for his name he told them that he did not wish, for obvious reasons, to disclose his name, but that he was positive that when they picked the man up they would find that what they had been told by him was factual.

As soon as they received this information, two detectives arrived at the dealer's home, just as he was leaving, and when they saw him they told him that they were taking him to the local police station for questioning, especially when they found that he did indeed have a large amount of cash in his pocket. The dealer tried to explain to the detectives that he always carried a large sum of cash in his pocket when he went to any auction sale and explained that he was at that moment on his way to Hurcomb's for their important auction of jewels.

Despite all of the man's protestations, the detectives insisted that he come with them.

When they arrived at the police station, the dealer all the while protesting his innocence, they started to question him leisurely. But by the time that they were satisfied that he was telling them the truth they let him leave, but by this time the auction was over.

The following day, the detectives, having already received many complaints from consignors about Mr. Hurcomb, began to think that perhaps the dealer had in fact been telling the truth and also that maybe the anonymous caller who had tipped them off the previous day may well have been Hurcomb himself. They then decided that they would call and speak with Hurcomb; the moment that they began to question him he admitted that his entire operation was phony and told them all about his nefarious dealings. They were quite astonished at his speaking to them without the slightest hesitancy. He explained to the detectives how he always knocked down items to his coterie of special friends and that later these items would be reauctioned at the local pub. He also admitted that the material that he had included in his long newspaper columns was all "imaginary" and without the slightest basis of truth.

When he had finished telling them all about his operation, they told him that he was under arrest for fraud and that they were going to take him back with them to the police station. They also advised him to take with him a bag of overnight clothes, as he would certainly be detained. It was quite soon after his arrest that he was brought up at the Old Bailey, and as soon as he was put up on the witness stand he admitted everything quite openly and told the judge all about his operation.

The judge then, after admonishing him for his misdeeds and telling him that on many occasions he had been robbing poor widows and orphans, sentenced him to a long term in jail.

As soon as he was committed, the auction house closed down, never to reopen. I never heard whether he passed away in jail or died after his release. In any event, if he did survive his sentence he must have been an entirely broken man.

Chapter 34

Gold Rush in England

Just prior to the outbreak of hostilities in Europe, it became essential for the British government to obtain as much foreign currency as it could possibly lay its hands on. With this in mind, the Bank of England tapped a hitherto untouched source of gold. It was announced by the bank that jewelers would be permitted to buy and sell any gold objects that they could get and also they were to be allowed to trade in gold sovereigns and other such gold coins.

Many people had, over the years, been hoarding such gold currency, but now they were being given the opportunity to sell any such that they owned with impunity, and at the same time they would be assisting the war effort. This being the case, the public began to sell whatever they had as though a floodtide had stricken them.

At this time the gold sovereign was worth roughly five American dollars, but as soon as people were allowed to deal openly with their gold hoards this value fluctuated daily. Amusingly enough, this period of gold selling became known as the "Gold Rush," and every day, from morning to night, crowds were lining up outside jewelers' shops, each with his little packet of gold for sale.

Many people had some very beautiful gold objects they wanted to sell, and although they were advised that what they had was worth considerably more than its actual gold content, most insisted that if they sold them they wanted the pieces melted down as bullion for the advantage of the government.

Since our shop was located on the main Piccadilly, we were daily besieged with gold sellers. Each morning when we opened up our shop there were always lines of people waiting outside. In fact, they looked like lines waiting outside to get into a hot movie.

As the people began to pour into the shop we would buy from them parcels of gold sovereigns, and also many pieces of gold.

When we purchased the packets of sovereigns we would collect them together until about two o'clock in the afternoon, at which time our man Andrews would take them down to a central control bank and hand them over to the teller. As soon as the teller had them in his hands, he would place them in specially prepared wooden boxes, and as soon as these were filled he would nail down the tops on each and send them off to the London airport, from there they were transported to Switzerland. In all of these transactions no checks were given by the bank, as the sellers always wanted their payment to be in cash, and we always needed to have plenty of this on hand for the following day.

In many cases some of the pieces of gold jewelry that we had to have melted down were beautiful, but we had no alternative but to comply with the sellers' wishes.

As many of these pieces of gold were of varying quality, each piece, unless hallmarked, had to be tested; this was done by rubbing on a touchstone and then testing with acid.

At the time of our father's death we naturally disposed of all of his clothing. In his wardrobe he had his old and almost unworn cutaway that he had worn only at weddings, funerals, and other such functions. Now our old manager, Mr. Christie, habitually wore a cutaway to business each day, and knowing that he and Father had been friends of very long standing, I asked him whether he would care to accept father's cutaway, especially as they were both of somewhat similar height and girth.

"Not only would I be pleased to accept it, but I would be honored to do so," was his response.

We then gave it to him, and the very next day he began to wear it. Now as each piece of gold that had to be tested on the touchstone had to be tested with acid, we set a bottle of acid near the touchstone on top of a safe that stood at the rear of the shop, so that both would be readily available for use.

One morning, shortly after Mr. Christie had inherited the cutaway, while he was in the process of testing a piece of gold one of our secretaries, who was in a great hurry passed quickly behind him, and in so doing she inadvertently knocked over the bottle of acid, some of which poured down the back of Christie's coat that we had given him.

At this moment he was quite oblivious to the fact that the acid had burned a yellow streak right the way down the back from collar to bottom.

The young secretary, knowing how he loved wearing his old friend's cutaway, was scared when she saw what she had done and coming over to me said, "I am afraid to tell Mr. Christie what has happened to his coat, but he has to be told, as he cannot possibly wear it as it is, and I beg you to tell him for me."

I was not afraid to tell him what had happened to his coat, but when he saw the damage he was very upset. But he accepted the situation and allowed me to tell the young woman that he forgave her.

What could I do? Christie had discarded his old cutaway and now this one was ruined and he was without a suitable coat to wear. I felt sorry for him, so I took him to my tailor in Savile Row and had a special suit custom made for him. This was, I am sure, the first and last time he had ever had a garment especially tailored for him and certainly not by a Savile Row man.

It was one morning while the Gold Rush was in full spate that a lady came in and showed Christie a very heavy gold bangle that she wished to sell on behalf of the war effort. She told him that when she had been in India with her husband, who had been an officer in the British army there, she had taken a handful of gold coins to a local jeweler and had watched him sitting on the floor of his shop melting the coins and then making them into the bangle. The bangle was quite solid and very heavy and could have been made of pure gold, as it was very soft, but Christie told the lady that he would have to make a cut in the side to be sure that it was of the pure gold it was purported to be.

The lady was quite adamant, but she had to agree to have him cut into the gold. The moment that his saw went into the bangle, it became quite obvious that it contained a thick core of pure copper and that the outside was but a coating of gold.

When the lady saw this she could not believe her eyes, but she realized that Christie had been quite right to insist that he cut into the bangle. The lady said that the jeweler in India must have been a magician, as she had watched him at work and had not for a moment taken her eyes off him.

Christie then told the lady that he had insisted because he had seen the same sort of thing many times previously when the customers had told him that they had watched the Hindu jewelers at work. The bangle was almost valueless.

This selling of gold continued unabated for about two or three weeks, and then all of a sudden it came to a halt. All of the owners of any such bullion had already disposed of their hoards.

Chapter 35

The Duke of Kent, Mrs. Sassoon, and Bert's Washing

It was shortly before war had begun and when England lived under the threat of possible imminent air attack, without warning, that a very strict blackout was imposed on the public. There were the severest of penalties attached for even the slightest infringement. This blackout was so strict that even the slightest streak of light emerging from anywhere was subject to penalty.

Everybody was conscious of the importance of these regulations and tried to accede to them at all times. Shades had been drawn on all windows before any lights could be switched on. In fact, anywhere that there might be a possibility of light it had to be covered in. Each evening when lights were to be switched on all precautions were taken by all.

In those days, it was our custom to travel after closing our shop by train to our apartment at Hove, a small town on the south coast, and we did this every evening, returning to London on the following morning. Our brother Bertram did not accompany us during the week, when he invariably remained in town, where he stayed at his club. But each Friday he would join with the family in Hove for the weekend. On these occasions it was his custom to accumulate his soiled laundry, which he always took to Hove with him for laundering.

It was one Friday evening when our man was on the point of closing the shop, when all of our lights had already been extinguished, that he heard a loud knocking on the door.

As our lights were already out, he had to open the door to see who might be there.

When he did this a lady and gentleman entered, and as soon as he had closed the door he was able to put on the lights to see who they might be. When he did this he saw that the callers were none other than the Duke of Kent, with an old lady who accompanied him. The assistant asked them to go upstairs, where I was still getting ready to make my departure together with my brothers, and as soon as I saw the couple, I recognized the lady as old Mrs. Sassoon, who for some reason or other habitually accompanied the duke.

As soon as I saw who they were, I asked them what I could do for them, and Mrs. Sassoon replied that they wished to see some of our collection of antiquities.

I then asked an assistant to open up our safes that had already been locked for the weekend and to bring out some trays of "things" for them to see.

Mrs. Sassoon seemed to be very intrigued by what we had placed in front of her and in many instances asked me to tell her about some of the various objects. For his part, the duke did not seem to be interested at all, despite the fact that Mrs. Sassoon was continually calling him over to see some particular piece. He did this with obviously blind eyes.

Now, as stated, my brother Bertram's habitual custom was to collect all of his soiled laundry to take with him to Hove, and this he collected together in a paper bag and placed on the top of one of the safes in readiness to be taken with him. The bag naturally contained soiled pajamas, handkerchiefs, socks, underpants, and any other item that required laundering. This Friday was no different, and his bag had already been placed on the safe top.

For some reason or other this bag took the duke's attention. He just stood in front of it and stared, fascinated. He did not just stand and stare; he seemed to be entirely transfixed. He then turned and said to me, "Please tell me what treasure you have hidden in that bag up there." He surely thought that we had some special treasure in the bag for some special client and which we did not wish to show them.

I tried to veer him away from this bag, by suggesting that he examine some other object, but to no avail.

He persisted, "Mr. Hill, you must be hiding something up there."

I then had no alternative but to tell him what the bag contained. "I must tell Your Highness that this bag contains nothing but my brother's soiled laundry."

For some reason or other, best known to himself, he did not believe me and, taking his walking cane in his hand, began to poke into the sides of the bag.

Our assistant, Andrews, who was standing nearby and who looked upon all members of the British Royal Family as something quite holy, tried to keep from laughing as, at the duke's insistence, I began to open the bag to take out some of the contents for him to see.

Also, for my part I had the greatest difficulty in refraining from laughter. Actually, I felt as though I might burst a gut at any moment, the entire scene was so comical.

After I had taken some socks and other things out of the bag, the duke seemed to be unconvinced that I had told him the truth and again began to poke into the bag with his cane. Eventually he must have realized that I was not lying to him and appeared satisfied that there were no treasures in the bag.

At this point he turned to Mrs. Sassoon and asked, "Don't you think that we have seen enough and should leave very soon?"

As they had already spent about an hour or so going through our trays, the lady agreed, and then both of them, thanking us for our courtesy, said their good-byes and left.

Why they had come to see us in the first place was a mystery that we could not fathom, nor could we tell why they had chosen to come so late in the evening. It was quite positive that they did not wish to make any purchases, as neither of them had even inquired the cost of any one item. Among the things that we showed them on our trays were some of the finest eighteenth-century gold snuff boxes of all types, and in this group there were some of the Louis XV and XVI periods that Mrs. Sassoon said she loved the most. She had discussed with me some of these boxes that had been made of golds of various colors known as *quatre couleur*. Gold can be made in varying tints by incorporation of various metals into the pure gold, which resulted in colorations that were delightful. Mrs. Sassoon also loved looking through our collection of objects by Fabergé, and she told me about some of the special pieces that she had collected over the years, which she said that she had in her home. After their visit, we never saw either of them again. Mrs. Sassoon, who was at the time quite elderly, must have passed on, and the poor duke was killed shortly after this visit in an airplane accident.

Chapter 36

My Visit to America

It was early in the spring of 1937 or about that year, and just as I was preparing to leave for a trip to America I was reading in the press about the fabulous French liner *Normandie* and I decided that instead of the Cunarder that I would normally have taken, I would cross on her. Actually, I had already booked passage on one of the Queen's but changed this in favor of what I expected would be a most enjoyable as well as interesting voyage.

About three days before my scheduled departure we were visited by some old friends and valued clients, Mr. David K. E. Bruce and his then wife, Ailsa Mellon. They told me that they wished to see what we had in very fine gold snuff boxes that they could add to their collection, which at the time must already have been quite extensive. Mr. Bruce told me that he had just finished reading our book, *Antique Gold Boxes, Their Lore and Their Lure*, which had been authored by my brother Henry and me, and Mrs. Bruce said that because she had been so fascinated with what we had written she had decided to augment their collection.

I then showed them the best of our collection of such boxes, and they both at once selected several of the finest specimens. The Bruces then told me that they were returning home on the *Normandie* and asked whether we could arrange to have the boxes delivered to them on board.

"Not only will they be delivered to you on board, but I shall have the very great pleasure of handing them to you myself, as I too am crossing on her."

We then spoke of the majesty of this great liner, and then after saying good-bye they left.

Having made all my preparations for the trip, I was ready in due time to make the crossing, and having taken the gold boxes for the Bruces with me, I contacted Villar, the purser, for the number of the Bruce suite as soon as I boarded. Instead of being courteous, as pursers invariably are, he was particularly unpleasant and very offhand. I could not make out why he was so obviously rude, but he gave me the suite number and I left.

To say that the Bruce suite was fabulous is stating the matter very mildly. It was indeed breathtaking.

I went to the special deck and then walked along a very wide carpeted area; it was just like the corridor that one might find at an exclusive hotel, and just toward the center of a row of suites I found the one that was being occupied by the Bruces. I rang a bell at the door, and soon this was opened by their uniformed butler who, as soon as I gave him my name, asked me to come in, as I was expected.

Their suite was furnished in the greatest of luxury and I was invited to join them on a balcony that overlooked the ocean, and it was here that, seated in a most comfortable armchair, I handed them their boxes.

We then had some drinks together and again discussed the beauty of the ship. While we were seated, Mrs. Bruce told me about her great collection of paintings, and naturally I knew that she owned some wonderful examples by the greatest masters. After all, she was the daughter of the great industrialist Andrew Mellon, who had donated his wonderful collection of art to the National Gallery of Art in our nation's capital, which had formed a nucleus for the great art it now possesses.

By the time I was ready to leave the suite, we had spent several hours in chatting and had become greater friends than before, and I arranged with Mr. Bruce to walk the deck with him next morning.

I then decided to explore the ship, and going down into the great lounge, I was astonished by its beauty. At one end there was a magnificent mural that covered, with images, the history of navigation. This mural was of glass and silver leaf and had been created by the artist Jean Dupas (1882–1964).

After the tragic burning of this ship in New York harbor in 1942, she was righted and towed away. Fortunately for us today, this great mural was removed unharmed and is today on exhibition at the Metropolitan Museum of Art in New York City.

Beyond this mural there were gigantic pillars of gold at each of the four corners of the area.

Then next morning I joined Mr. Bruce in a most delightful walk around the deck, and while doing so we discussed all manner of topics, with special emphasis on the state of the world at that time and the certainty of an approaching terrible conflict. This was a subject uppermost in most people's minds at this time, particularly a person in Mr. Bruce's situation in American politics.

After we had spent some time together, he told me that he had to return to his suite, where they would be lunching, and then after we arranged to meet again next morning, he left me.

I then went down to my stateroom, which by that time had been changed from a bedroom to a sitting room, with a table upon which I had arranged to have my typewrite set in the center. I then put a sheet into the machine so that I could commence writing, when suddenly the boat seemed to make a ninety-degree turn and I was flung across the room and the typewriter followed on top of me. Many other pieces of furniture were similarly flung around. How I managed to escape serious injury I do not know; also, my machine was not damaged.

Then just as suddenly the boat righted itself and I was about to stand up and replace the furniture and the machine on the table.

I could not understand what had occurred, as the sea was as calm as a lake, and I could not again settle down to do my writing. I felt that I had to go up into the great lounge and see what had happened.

When I arrived in the lounge I saw that most of the first-class passengers had similarly congregated there to find out what might have caused the trouble. My friend Mr. Bruce was already there, also wanting to discover the cause.

I then heard that a very pregnant lady who had been seated in one of the very large armchairs at one end of the room had been flung right across and the chair upon which she had been sitting, which had been attached with chains underneath, had broken away and been flung across on top of her.

Although we tried to find out what had happened, none of the sailors would speak.

Nor could we discover the fate of the lady, whether she had died or lived; it was certain the baby she was carrying must have been killed in the accident. It was Mr. Bruce's thought that there had been some quarrel on the bridge, which must have caused the boat to turn with such violence. Since we later discovered that the purser, Villar, who had been so very unpleasant, had been named Ministre de la Marine in the ill-fated (Nazi inspired) Laval government, I assumed that Mr. Bruce had certainly been correct in his thinking. Whatever the connection, there may well have been some connection between the accident on the boat and the eventual burning in New York harbor early in the war.

Beyond this occurence, the crossing was quite uneventful, but there was one episode that was quite amusing.

There had been set up in the enormous dining room a very large round table that seated twelve gentlemen. Each was the president of some gigantic corporation or other and traveling alone. I was invited to join their number and be seated at this table. I did this. Mr. Bruce was not among us, as he had all of his meals together with his wife in their private suite.

After we had been at sea for about two days, the ship's chef, who considered himself one of the world's greatest cooks, which he in all probability was, came to our table at lunchtime. "Messieurs, I would like to make you a proposal that I am sure you will find most interesting. I suggest that each of you write down on a piece of paper that I shall hand you your favorite dish and one that you would like me to prepare for you. Then in the very unlikely situation that I am not able to make it for you, I shall be the loser and I shall have sent to your table as much caviar and Dom Perignon champagne as you can possible consume during the entire length of the voyage."

All at the table decided to join in this, and each took the piece of paper from the chef.

Coming from England and never previously having been in the States, I wrote my challenge, which was a salad of hearts of palm. This was something that I had read about but had, at the time, never seen. How was I to know that hearts of palm could be purchased at almost any grocery market in the States? Thus I failed miserably, as did most of the others.

However, there was one Southern gentleman who stumped the chef. He had written on his paper: "Country dirty rice."

The chef took the papers and after reading them left us with a very disturbed look on his face, as he had no idea what the

Southerner had ordered that he prepare. We were then laden at each meal at the table with the champagne and those very large blue and white cans of the finest beluga caviar.

"It is very simple. It is chicken livers sautéed and served on a bed of rice, and the rice and the livers get a somewhat dirty color. Beyond this, it is a very ordinary dish down south," the Southern gentleman explained.

I awakened very early in the morning of the day that we arrived in New York City, as I had been advised by Mr. Bruce to do, so that I could see the Manhattan shoreline, which he had told me was something quite exceptional.

I did this and gradually as we approached saw the enormous skyscrapers appear on the horizon, and to my mind it was as though I were arriving in a fairyland. As this was my first visit to the States, I made up my mind to visit a number of cities on the east coast. I knew that I would not have time to go out west, as in those days it took about four days to cross the continent and then return, and I had planned to stay in America no longer than a month.

I decided that California would have to remain for some subsequent visit. My first trip took me to Chicago, where after spending quite some time at the magnificent Art Institute and later the famed planetarium, I went to visit my old friend Harry Blum at the store that he owned on Lake Shore Drive.

During my visit with him, during which I conducted some business with him, he turned to me and said, "Don't you ever look into a mirror? Your hair is a disgrace and needs cutting."

Laughingly, I agreed with him and left the store to go straight to the barber he had suggested. When I arrived at the barbershop I told the man what I wanted him to do for me, and then just as he was finishing I said to him, "Would you mind curling my mustache for me?" In those days it was quite the fashion in England for one to sport what was known as a "guardsman's mustache," and I followed the fashion. In order to control such a mustache it is necessary to roll up the ends with a pair of very narrow hot curling irons. In England this was a very ordinary request, all barbers being well versed in the operation.

The young barber looked at me as though I must be out of my mind, as he had never previously been asked to do such a thing, but not wishing to appear ignorant, he said, "Certainly, sir."

I saw him approach another elderly barber, who it appeared did know what I wanted and explained to the man what he had to do. I then saw him climb up a short ladder at the other end of the room and bring down with him a pair of curling irons in his hands. He then proceeded to place these into a flame, and when they were red hot he approached me with somewhat trembling hands. The irons that he had in his hands looked to me as though they were more serviceable for a horse's mane than for any human head. Not wishing to be entirely burned across my face, I told the young barber that I decided to leave my mustache to be curled upon my return to London, and it was quite obvious that the young man was very much relieved at my suggestion as he put the irons away.

The following day I returned to New York and then decided to visit Boston, this being the second city on my list, as I wished to see the Boston Museum's collection and also several pieces of fine American silver that we had sold that institution over the years.

While I was seated at lunch on the train, and in those days railroad dining was a delightful experience, a gentleman seated opposite me began to speak with me. Hearing my accent, he inquired what part of England I came from. I told him that I was a Londoner and that this was my first visit to the States, and also that I was on a sort of holiday.

"Then," he said, "you have never before been to Boston."

I told him that was the case.

"If you would care to be my guest tomorrow, it would give me great pleasure to drive you around my native city and show you some of its sights."

I must say that I was quite taken aback by his suggestion and told him that I would enjoy that immensely.

He told me that his limousine would pick me up at eleven o'clock at the Copley Plaza Hotel, where I had informed him I would be staying, and soon after we arrived at our destination and I left. I did not even know his name, as I had forgotten to inquire.

Next morning, true to his word, there was the gentleman with his chauffeured limousine waiting for me out in front of the hotel.

I got into the car, and we were off; we went all over the city, and he pointed out to me many places of historic interest until at one o'clock he invited me to be his guest at lunch at a very old seafood restaurant located just over the site of the famous Boston Tea Party. It was here that he introduced me to Boston scrod, a fish as far as I know quite unknown in England. After we had finished our lunch, we continued our journey, and in the course of the ride he pointed out to me a very large building that he said was the headquarters of his corporation.

By then it was approaching four o'clock in the afternoon and he dropped me off at my hotel and as we parted he handed me his card, which I put into my pocket. At least, I thought that I did so. I then thanked him for his great kindness to me, and as soon as I left him I went straight up to my room to write him a letter of my thanks and also to invite him to be my guest at any time that he came to London. But despite my searching, I could nowhere find his card. I must have dropped it on the floor of his car when I left him.

But beside this, what was more frustrating was that I had forgotten his name, so that I could not even telephone him my thanks.

To this day, it is now some forty years later, I still hope that perhaps sometime we may again meet, when I shall be able to apologize for what must have appeared to the gentleman to be utter rudeness on my part.

The next couple of days I spent in Boston, and then upon my return to New York I decided to visit Baltimore, where I wished to visit Walter's Art Gallery. Upon my arrival at the gallery, the then director offered to take me through and pinpoint some of their great acquisitions.

While we were strolling round viewing many of their great objects of antiquity, he remarked, "Isn't it a shame? We get visitors from all over the world to view our collections, but it seems to me that Baltimoreans themselves are much more interested in horses than they are in some of the wonderful things that we have on display here."

198

Just for the record today, things have changed radically at Walter's, which has been entirely rebuilt, and now it has a continuous stream of locals who do come and visit.

After spending most of the day with him, I told him that I had to return that same day, as I had invited some guests to dinner for that evening and could not possibly be late.

Arriving at Baltimore's Pennsylvania Station I descended the long staircase that leads down to the trains, and as I did this I saw a large group of young people all wearing caps with the word "Orioles" across the front. Being somewhat a lover of bird life, I was fascinated that Baltimore should have such a bird society.

That evening at dinner, where my old friend Victor Hammer was one of my guests, I remarked how interested I was to find so many young birdwatchers in Baltimore. Everybody seemed quite stunned at my announcement, and when they realized what I meant they all became convulsed with laughter. How was I, an Englishman, to know anything about the Orioles being a Baltimore ball team?

Finally, my month's visit drawing to a close, I decided that I should visit Washington, D.C., and go through the National Gallery that the Bruces had been speaking to me about on the *Normandie*. So I arranged to do this the following day.

As soon as I was settled in my Pullman chair on the train and we were en route, I noticed that most of the passengers were ordering Bourbon and branch water. So doing in Rome as do the Romans, I similarly ordered this drink, which I had never previously tasted. Being quite thirsty at the time, I drank the liquor down quite rapidly, and this resulted in a violent headache.

Despite the headache I visited the National Gallery, the Corcoran, the Phillips, and the Smithsonian Institution.

I decided that I would not visit the White House or the many other government buildings for which the capital is so famous until a subsequent visit.

Many years then passed and one day while I was at lunch with Victor Hammer, he suggested after our meal that I try a glass of Bourbon. He told me that his two brothers, Harry and Dr. Armand, had at that time just bought the Dant Brewery Company. I then told him of my experience with Bourbon on the train to Washington, but he was insistent that I would never get a headache from their Dant Bourbon. I must say that I drank a glass, much more slowly than previously, and thoroughly enjoyed it. Nevertheless, to this day I still fight shy of the brew.

Then, following upon my visits to Chicago, Boston, Baltimore, and Washington, D.C., I felt that I had a fairly good idea of what made America tick. Having made this decision, I left for home, and having enjoyed every moment of my stay, I told myself that the very next time I crossed I would make a point of visiting the West, and that is precisely what I did.

Chapter 37

Return to England on French Liner

Having spent the month that I had allotted myself for my trip in the States and having visited the various cities of the East, I decided to leave for home. Since I had originally crossed on the *Normandie*, which journey I had thoroughly enjoyed, despite the very unpleasant occurrence on board, I arranged to return on another French liner. Today I have completely forgotten its name, but I do recall that it was one of the flagships of the Compagnie Generale Transatlantique.

All that I can now state is that this crossing was one of the most enjoyable that I had ever made and everything about the ship was truly delightful.

There were several occurrences on this crossing that stand out quite clearly in my memory and which I shall never forget; two of them were replete with humor.

At this period I was still a bachelor and marriage was completely outside my thinking. I was enjoying my life too much to even consider getting myself embroiled in any such state as that of matrimony. On this particular crossing there were quite a number of unmarried and unattached men and women traveling alone, and for this reason it was, I suppose, quite natural for us to get together on most days.

The sea at this time was as calm as a lake, and one morning after we had been at sea for some three days I was walking round the deck taking my regular exercise when I noted that a table-tennis match had been scheduled for that day at noon. When I read this notice I saw that my name had been included as one of the players. Although I am not nor have I ever been any sort of an athlete, I felt that I could handle myself fairly well with a table-tennis paddle. I then saw that the match had been scheduled for that day at noon. Then I began speaking with another young man who similarly had found his name on the bulletin board and said

201

that as it was so beautiful out on deck he could not wait to play. I then decided that I would eat a very light meal at lunch before the game so that I would be ready for the fray.

Shortly after this meal I went onto the deck where the matches were to be played and met there most of the other unmarrieds, who were waiting either to play or merely to watch. Everyone seemed in a particularly friendly and happy mood. At the time I thought nothing of this, and it appeared to be the most natural way for everybody to be. There was one young man who very nicely indeed wished me luck in my game.

As soon as I was called for my turn at the table, I noticed my opponent standing at the opposite side of the table. She was a young lady whom I did not recall having seen previously.

We then began to play, but when I was at the left of the table the ball was at the right, and when I was at the right it was at the left. It seemed to me that the only time I had any contact with the ball was when it came my turn to serve. Seeing what was happening to my game, it did not take me too long to see that I had been set up unmercifully, and I then realized that when the young gentleman had wished me luck he knew what was going to occur. Thus the game was soon over, and to my utter disgust I noticed that all of the onlookers were doubled up with laughter.

I then discovered that I had been set up to play my match against, as I think it was, Alice Marble, the world's great tennis champion of the day.

I must say that at this point I was not in any way amused, but I soon realized that the entire episode was very funny and I joined in the fun together with the others.

It was at about midday on the following afternoon that I was seated in the lounge with about half a dozen others to have a prelunch apertif. In this group there were two ladies, one a highly respected art dealer of German descent, Madame Drey, and the other her daughter, who at the time must have been in her late teens. This young lady was in my mind as beautiful a thing as I had ever set eyes upon; to my mind she could have been compared to a piece of Meissen porcelain.

Seated next to this young lady was a Frenchman who was trying to make conversation with her, but who apparently found himself at an impasse, as it seemed that she did not speak any French and he very little English.

Opposite him and to my left there was a gentleman who, despite the fact that we were crossing in midsummer, wore a beret at a somewhat rakish angle and also a wide flowing black cape. This gentleman had a longish beard entirely gray, and although I later discovered that he could not have been more than in his fifties, he looked to be a man in his seventies.

I do not recall who else might have been round the table in this little group. We then began to introduce ourselves one to the other. The bearded gentleman was none other than the great French Cubist artist, Monsieur Braque.

Naturally, being in the art business, I was quite enthralled at being able to chat with so eminent an artist, and we then spent some little time discussing art in many of its various aspects.

I did notice that all the while that we were chatting together Braque had his eyes focused on this young lady. He seemed to be transfixed by her. I must say that not only was he looking at her so seriously, he was doing so with quite a lecherous leer on his face.

Then he suddenly turned to me. "Monsieur Hill, would you mind passing the wine list over to me?"

At the moment I had the list in my hand, deciding what to order for my prelunch drink.

As it happens, such wine lists, especially on French liners, are quite large and all apparently have one side that is completely blank and white.

I at once passed this list over to him; then he asked me whether perhaps I had a pencil.

I told him that I had, and he asked me whether I would lend it to him. As it was quite an expensive pencil, I at once handed it to him with the proviso that he return it to me when he had finished with it. He agreed to do this. Then with pencil in one hand and the back of the wine list in the other, he began to draw.

I was fascinated to see what he might be doing when I noticed that he had drawn a straight line down on the middle of the sheet from almost the top to the bottom. He then began to study the young lady again with great interest for several moments, and then he drew a half-circle that almost, but not quite, touched the center of the straight line.

When he had done this he stared at it for some little time and then, apparently satisfied with what he had done, placed a dot in the center of the half-circle and then at the bottom right hand placed his signature: "Braque."

He then passed the drawing over to the young lady and said to her, "Mademoiselle, do you know what I have drawn for you?"

The young lady answered quite simply, "No, monsieur, I do not."

He then said to her, "Mademoiselle, keep this very carefully, because it is your portrait as I see you, and one day you will thank me, as it will be worth a lot of money."

At the time I recall I wished he might do something for me, but I did not, perhaps foolishly, have the nerve to ask him.

I do not know whether or not the young lady did, indeed, keep the drawing, but as her mother was an art dealer the chance is that she did, and in fact she may still have it in her possession. If she does, then it certainly is quite a treasure and one that I can state categorically I saw being drawn by the great Braque.

As I write these lines I remember that a couple of days later we landed at Southampton much to my regret. I also ponder the fact that such transatlantic crossings are virtually no more and that the aircraft has taken over most of such, together with all the romance that always accompanied these voyages.

Chapter 38

Baron Georges de Menasch and Jade

One of our very good friends both in London and later in New York was a gentleman of Anglo-Egyptian heritage named Baron Georges de Menasch. Although he was born in Alexandria, Egypt, he had resided for most of his adult years in London, where he still remained after his divorce from his wife, the baroness, who was then residing in New York. Georges was a gentleman in every possible respect and also a great aesthete where art and antiquity are concerned. His claim to fame, and a matter of which he was inordinately proud, was that during the nineteenth century his family, who had been prominent bankers in Alexandria, had been commissioned by the great Disraeli to act as their agent with regard to the passing over of money for the British purchase of the shares in the Suez Canal. It was to his forebears that the now historic coded telegram had been sent by Disraeli, the British prime minister of the day, reading: "A ditch dug in sand is the best soil for celery," which cryptic message contained the instructions to proceed with the purchase. At the time that I knew Georges, he still had this telegram in his possession and treasured it enormously. Now that Georges has passed on I often ponder the fate of this telegram. Maybe it is still in the hands of a relation.

As a great connoisseur and collector primarily of the applied arts he loved color beyond all else, whether it be in paintings, in jewels, or in objects of art. In regard to color, one of his greatest loves was a collection of diamonds of varied tones for which he had ordered made a special leather wallet so that he could carry these little gems with him wherever he might happen to be going. As is possibly not too well know, diamonds are found in a variety of different colors and of these some are exceedingly rare and very difficult to find. In his collection he owned diamonds that were canary yellow, blue, pink, green, deep chocolate, and violet; he also owned one of the rarest of all, a red diamond our brother

Bertram had discovered when he had been traveling on holiday in Buenos Aires, which he had then acquired. The moment that he arrived back in London he had called the baron and told him of his discovery, and Georges was round at my brother's office even, it seemed, before he had replaced the telephone on its hook. The baron bought the stone immediately with the remark: "I think that I now have every possible color that I could ever buy anywhere." Each of the diamonds that he now owned weighed about one carat. The very fine blue white diamonds that are usually bought by people who wanted to own diamonds for personal adornment did not interest Georges in the slightest degree, at least certainly not for his collection.

Shortly after he had acquired the red stone, we purchased an entire necklace all of blue diamonds. They had been collected by somebody and consisted of every possible shade of blue, from the darkest inky blue to the palest of sky blue. Despite what Georges had said, that his collection was now complete, I called him so that he could see this very rare and unusual necklace.

The moment that he saw it he said that he would like to buy from us two varieties of blue diamonds that would go into his collection, and I allowed him to choose one very dark and one very light blue that would fit well into his group. May I say that he chose very well indeed?

Many years then passed and we saw Georges at odd moments, sometimes in London and sometimes in Paris. After we had established our offices on 57th Street in New York City in the early 1940s he arrived one morning to visit with us. He told us that owing to the frightful conditions existing at that time in England, and in fact all over Europe, he had decided to spend the war years in America, and having been told by our brother Bertram in London that we were over here, he said that he had decided to make us his first port of call.

As we sat and chatted about the political situation and about the good old days, he said to me, "You know that I propose continuing my search for gems over here. At least I shall have something to occupy my mind." He then added, "You know what I have been dreaming of for many years?"

I replied that I supposed that he was talking about other possible diamonds for his great collection, but he replied, "No, for many years now I have been trying to find a piece of rare Chinese Imperial jade that I would love to wear on my finger mounted as a ring. I have been searching for such a piece in London and also in Paris, but I have never seen anything that I thought would be good enough to satisfy me. Now that I am over here I would love to try and buy such a piece. I think that maybe I shall go out to the West and see whether perhaps I can find a fine piece out there."

Now I knew very well that such Chinese Imperial is inordinately rare and, in fact, it can easily be mistaken for fine emerald, and I also knew that the Chinese consider wearing such a gem just for good luck. I told Georges that if anything ever came through our offices I would call him immediately, and then after giving me his address in the city, he left.

It could not have been more than half an hour after Georges had left that a gem dealer friend of ours happened in our offices on some business or other and while there he told me that he had something quite special that he would like to show me, as he thought that I would be interested. "It is not something that you would ever want to buy, but I know that you will enjoy seeing what I have," he said. Then taking a small packet out of his pocket, he placed in my hands one of the finest pieces of Imperial Chinese jade that I had ever laid eyes on, which had been polished ideally for wearing mounted as a ring. The moment that I saw this gem I knew that it was precisely what Georges said he had been searching for over the years. I then asked the dealer how much he was asking for it, and when he told me I bought it from him at once. I knew that even if Georges did not buy it, it was something that I would want to own myself.

As soon as the dealer left with our check I telephoned Georges, who had by that time arrived back at his apartment, and told him that we had just purchased a piece of superb Chinese jade that he could have if he liked it as much as we did. I told him that if he did not find it as fine as he wanted, then I wanted it for myself.

Georges then asked me to hold the piece for him until he could see it first thing next morning, when he said he would be round.

When I arrived at our offices next morning there was Georges waiting outside the door. He said that he had been awake all night dreaming about the piece of jade that I had mentioned to him.

We then went into the office, and I took the jade out of our safe and handed it to him.

Georges picked it up as though it were a delicate little baby, and as he looked at it I could see that he was almost trembling with excitement. "But this is exactly what I have been searching for over so many years, and I don't really care how much you want for it; it is mine."

We then discussed the mounting of the stone as a ring.

"I want to do nothing with it for the present. I just want to have it in my pocket for a few weeks. Then after that I will ask you to have it mounted up for me to wear."

It was about a month later that he was again in the office and brought the jade in with him and said that he now wished to have it mounted up as a ring so that he could wear it. "You don't know how happy you have made me with this gem."

I promised to put the thing into the hands of our jeweler immediately and call Georges as soon as it was ready for him to collect.

"I will be visiting with my ex-wife the baroness at her apartment on Park Avenue, and I wonder whether you and your brother would care to be my guests there."

I replied that we would be delighted to join him there. He then gave me her address, and we arranged to be there the following afternoon at teatime.

When we arrived we saw that the baroness lived in one of those oldtime enormous apartments on Park Avenue, and when we entered we saw Georges sitting quietly in a corner on a stool. In contrast to the lady, who was very fat, Georges himself was very short and slim; in fact, when married they must have made an entirely incongruous couple.

The lady sat enthroned in a very large chair set in the center of the room, as though she were queen of all that she surveyed. Georges for his part seemed afraid to even open his mouth.

The entire scene was to us exceedingly funny.

The baroness then asked us whether we would care to have a drink, and on our replying in the affirmative she suggested either lemonade or ginger ale. I then replied that I was not particularly thirsty and both of us made a hasty retreat so that we could get back to our apartments and have a Scotch. For my part I felt that I needed one. Upon reflection, I decided that perhaps the baroness was a Moslem and if this were in fact the case, it would account for her reluctance to serve any alcoholic beverages.

The following day Georges was again up in our offices to apologize for what he termed his ex-wife's boorish treatment. "You can now see why we are divorced."

It was just at about this time that my sister-in-law had arranged to have a dinner party at her apartment, and she telephoned Georges, whom she knew quite well, and invited him to be one of her guests. Georges said that he would be delighted to come.

On the evening of the dinner party Georges arrived, and after getting a drink, he was introduced to the other guests and we then entered the dining room and I saw that she had placed Georges at her right side. In all there were twelve guests round the table.

Everybody seemed to be delighted when Georges told them about some of his experiences in the world of jewel collecting, and after he had finished telling about his colored diamond collection, he related how we had found for him the piece of exquisite Imperial Chinese jade that he now wore on his finger, which he said he had been searching for over these many years both in London and Paris without success.

One lady seated at the far end of the table asked whether she might see the ring in her hands, and without a second thought Georges removed the ring and had it passed around the table for the lady to see. As it went slowly round the table everybody remarked on its extreme beauty and told Georges how lucky he was to own such a rare gem. Georges was beside himself with pleasure as he heard all these raves about his jade.

After a short time had elapsed, the ring returned to the hands of my sister-in-law, who is inclined on occasion to be a bit of a jokester. Of a sudden she exclaimed in a very loud voice, "A terrible thing has happened! I have swallowed the ring!"

Georges was extremely upset, but all that he could do was sit and tremble. He could visualize the progress of the ring through her body until it would eventually emerge and exit via her asshole. This thought was naturally most unpleasing to his aesthetic soul, but there was little he could say or do.

The company present then began to discuss the probable time that it would take for the ring to pass through and exit, and as each member of the company present gave his or her opinion poor Georges became more and more disturbed.

Seeing how intensely upset he was, my sister-in-law then gaily announced that she had the ring in her hand and she had not swallowed it and it was all a joke. She then handed the ring to Georges, and as soon as he had it in his hands he rose as quickly as he could and, saying goodnight to the company in general, quickly made his exit.

As he left, the company were all laughing merrily.

After this evening Georges did visit with us several times during the ensuing months, but somehow he never seemed to be quite as friendly as he had been over the years.

It was soon after the last visit we had from Georges that the war came to an end and he was in to say good-bye, saying that he hoped to see us again at some time later when he was again back in his rooms on Jermyn Street in London. He said that he could not wait to see whether his other paintings and other things were still intact or whether they had suffered any severe was damage. As soon as he arrived back in London he wrote to say that despite the terrible bombing, he had found everything in his apartment untouched and all was in perfect condition. Three weeks after we received his letter it appears that he left his rooms to visit his tailor and, knowing that he would have to undress for his fitting, left all of his gems in his room locked in a desk drawer, including his diamond collection and also his jade ring. While he was out, his rooms were entered by some thieves and he was robbed of all of his valuables.

Shortly after this occurence Georges took sick and passed away. We always felt that he had died of a broken heart. He had always mentioned that he had for many years had some slight heart ailment, but he had said that his doctor had told him that he had nothing to worry about in this regard. There is somewhat a slight moral to be drawn from this story of the jade ring, and that is that it is very ill advised to remove any piece of one's jewelry for one reason or another outside the confines of one's own home. So many jewels and particularly rings have been lost by ladies who remove them when they wash their hands in hotel or restaurant or even theater powder rooms, when they are frequently picked up by others who see them after the owners have left.

Chapter 39

Volunteer Orderly at a Joint Disease Hospital

It was during the midforties, when the war was at its height, that a cousin of mine came up to see me. He had a son who was spastic, and for this reason my cousin was interested in all medical matters that could pertain to this condition. He told me that he had decided to volunteer to act as an orderly at the Joint Disease Hospital in New York City and, knowing of my interest in medical matters, asked me whether I might care to join him, so that in any case we could be together. He said that he knew that I had been giving blood as often as I was permitted to do so over the past several years.

At this time the hospital was sorely in need of male orderlies, as so many men were already in the Armed Forces. Upon little reflection, I told him that I would be pleased to join with him. It was then arranged that we would meet with the matron at the hospital on the following afternoon, so that we could then volunteer our services officially.

As soon as we arrived we were ushered into the matron's office, and after we told her that we had come to volunteer she said, "You cannot imagine how much we need your services," and then asked us to go downstairs to see another of the nurses, who would indoctrinate us into our duties. We then met with this young lady, who spoke with us, and after about half an hour of instructions we were apparently fully qualified orderlies.

It was arranged that we would work every evening from five o'clock in the afternoon until eight.

I was immediately after this "lesson" sent on to my first assignment, and that was to see a patient in a private room awaiting a hernia operation set for the next morning, and I was called upon to prepare the gentleman for this operation.

Not quite knowing how to handle this situation, I decided that I would see the patient and then see what I could do for him. Naturally, I had never previously been asked to do any such thing.

The patient I saw as I entered his room was quite elderly, and when I saw him I became quite nervous. I had to shave all around his private parts. Now this was quite an ordeal for me. I went over to the gentleman and introduced myself, and he, knowing what had to be done, at once removed the covers from his bed and lay naked in front of me.

As he lay unclothed I saw that he had quite a prominent potbelly, and this in no way eased my mind. Little did the gentleman know that what I was about to do for him was a first as far as I was concerned.

Then with trembling hands I picked up the razor and began to shave off all of his pubic hair. How I managed this without first castrating him I shall never know. Suffice it to say that I did an admirable job and as soon as I had completed my work the gentleman thanked me profusely. He seemed delighted with what I had done for him and was full of smiles when I left.

As soon as I had completed this chore the nurse called me on their intercom public address system and asked me to go through the male wards and make the patients as comfortable as possible for the night. By this time it was well past my allotted period of four hours, but I could not refuse. At that moment I knew that I would be involved every evening for much more than the time that I had originally suggested.

As there were sixteen beds in the ward and each bed was in use, this duty of readying the patients for the night was quite onerous, and I did not leave the hospital until well after ten o'clock.

Entering the first ward, I was almost floored by the series of most unpleasant smells that assailed me. No doubt any regular nurse would have been inured to this, but I was not in any way. I then decided that the following evening I would bring with me a large bottle of inexpensive toilet water that I could rub on the men's backs.

And so the following evening when I went through the wards I used this toilet water with abandon and at the same time straightened out their bedclothes and pillows. As I poured the toilet water all over the place I saw that the men were delighted at the pleasing aroma and I noticed their noses twitching with pleasure. Many of the patients tried to slip me a dollar bill so that I would pour more of the lotion on them, but when I refused their tips they could, none of them, understand me. To refuse money, this was something quite new to all of them.

When on the second evening I had finished in the wards and was extremely tired, I again heard my name being called on the intercom and I was asked to go up to the nurse's room, as she had something to tell me.

"Before going through the wards tomorrow afternoon I would like you to sit at the telephone and answer any questions from people who will be calling in regard to their dear ones."

When I told the nurse that I understood and would do what she asked me to do, she replied, "There are four set replies that you can answer at will." And as she said this she handed me a paper on which these replies were set out. They were:

He is doing as well as can be expected.
He is doing nicely.
He is holding his own.
He is very comfortable.

The nurse said that I did not even need to look at the patient's chart before answering, as she said that in the end it would not make any difference one way or the other. If the patient recovered all would be well, and if not, then that would be that.

One evening shortly after I commenced working—I had by this time been there for about two months—I was asked by the nurse to go through the private rooms, where some of the patients might need some assistance. At the time I was quite exhausted, but I felt that I could not refuse her.

In the first room that I entered I saw a very tall, lanky man lying on his bed with one leg up in traction, and as far as I could see there was little that I could do for him except puff up his pillows.

He looked up at me and said in a very offhand tone of voice, "Go round the corner and buy me some ice cream."

I at once refused and told him that there were other patients who needed my services more than he, when he replied, "But I am Dashiel Hammett."

"I don't care who you are, I am a volunteer and not a messenger boy, and I am here to assist people get well, not to run errands for them and get them ice cream." I then looked at him and thought for a moment. "If you want ice cream so badly, just get up and get it for yourself."

Hearing my remark, he started to laugh loud and long, realizing how ridiculous was his request and also my reply. From that time onward and until he was released from the hospital we were good friends, and this ended by his calling me Sidney and me calling him Dash.

This was quite amusing, but there were many other moments while I was serving the hospital that were full of pathos.

One of my other duties was to allocate beds for any newly admitted patients. As the beds in my wards were all for men, I could choose when and where I could put them.

Almost invariably the patients arrived with mothers, wives, or sweethearts, who always attempted to hand me dollar bills to find good beds for their beloveds. Similarly nobody could understand my refusing to take their money.

When I arrived each afternoon I was required to go down to the laundry room to get my whites and then change out of my city clothes before entering the wards. Here there was no question of size, as I had to accept whatever was handed me. One evening I attempted to reject some article or other, but without any result. I had to take what they gave me. I might be handed a short shirt with sleeves long enough for a fully grown gorilla, or again I might get one that could have sufficed for a midget. The pants were always a joke as far as I was concerned. These would always be ideal for a dwarf or for a man about seven feet tall, possibly a basketball player. When I suggested that I would like to bring my own whites and then have them laundered myself, I was informed that this would contravene all hospital regulations, and I had to presume that they had some very cogent reasons for this.

As my cousin and I were the only two male orderlies working at the hospital at that time, when anybody called up to speak with me on the telephone I was invariably referred to as the "nurse's aid in pants."

I continued working at the hospital for the better part of two years, and I must say that the experience was quite rewarding.

215

But one day I seemed to pick up some eye infection and went to see my eye doctor about this and he told me quite succinctly that undoubtedly I had picked up some sort of condition from one of the patients. He insisted that I immediately cease my services there and resign. If I did not, he said, I might lose the sight of one of my eyes.

This then was a most serious situation for an art expert, and I at once went back to the hospital and resigned.

Although I found the work at times quite onerous, I really enjoyed what I had been doing, but I had no alternative but to stop. The nurses were quite sorry to see me leave, but all agreed I had to.

Chapter 40

Golden Boy Christ

It was quite early in the war that while passing an antique jeweler's establishment on Fifth Avenue, we saw on display in their window what appeared to be a superb figurine of the boy Christ in gold. It stood about eight inches in height, on an engraved rock crystal pediment overall about twelve or fourteen inches high. We at once went into the shop and bought the piece and then asked the jeweler to tell us anything that he could about the origins of the piece. He told us that he had bought it quite recently from an émigré from Austria who had managed to bring it out from his native town by wrapping it in a piece of thick cloth.

We then took the piece back with us to our offices and began to study it in some depth. The little figurine was of enameled gold, the Child's head covered with long golden tresses. He wore a red cloak, and the face was enameled in naturalistic colorations.

There was something that did not quite sit right, but we could not quite make out what was the matter with the piece.

It was just at that moment that Dr. Sandoz came into the office, and as soon as he saw the piece he exclaimed, "I don't care how much that piece is going to cost me, but it is mine! I have to own it not alone for its beauty, but because any representation of the boy Christ is of the greatest rarity, and as I look at him I see the piece centering my entire collection at home in Switzerland. Now as I see the piece there is something not quite right about the setting of the Child, and as I look at him I can see what is wrong."

We then told the doctor that we similarly saw something wrong in the Child's stance.

"We have to remove the base and turn it round, and then we shall see the Child in correct position."

We at once saw that the doctor was right and, turning the base round, saw that for some reason or other it had at some time

217

been incorrectly poised. Now that we saw Him, we saw that we had a great rarity in its fullest splendor.

Upon examination we came to the conclusion that the piece was almost certainly of German origin and probably produced during the latter part of the seventeenth or possibly the eighteenth century.

There next arose the question of payment, and the doctor said that here he had a serious problem. He explained that all of his liquid assets were at that time tied up in Canada and the Canadian authorities with whom he had recently been in touch on another matter had refused to allow him to withdraw any of his funds. As he was Swiss, they explained, any funds he might wish to withdraw could ultimately land in the pockets of Nazi interests, and this they could not in any way allow. The doctor then told us that he had explained to the Canadians that he hated the Nazis as much as they did, but they were adamant and had refused any of his arguments.

My brother then told him to explain to the Canadian authorities that if they allowed him to withdraw the cost of the Christ statuette, then they could themselves relay the funds directly to London on our behalf.

The doctor then said that he would contact Canada and see whether this would make any difference to them.

A few days later he was again up at our offices and told us that the Canadians had again refused to take any notice of his request.

"Despite everything I want the statuette desperately, and I must have it."

My brother then suggested that he himself, being a British subject, would fly up to Ottawa and see the head of the bank there and perhaps be able to arrange something on the doctor's behalf. And it was then arranged that my brother contact Ottawa and make an appointment to meet with the banker there on the following day.

On the telephone the banker was most polite and agreed to see my brother at noon on the following day, and my brother then arranged to fly up and discuss the matter with him. Meanwhile he told the doctor that, in any case, we would hold the piece at his disposal.

Next day my brother was in Ottawa and went to the bank as arranged, but the banker's secretary apologized and told him that the banker had forgotten the appointment he had made and had left for another luncheon engagement. My brother then told the young lady that he would go out and get a cup of coffee, after which he would return and await the banker's return.

In due course, after my brother had been waiting for the banker's return until about three o'clock that same afternoon, the banker returned. The gentleman had certainly partaken of the traditional three-martini lunch and seemed to be in a very jovial mood when he came in. He told my brother that he was very sorry indeed that he had had to wait for him for so long a time, and they then discussed the question of the payment out of the doctor's funds. The banker then explained that naturally Canada was in the war up to the hilt and with every man, but that money was an entirely different proposition.

Despite this my brother then explained that the funds could be transmitted directly to London on our behalf and that there was no way in which they could ever possibly fall into the hands of the Germans.

The banker then stated that because of his discourtesy to my brother he would arrange for the funds to be transmitted immediately to us in London, but he told my brother that he should tell the doctor that he could not use this facility again at any time in the future and that his funds were blocked for the duration of the war.

Later that same day my brother returned to New York and told the doctor what he had arranged and also explained to him that the only reason that the Canadian banker had allowed for the transfer of the funds was that he said he had been so discourteous in making him wait for his return from lunch.

The doctor, naturally, was delighted to hear what my brother told him and was quite amused, remarking with a smile, "Maybe it was through the influence of the young Christ."

Chapter 41

Dixon's New America

It was our brother Bertram who, living in London, was always on the lookout to see what he could find for us in the field of Americana. He knew that anything in this area would always find a home somewhere or other in the States. He was particularly interested in old books and used to make a point of visiting with antiquarian booksellers at least once every month.

While Bertram was speaking with one of his old bookseller friends, the dealer remarked, "I have just purchased two volumes that I think your people in New York might like to have." And as he spoke he drew from his shelves two volumes, each beautifully bound in blue Morocco leather and titled *Dixon's New America*.

My brother had never heard of these books but became quite intrigued and began to leaf through some of the pages, and as he opened the books he saw that they contained bound holograph sheets that had been compiled by two Englishmen while crossing the States from Lawrence, Kansas, out through Utah. He naturally concluded that this was something that we would be delighted to have and at once bought them from the dealer.

After buying them he included them in a shipment of various other antiquities and shipped them off to us in New York. As soon as my brother and I saw them we similarly became most interested in them and began to study the contents. According to the preface it appears that at about 1867 two adventurous young university professors, one William Hepworth Dixon and his friend Charles Wentworth Dike, of Trinity College, Cambridge, decided that they wanted to travel across the States to study conditions there and also see what made America tick. Both these men were quite well versed in life in America, having read as many books on the subject as they could find, but beyond this they wanted to see for themselves. They wanted to see how people lived and loved and also how they traveled. After giving the matter some considerable thought, they took ship across the Atlantic and landed over here in New York City.

Having been introduced to many scholars through their university interests and affiliations, the two discussed their project with these scholars, and they were advised to start their travels from Lawrence, Kansas. They were told that this would be an admirable focal point for them. Having received this advice, they obtained transport to Lawrence and decided that until they arrived there they would travel very light, as they were informed that upon arrival they would be able to buy anything that they might need for their further journey to the west. It was their desire to write a journal of their journey for eventual publication, incorporating as many details as they thought might be of interest to their eventual readers. In due course, upon their arrival at Lawrence, they met many Kansans to whom they had taken letters of introduction, and they found that they were being most cordially received on all sides.

After considerable conversation with their newfound friends, they decided that they would travel west via Salt Lake City and visit with some Mormons, for whom they had been given many introductory letters by their new Kansan friends. They found that at Lawrence they could quite readily buy horses for this part of their journey, and they were informed that when they had finished with the horses, they could easily be resold, and they were jokingly informed that of a certainty they would not wish to take the animals back with them to England.

Among these letters they received some were addressed to the heads of the Mormon church, and they were soon off on their travels.

After an uneventful ride, they arrived at Salt Lake City, where they met with several of the people for whom they held letters, and they were received most hospitably by them. Their hosts invited them to meet their families and were taken by them to meet their several wives and innumerable children.

It was this sort of fact that they wished to note in their diary as an important aspect of life in America. They knew that in England very little, if anything, was known about Mormon life and knew that such reading would be most acceptable to the public.

After I had finished reading the manuscript now in our hands, I decided that this must be a most worthwhile piece of documentation for American libraries. Upon speaking with several of my local bookseller friends, I found that this diary had been published in America and had gone through several editions. I felt that I should discuss these volumes with the librarian of the New York Public Library, and he told me that he had never heard of this diary, nor did they own a copy in their collection. He was quite excited at the thought that I would be pleased to show the two volumes to him, and I decided that I would go down to the library and take them with me. When I arrived at the library and showed him the two volumes in which the holograph sheets had been bound, he said that he thought that these manuscripts would be a most admirable addition to their shelves and asked me to leave them with him so that he could show them to his principals, which I was happy to do. He then, after some little study, said that although at some time or other he had heard mention of this dairy, he had never actually seen a copy. He then told me that as soon as his principals had an opportunity of reading through the sheets he would be in touch with me. On this note I left.

About a week later the librarian called me. "My principals have decided against the acquisition of the Dixon diary, because they say that it was compiled by two Englishmen and not by Americans." Confidentially he added, "I personally think that they are quite wrong, but there is nothing that I can say or do."

I told him that I would pick up the volumes myself at some convenient time.

As soon as I had the two volumes back in my hands, I decided that perhaps I would keep them back from sale for my own library, as I was so very fascinated by the contents, but I thought that before I make any definite decision I should write and offer them to the head of the Mormon church in Salt Lake City and give them the opportunity of making the acquisition. After all, they did contain much about the life of the Mormons at that time.

I thus wrote to Dr. Young at the Mormon church and told him all about these two volumes, and he replied most courteously to tell me that he was most pleased to hear about the volumes and said that they would like to buy them for their library, and he asked me to have them shipped out to him together with our bill.

In my original letter I had quoted him twenty-five hundred dollars for the two volumes; it was for this sum that we sent the bill.

Then after they received the books at the church we received a letter from the doctor enclosing their check for twenty-five dollars in payment. We at once returned the check to him, mentioning that they had made a twenty-four-hundred-and-seventy-five-dollar error, and I asked him kindly to return to us the volumes at his early convenience.

We received the two volumes back just as my eldest son, Lawrence, was about to celebrate his birthday, and so in consultation with my brother Henry we decided that as the authors had commenced their journey and diary at Lawrence, it would be fitting for us to present them in his name to the library of the University of Kansas situated in that town.

We then wrote to the then librarian of the university, a Mr. Vosper, and made him the offer of the volumes as a gift. He replied to say how delighted they would be to accept our gift. He also said that he much appreciated our reason for the presentation to them.

Some many years passed and one day my brother Henry was traveling to Europe. At the time being seated next to a gentleman at one of the airports en route, he became engaged in conversation with him. They then introduced themselves the one to the other and the other gentleman then stated, "I am Mr. Vosper, the librarian at the University of Kansas at Lawrence."

When my brother heard this he at once recalled that we had made the gift of the Dixon diaries to the library and told Mr. Vosper so. Mr. Vosper said that he was delighted to meet my brother and told him that the two volumes were being held in their rare manuscripts department and that they considered them as one of the shining jewels in their entire collection. He also told my brother that many of the students had studied these volumes and had found them most useful in their study of American history.

Chapter 42

Farouk and Rommel

While in Paris, ever on the search for rare objects that I knew would fit harmoniously into one or other of the varied collections of King Farouk of Egypt, I spent much time walking the streets of the Left Bank, primarily in the area around the famed Sorbonne, where there were, and still are, for that matter, innumerable small antique dealers' shops. Here I could never tell what I might find at any one of them. It was almost like looking for the proverbial needle in a haystack. But one could never tell. It was always this sort of thing that makes the art and antiques fields so fascinating. One way or another I always knew that I would never return to my hotel empty-handed.

Despite the fact that I enjoy walking, I always had a taxi following me so that whenever I felt tired I could relax in the cab. Also whenever I made a purchase I could leave my package on the seat. Usually when I returned late in the afternoon to my hotel I would have a small heap of such little packages. In those days I always waited in the morning until I saw a taxi that was reasonably clean-looking and then made a deal with the driver. I used to say to him, "I want you to stay with me until I discharge you later this afternoon, when I will pay you double whatever might be shown on your meter." This proposition never failed to delight the man, and as far as I was concerned, the franc in those days stood at about two dollars for a thousand.

It was on one day in spring when the air was clear and fresh that I set out on one of my jaunts, having made my usual arrangement with a taxi driver, and as soon as we were over the bridge and on the Left Bank, I got out and decided that I would walk.

After I had been in and out of several shops, and having made several nice purchases, I decided that I would like to rest awhile and relax over a cup of coffee, when while seated I noticed the towers of Notre Dame looming high in the near distance.

So as soon as I had finished my coffee, I told my taxi driver to go toward the cathedral, where I knew that I could sit and possibly enjoy some of the wonderful organ music that was usually played at midday. On arrival I entered the cathedral and saw that it was almost deserted. There were perhaps just a handful of people sitting in its pews, listening to the delightfully restful music.

While I did this I fell into a sort of *dolce far niente*. Then looking around me, I noticed some activity around the curtains of one of the confessional boxes and presumed that this must be the hour when the Fathers were readying to take confessions.

Seated at one end of a line of pews I saw three very glum-looking young women. They were all wearing very, very short skirts and extremely low-cut blouses, where their bosoms were very much to the fore, and I then concluded that they were positively hookers who were wishing to make their peace with their maker, if only temporarily. After watching these girls for several minutes, I saw one of them rise and kneel before one of the confessionals, and I saw that she was speaking through the curtained grille.

She could not have been there for more than perhaps five minutes when I saw her rise and leave the cathedral with a broad smile on her face. No sooner had she left then the second of the trio rose and did precisely what the first girl had done, and after finishing she similarly left with a broad grin on her face; she was then followed by the third, who did exactly what the other two had done. This was surely a regular operation for them.

Naturally, I did not know where they were going after they had left, but I do recall making a small bet with myself that they were all three of them off to reenter the "Love for Sale" mart.

After I had been in the cathedral for maybe an hour or so, feeling much refreshed, I left and, finding my taxi waiting for me outside, told the driver to follow me as usual.

I then began to stroll leisurely through some narrow street, where I noticed an antique dealer's shop that I had never seen previously and decided to go in and see whether perhaps he might have something for me. When I entered I introduced myself to the man, who presumably had heard about me, because he at once began to bring things out to show me. Despite this I saw nothing that could in any way have appealed to me.

I then said to him, "Have you by any chance anything in the way of automata?"

And looking at me he said, "I have only just this morning purchased an antique gold box that I would very much like to show you. It comes to me from a very elderly gentleman who told me that it had been in his family, certainly since the time of Louis XVI." He then waited a few moments and continued, "I am rather hesitant about showing it to you because it is very, very expensive."

I told him that if I approved the piece I would not let price stand in my way.

After the little conversation, the dealer opened his safe and took out what I saw immediately must be one of the rarest antique gold snuff boxes that I had ever seen. It was an automaton. Not only was it a snuff box, but it contained a secret compartment concealed under its lid, which when opened by pressure on a very tiny lever hidden to one side came into view. Here was an entire scene in highly colored enamels of a young boy and girl seated in a garden in an amorous embrace. When another tiny lever at one side was pressed the girl's skirt moved slowly to one side and at the same time the man's pants opened at the fly, and they then began playing with each other sexually. All the while a music box played a pleasant little tune. This was one of the most exciting and exotic objects of its type that I had ever seen in all of my experience. It was something that I knew would delight the king. Not was this because of any sexual aspect, but because of its rarity as an example of the clockmaker's art.

Despite the fact that the dealer was asking a very high price for this box, I knew that I had to buy it; as far as I knew, the cost would not in any way affect the king's desire to acquire it.

This being the case, I at once paid the man with a wad of francs that I always carried with me on these trips, as to the French checks were almost unknown, for one reason or another.

After I had paid for the box I asked the dealer to let me have as many details as he could about the origins of the piece, so that I could record all this when sending the box out to Cairo. He had little more to tell me after he had told me about the original owner, and I had to be satisfied with that.

226

After this acquisition I at once returned to my hotel so that I could make a record of what the dealer had told me; I did not wish to forget any detail, as I knew that the king loved to read all about these little aspects of his purchases.

I then thought to myself that while I was in the cathedral maybe I had been praying silently for some such find.

When I returned to my hotel, I decided that instead of sending the purchase off to the palace in Cairo from Paris I would take it with me to New York so that my brother could see what a rare little gem it was.

As soon as I was back home in New York a package of my new acquisitions was prepared and shipped to Cairo, and as all such shipments were made through the government bag, it was in the king's hands within two days. When the king saw the box he was so enthralled with it that he sent me a special cable thanking me and telling me that he found the object quite extraordinary and also that it would make an excellent addition to his already famous collections.

It was just a couple of days after he had received the box and after we had received his cable that the Nazi general Rommel was rushing madly across the Egyptian desert with his Nazi hordes, and it seemed that it could not be too long before he reached El Alamein, from whence the road to Cairo would lie wide open to him.

Just at this time we were again preparing another shipment to be carried to Cairo in the government pouch from Washington, and in this package there were similarly some lovely and desirable objects, which we knew that the king would want. However, the news from North Africa was indeed very gloomy and we felt that perhaps sending any further shipment would be fraught with danger. The question then arose in our minds: *Shall we or shall we not make any further sendings at this time?*

Then after some consideration we telephoned our old friend, the Egyptian counsul general Chawky Bey, at his office on Fifth Avenue and told him that we wished to speak with him about the Rommel situation in Egypt. He told us to come right over and said that he would be waiting for us.

When we arrived in his office we could see that he was as perturbed as we were by the news.

"Chawky, do you think that we would be ill advised to ship anything to the palace just at this time?"

And he replied. "I am afraid that I cannot give you any advice one way or another; you know just as much as I do about the situation." And then, with a most theatrical gesture, he went to his desk, opened a drawer, and took out a small pistol, saying as he did so. "If Rommel succeeds I am finished and I shall shoot myself."

After this most unsatisfactory visit we returned to our offices and tried to decide for ourselves what we should do. After due reflection, we decided to cable the king in Cairo and see what he might have to say. After all, we felt that he would most likely be on top of the situation. In this cable we asked him for his opinion, whether he thought we should ship another package or perhaps wait for calmer times.

A few hours then passed and we received a reply cable from the king, which was sent as speedily as possible on a government priority basis. The cable read: "Ignore everything and ship as usual."

When we received this cable we were very elated and decided that the king must know something that we did not, and we felt that something was in the air that he knew about, which might change the entire picture.

We at once again telephoned Chawky Bey and told him that we had just received some news from Cairo that could potentially be of very high importance for him. We again arranged to meet with him at his office and went right over with the cable in our pockets.

As soon as we were there and showed him the cable he began to laugh. "The king knows something that we do not, he stated. And as he said this he again did a little dance around his desk, saying as he did this, "I think that I can now throw my pistol away."

We left him in a very happy mood and decided as soon as we were back at our office to prepare our shipment to Cairo as the king had suggested we do in the cable.

True enough, next morning we heard the news that the British forces under General Montgomery had halted the Nazi advance at El Alamein and that Rommel and his forces were in fullest retreat back across the desert. The following day our shipment was in Cairo, and we again received a special cable from the king, saying how delighted he was with our continued efforts on his behalf.

As it later transpired, this Nazi retreat was the turning point in the entire war and heralded the beginning of the end of the Nazi threat to all, both European nations and those of the Middle East.

Chapter 43

Bernard Baruch and His Box Collection

As has so often been reported in the press, Bernard Baruch, renowned politico of the Franklin D. Roosevelt era, was accustomed to seat himself on a park bench, be it in Central Park in New York City, in Washington, D.C., or, in fact, anywhere that he might be traveling. It appears that he always seemed to enjoy speaking with anybody who might be seated on the same bench as he and who would be prepared to listen to him expound on all sorts of matters, be it politics, life, or what you will. It never mattered to him in the least if his companions were black, white, or Hispanic, young or old, and I do not believe that he was in the slightest degree interested in any replies that he might receive from any of his listeners. Basically, he loved the sound of his own voice. As a man he was quite tall, maybe six foot plus, slim, and very good-looking and as a personality quite an unmistakable figure.

During the many years that we were located on East 57th Street he would quite frequently come into our offices and, seating himself on the edge of our receptionist-secretary's desk, talk to her. Blanche, our secretary, was naturally very flattered by attention, except that he invariably arrived just at our closing time, and in the event that she had a date for that particular evening she would be quite perturbed. Why he always arrived at this particular hour she could never figure out. How could she, a mere secretary, tell so famous a personality that although she was flattered by his attention, she would like him to leave so that she could make her date on time? She had a problem.

These evening visits occurred over quite a few years, and whenever he did come he seemed to follow a similar pattern. Never once did he discuss any matters of business with her or with me whenever I met him. Until one day at about lunchtime he came up again, something that he had never previously done, and asked Blanche to tell me that he wished to speak with me on a private matter.

Blanche then asked him to wait a moment while she went into my private office and told me that he was waiting to see me.

I told her to bring him in, and this she did.

As soon as he was seated at our desk he began talking. "I have just recently been told that you and your brother have coauthored a book titled *Antique Gold Boxes, Their Lore and Their Lure*, and I must tell you that I managed to get hold of a copy, which I have just finished reading, and as soon as I had finished reading it I tried to buy a copy for my library, but found that it was all sold out and no longer available. I became so excited by what I read that I have decided to start a collection of these boxes."

I thanked him for what he had said about our work, and I told him that the writing had been a labor of love. He then asked me what we had to show him so that he could start right away with his new collection. At that moment we had some fifty or sixty boxes in our collection of all types and various nationalities, and at his request we brought out onto our desk all that we owned, all laid out on trays.

"Now please tell me all that you can about the subject of these gold boxes, where they were made and when they were made and also any particular histories pertaining to each. In fact, I want to know anything that might be of interest to me as a new collector," he requested.

I then proceeded to give him a brief résumé of all that I knew about the subject. I told him about the high period during the reigns of Louis XV and Louis XVI of France, when some of the greatest examples were made to coordinate with the costumes of the day and that some of them were created for use during the winter months and others of lighter color for the summer.

I also told him how many of the fashionables of their day would sometimes order several boxes at a time so that they could alternate them, as men do today frequently with their cuff buttons.

I also related how Napoleon Bonaparte ordered gold boxes to be made for him in very great quantity, some to be emblazoned across the lids with the Napoleonic bee in diamonds, and others with the initial "N" similarly in diamonds. I explained how the

Emperor used these to be given to ambassadors or other luminaries, particularly when he wanted to receive any favors from them, much in the manner that bribes are today given by large corporations to influence customers. This latter Baruch appeared to appreciate to the full, and he said that he understood.

I also discussed the wonderful gold boxes that were created in England during the period of King George III and which were used for somewhat similar purposes. He seemed most interested when I described the so-called "Freedom Boxes" that were made to be presented to people together with documents of Freedom of the City. There is today the great collection of these housed at Apsley House in London, which had been the home of the Duke of Wellington. These boxes had been presented to him by the various cities that he had passed through on his triumphant march to London after the defeat of Napoleon at Waterloo.

I then told Baruch about some of the great specimens that we had acquired for king Farouk of Egypt, exclaiming that in these cases most of the boxes were associated with some special mechanical or musical mechanisms.

We went on to talk about some of the great examples that had been created in Switzerland toward the end of the eighteenth century and more particularly during the early part of the nineteenth century and how in this case the enameling was perhaps the most prominent part of the whole.

While I was speaking he listened to every word that I uttered and seemed to be eating up my words. Never once did he interject a single comment. After I had been speaking for maybe two hours or so, he interrupted me.

"Are you quite sure that these boxes that you have laid out on these trays are all that you can show me?"

I assured him that these comprised our entire collection.

He then said to me, "Would you please let me have a small tray?"

When we had given him the tray he began to study each of the boxes with great care, and then after some time had passed he had placed about twenty of them on the tray.

"As you will have noticed, I am sure, I have not asked you the price of any one of these, because I do not want the price aspect to enter into my thinking," he began, and then he continued, "Now I want you to write me a short history of each of the specimens that I have selected and also at the same time give me any information about each of them that I could find of interest to me as a collector."

"I understand quite well what you mean," I told him. "For a collector all these aspects would certainly be of interest."

He then continued, "When you have done all this for me would you please set all out on a sheet together with the cost against each item and also place a small ticket in each of the boxes so that when I decide on any of them I will be able to open the box and read what you have written? In any case, please reserve all these for me until I give you my final decision. When you have the sheet prepared please send it over to me at my hotel."

I explained to him that it would take us about two days to prepare the documentation he requested, and then he told me that he was in no great hurry and, saying good-bye, left.

Next day, together with Blanche, we prepared the lists that he requested. Blanche, having worked with us on the book, was almost as knowledgeable as we were on the subject.

When typing up the lists together with all the documentation and prices, she found that it was necessary for us to use three sheets. The last of these sheets had just one of the items at its head. However, on this final sheet we made a grand total, although each of the first two sheets were totaled at the bottom.

As soon as all was ready we sent the lists over to Mr. Baruch at his hotel as we had arranged to do. As soon as these three sheets were in his hands, he wrote us a letter making us a very close offer for the entire group, but he based his offer on the total at the base of the second sheet, completely ignoring the top of the third sheet.

We replied to him, explaining that he had missed the overall total as set out on the top of the third sheet. He again replied, ignoring what we had written him about the third sheet but repeating his original offer. He also wrote: "Please forget all about what I told you about my desire to become a collector. After you have accepted my offer I shall write you and tell you that I want you to send each of the boxes to a different recipient."

Never previously having done any business with the gentle-man, we wrote him that we were accepting his offer on his terms, as we wished to retain him as a client in the future.

A few days then passed, and we received his further instructions together with his check. He wrote: "One of the boxes that I have marked on your sheet is to be sent to Eleanor Roosevelt; another is to go to Anna Rosenberg," who at that time was a member of the Roosevelt administration. Beyond these two personalities I do not recall the names of the other recipients, except that each was either in the government or in one area of the arts.

As far as I now recall, the box that we sent to Mrs. Roosevelt was of the Louis XVI period and beautifully enameled.

In due course, most of the recipients wrote asking us to advise them of what figure they should insure them for. Presumably they wished to know how much had been paid for their gifts by Mr. Baruch without putting the matter in so many words.

As soon as we received these requests we called Mr. Baruch and asked him how he wanted us to reply.

He replied quite tersely, "Just write and tell them the truth."

At this time I do not remember how much we received for the collection that he bought from us, but I do know that in today's market each of the boxes would be worth a minimum of ten times its original cost, if not more.

After we had concluded our transaction with Mr. Baruch, we replaced the balance of our collection in our safes and proceeded to seek further specimens to remake our group. We had in the transaction placed about twenty items with him.

Chapter 44

Antique Show at Armory

A few weeks after we had resumed our search for further specimens, we were approached by the directors of a forthcoming Armory antiques show on Park Avenue and invited to take a booth there. At first we were rather disinclined to show our things at such a show, but after a while we decided that we would do so. We were leased a booth, deciding that we would display a collection of antique jewels as well as our collection of gold boxes.

It was during the early forties, and finding that antique shows were beginning to make an important impact on the world of art and antiquity and having already decided to take a booth at the forthcoming Armory show, we commenced arranging for our display.

When we arrived at the booth we saw that it would be necessary to dress it up a little, and we watched others doing the same thing at their booths. However, when we saw what most of the others were placing on show for sale, we felt that we had been quite ill advised to reserve our booth, as what we had to show would be quite out of place, but having done so we had to go ahead. In our showcases we proposed displaying our group of fine antique gold snuff boxes, for which we were quite renowned, and also some very fine specimens of horological interest. Beyond this we showed many fine piece of antique jewelry from the period of the Renaissance through the Victorian period.

The question then arose, What shall we use as a backdrop, the security being what it was at the Armory, that would not encourage any thieves? All of the valuables were to be placed in secure vaults overnight, so that these would be quite safe.

Just at that time we owned a portrait of a man, just the head and shoulders, that had been painted by the nineteenth-century British artist Beechey, and we felt that this would be an ideal thing to hang.

The portrait was not valuable in the least, and particularly as the sitter was so ugly, we considered that nobody in his right mind would even give it a glance, except perhaps to laugh at it. The man had an enormous bulbous nose, and this together with his other features made him look quite grotesque.

We then opened up our booth, and after the show had been in progress for a couple of days, we realized that we had been quite wrong in going ahead with it. Several people did pass by our cases and admire what we had on display, but beyond this there were no sales.

While seated at a desk at the rear of our booth one morning, I noticed a lady standing and staring at the portrait. It seemed to me that she was almost transfixed as she stood. Without saying a word she must have been there for some ten or fifteen minutes, and I had completely ignored her, when she came over to me.

"I have been looking at that portrait hanging at the back of your booth, and I am wondering whether you can give me any details of its possible history," she inquired.

I told that as far as I knew we had received no history when we had originally purchased the painting at an auction in London, where it had been sold together with several others from an anonymous source. I told her what I knew about the artist, Beechey, and about his period, and I also told her that the portrait had obviously never in its life been cleaned or in any way touched. I also told her that if it were to be cleaned a signature might appear, although I told her that one could not count on this.

Then to my utter astonishment she said, "I can tell you something about the origin of this portrait, as the sitter has my family nose, and as you can see, this is the most prominent detail in the entire painting. Beyond this I cannot conceive of anybody else having so interesting a nose."

This entire conversation was to me so ludicrous that I would have been delighted to hide myself in a corner and have a good laugh, but there were no corners in the booth. The lady then continued to stare at the portrait, and then as an afterthought she inquired how much we were asking for it. "Must buy it at any price," she said.

For my part I would have given it to her, but I did quote her a figure and she at once wrote me her check.

236

"I am writing this check right away, as I don't want to take the risk of losing the painting," she told me.

The thought that anybody else might want to buy it never for a moment had entered my mind. She then said to me, after writing her check, "Am I the lucky one! Never did I think that I would ever be able to buy my ancestor's portrait, and now I want to hang it in my home and leave it for my family after I pass away. Would you please have him packaged up so that I can take him home with me in a taxi, as I cannot wait to show him to my sons and then to see the pleasure on their faces as they see what their forefather looked like."

I told her that she would have to wait until the show closed before we could take the painting off the wall, as I told her it would ruin our booth to do so. But she was quite adamant; she had to have him immediately. Knowing that we would have no difficulty in replacing the painting on the wall, I allowed her to take him home with her.

At the end of the week the show closed, and I must say that for me it was quite a relief. As far as I was concerned, the entire booth had been a mistake.

After I had been back at our galleries for a few days the lady came in to see me.

"I have come in to thank you for selling me that portrait of my ancestor; when I got home and showed him to my sons, they all declared that as far as they could tell there was no doubt in their minds that with the family nose it had to be him." She told me that a long discussion had ensued among her children as to whether or not it was the portrait of their Uncle John or some other member of their family. They knew, it appears, that one of their ancestors was recorded as having had his "likeness" done during the midnineteenth century. I trust that the family still retains the portrait and they continue to derive much pleasure from its acquisition, at least as much pleasure as we had in parting with it.

Chapter 45

Renoir and the Madame Stora Painting

Virtually week after week there is a continual stream of oil paintings of every conceivable period and nationality being offered for auction at salesrooms throughout the international art market: Christie's, Sotheby's, Phillip's, Doyle's, and so on over here in New York, Christie's and Sotheby's in London, the Salle Drouot in Paris, and so forth. From time to time a particular painting will appear that seems to stand apart from all others for one reason or another.

And so it was that while viewing a group of paintings at one of New York's auction galleries—at this time I believe that it was Christie's—I noticed a painting titled *L'Algerienne* painted and signed by the great Renoir, the outstanding personality of the French Impressionist era. There was a label attached stating that the sitter had been a Madame Stora. This portrait was very prominently displayed on a wall, and as I gazed on its great beauty and majesty I began to ponder as to whether the lady might have any relationship to my old friend Monsieur Stora, the art dealer from Paris who had settled over here in New York during the war.

Monsieur Stora was a gentleman of the greatest erudition, not only in paintings, but also in many other fields of antiquity, and it had always been a great pleasure for me to be in his company and discuss some detail or other in one of these various areas. He would frequently expound on some of his antiquarian glories of years gone by. During the fifties many New York and other antique dealers would lunch at the downstairs restaurant of Stouffer's on East 58th Street, where no women were permitted unless accompanied by a man. Here in the center of the room a large round table had always been set where many of the dealers would foregather and where all were welcome. At this table one could never tell just who might join. There were Egyptologists and dealers in paintings, porcelains, silver, and jewels, and the conversation was always most stimulating.

238

"L'Algerienne, Madame Clementine Stora," 1870, by Pierre Auguste Renoir (reprinted courtesy of the fine Arts Museum of San Francisco: gift of Mr. and Mrs. Prentis Cobb Hale in honor of Thomas Carr Howe, Jr.).

At this table Monsieur Stora usually ate his lunch whenever he was in town.

A couple of days after I had seen the portrait of Madame Stora, he came down to lunch, and being seated at this table, I told him about the beautiful painting that I had seen and inquired whether he knew anything about the portrait and whether perhaps the lady had been any relation of his. After all, his name, Stora, was quite unusual as far as I was concerned.

After I had finished speaking, he looked up at me with a very wistful expression on his face. "But of course I know the painting very well indeed. It is of my mother, who was known affectionately as 'L'Algerienne.' "

Being much intrigued at his reply, I said, "In that case, you should buy it and hang it in your apartment."

"I could not buy it for several very cogent reasons. First, I could never afford to pay the price that it will command, and second, because even if I did buy it, I have today nobody I could bequeath it to." He then continued, "Despite these negatives I would dearly love to have it back and hanging on my wall so that I could feed my eyes on my mother's great beauty, although being as old as I am this could not be for too long. But perhaps you would like to know why the portrait is no longer in my possession and on the market for sale?"

I told him I would love to hear what he had to tell me about it, as it is always most interesting to hear any story about a painting, particularly if it is a famous one, and this was certainly in that category.

"When I was a very young boy—I must have been about ten or eleven—at this time I lived at home in Paris with my father and mother. I was an only child. My father was one of the leading antiquarians of his day, and the three of us enjoyed a very close and happy relationship. My father was very fond of relating to us over the dinner table stories of some of his discoveries, and both of us enjoyed listening to him tell about them. It was my father's wish that I have the best schooling available in those days, and they enrolled me at the Lycée, where I did very well.

Now among his friends father numbered some of the great French artists of the day, many of whom would on occasion dine with us, and among these Monsieur Renoir was perhaps one of his closest friends."

At this point Monsieur Stora stopped talking to take a sip of the wine that he habitually drank with his lunch, and after a while he continued.

"One evening Monsieur Renoir when dining with us was looking over at Mother, whose beauty he had always admired, and said to Father, 'Monsieur Stora, Madame is so very beautiful that with your permission, I would dearly love to paint her portrait, so that it can hang over on your wall and, for myself, I can always admire her when I'm here even when she is not present. If you allow me to do this I would title the painting L'Algerienne.'

"Father said that he would be delighted and would treasure such a portrait, especially as it would have been painted by one of his dearest friends.

"Thus as soon as dinner was over Renoir said that he could not wait a moment to start work on the painting and asked my mother to go into her bedroom and change into her native Algerienne costume, and this is what she at once did, especially as she told Monsieur Renoir that she would be very proud of such a portrait.

"After this beginning it did not take Monsieur Renoir too long to finish the painting. Incidentally, all the while he spoke to me, Father seemed to insist on the 'Monsieur' when referring to Renoir. Mother had been over at the artist's studio a couple of times, and soon afterward Renoir told my father that the portrait was ready to be hung.

"As soon as Father heard this, he invited Monsieur Renoir over to dinner and asked that he bring the portrait with him so that he could himself hang it to the best advantage. Father told Monsieur Renoir that as he was the painter of this great gift, he wanted him to have the privilege of arranging for its hanging where it could be viewed in all of its splendor.

"When Father saw the portrait for the first time he was enchanted with it and after dinner was over asked the artist where he thought it should be hung.

"Monsieur Renoir said that he himself was entirely delighted with the result of his work and, taking a hammer and nail from Father, got up on to a chair, knocked a nail in the wall, and hung

241

the portrait. He said that he had placed it in a position so that whenever he was invited to dine with them he could look up at his work.

"After this the years passed very pleasantly, artists and friendly dealers always in evidence around the house. However, one morning Father was discovered dead by my mother; he had passed away peaceably in his sleep.

"I am afraid to say that my father was a most generous man and when he passed away left Mother and me with very little money with which to carry on.

"A few weeks after his death Mother had to pay for a new semester at the Lycée, where the fee was five hundred francs. For my part I told Mother that I thought that I should stop going to school and try to follow in Father's footsteps and perhaps be enabled to bring in some money from antique sales.

"Mother was quite adamant. 'Father always wanted you to have the best schooling, and now because of his death I am not going to allow you to stop school,' she insisted.

"In those days five hundred francs would have been the rough equivalent of one hundred dollars in American money. Naturally, Mother knew many of the art dealers of the day and asked several of them how much they considered her portrait would fetch. Most of them told her that it would be worth about five hundred francs.

"This being the case, she called one of her friends and sold him the portrait that you have just seen at auction for the five hundred francs that she used to pay for my semester."

As Monsieur Stora spoke and told me this story he seemed to be quite nostalgic, and I really believe that until I mentioned the matter to him he had completely forgotten all about the painting and the story behind it.

On the day of the auction I went to the Galleries to watch while the portrait was sold, and while there I noticed Monsieur Stora seated at the very rear of the room. In due course the painting was offered, and being a beautiful example of Renoir's oeuvre, it was sold for a considerable amount of money. I could not tell what the old gentleman's feelings were when he saw this. In today's market the portrait would certainly be worth even considerably more than it realized at this auction. *L'Algerienne* is now in the collection of the Fine Arts Museum in San Francisco.

Chapter 46

Senor Gonzalez Gordon and His Portrait Collection

There was a very wealthy Cuban gentleman living on a vast estate in Havana who was a direct descendant of the famous family of the Dukes of Gordon. This Gordon family was very old and highly renowned throughout the world, and there were, and are still today, many members spread all over the world. Particularly were the members of this famous family settled in Spain and Portugal, where they were associated with the port wine and sherry industry.

The gentleman's name was Senor Gonzalez Gordon, and he was one of the directors of the famous firm of sherry distillers Gonzalez Byass & Company. One day we received a letter from this gentleman in Havana in which he wrote that he had been given our name by another member of his family resident in England, who had advised him that we would perhaps be the best firm of art dealers to assist him in a project that he had in mind. In his letter he wrote that he wished to obtain as many portraits of various members of the Duke of Gordon family as he could lay his hands on, extending over the past several centuries. His project was to establish a museum in Cuba to honor his family.

In this same letter he stated that he was a direct descendant of the family. He also stated that he had already found a suitable site for the projected museum.

On receipt of this letter we replied that we already knew of several suitable portraits that we could let him have immediately, also that we knew we would be able to buy others from time to time that we would be able to offer him. We told him that our representative in London would be advised of his interest and would be in continuous touch with us in this regard.

In this same letter we enclosed a photograph with details of one Gordon portrait that we already owned.

As soon as he received our letter he replied enclosing his check and asking us to ship the painting as soon as possible so that he could hang it together with several others that he already owned.

From that beginning we were able to supply him with several others that came our way, including some that dated back to the seventeenth century. Whenever we wrote him about any of these he at once mailed us his check and asked that they be shipped immediately. He then wrote that his collection was growing beautifully and he could not wait for the day when he could build his museum and place it on its walls.

I then wrote him that I would be going to arrive in Cuba the following week on a vacation, and he replied that he would, unfortunately, not be able to receive me, as he would be traveling, but that Senor Lobo, the millionaire sugar planter, a great friend of his, had asked that we contact him on arrival and would be happy to introduce me to the famous Havana Yacht Club, where we could lunch as his guests.

After my return to New York from this vacation in Havana, we received from London a portrait of one of the seventeenth-century Dukes of Gordon, which was, as far as we could see, the finest of its type that we had so far been able to lay our hands on. We had it photographed in color, as the duke had been painted in his red ducal robes, and mailed it to Senor Gordon. This was the most expensive portrait that we had until that time been able to offer him

As soon as this letter and photograph were received by Senor Gordon, he replied asking that we hold it aside for him to see, as he wrote he would be arriving in New York the following week, when he could then decide, one way or another, as he wrote this one was much more expensive than any of the others he had already in his collection. He also wrote that this painting, however, looked to be quite superb and despite the cost he would almost positively buy it from us.

When the gentleman arrived, there was no doubt about who he was; his face could have been the one that had been painted in the present canvas. It could have been his portrait; so much for the Duke of Gordon's family genes. The moment that he saw it, he said that this would certainly be a central feature in the museum.

The portrait was in a very delicate frame that looked as though it had been made by Chippendale and was itself a work of art. Seeing this, he said that he wanted to carry it back to Havana himself so that he could see that no harm came to the frame. He jokingly said that he thought that he would reserve an extra seat on the plane so that he could have it next him until he arrived home in Havana.

Very shortly after this visit came the Revolution in Cuba under Castro, and the shades obviously fell on the island, certainly as far as Senor Gordon was concerned. We wrote him several letters but never received any replies from him. We then met with several émigrés from Cuba in New York and asked them whether perhaps any one of them might have any idea of Senor Gordon's whereabouts. All that we could find out from these people was that they knew that many of the very wealthy had already been liquidated.

We again wrote him another letter, and this time we received it back marked "Undeliverable."

To this day we have never been able to discover anything about his fate and can only assume that he was one of those liquidated.

Some months after the Revolution, we met Senor Lobo in New York, who from being a very wealthy sugar merchant, seemed to have become an entirely broken man.

Positively the Gonzalez Gordon Museum had not been built, and it is virtually positive that it now never will be. What happened to the collection of Gordon portraits is anybody's guess.

Chapter 47

Trip to Havana

While on this trip to Havana accompanied by my then wife, I went to many of the night spots that abounded high on the hills outside of town, many of which were beautiful in the extreme, with flowing waterfalls rushing down over the rocks. It is possible that some of these still exist.

However, despite the beauty of the surroundings, the food served in the various restaurants was not at all to our liking, and one morning when standing at the entrance of the Nacional Hotel where we stayed, I was complaining about this to Mr. Bloomingdale, who said that he similarly detested the food that was being served. He told me that he had found one restaurant downtown in the old section of the city that was to his mind superb; it was, amusingly enough, named Moise Pipik. He advised that we try it. That same evening we went there and found, to our delight, that he was perfectly correct in his judgment. After all, he was one of the owners of the famed department store of the same name in New York and should be able to judge quality.

While we were seated in this restaurant a gentleman, obviously a refugee from Nazi Germany, came over to our table and offered me a lottery ticket. I told him that I was not interested, and he left. At that moment I had some second thoughts about the matter. *Here*, I said to myself, *is this poor fellow trying to eke out a few pennies and I refuse him*, and this I could not let go by. Then, calling the man over to our table again, I asked him, "How much is a whole lottery ticket?"

He seemed very surprised at this question, as probably people were buying small portions of a ticket. He replied, "Five dollars."

I then told the man that I had a proposition for him. (Fortunately, I spoke German, as the man spoke no English.) I then told him that I would buy a whole ticket from him for the five dollars, but only on one condition. He then asked me what the condition was, and I told him, "You must put your own name on the stub of the ticket, so that if in the eventual drawing you win anything I want you to keep it for yourself."

The man seemed to be quite stunned by this and replied after some short consideration, "With regard to any prize money that I may win, if this is a very large sum then may you and your wife be blessed, and depending on the value of any prize money downward so will my blessings be reduced proportionately."

Whether this man did win anything I will never know, nor do I know whether any of his blessings have or have not done me any good. I do recall that at the time there were what appeared to be thousands of émigrés from Nazi Germany waiting to leave Cuba and go to Israel or the United States and these people were kept penned in behind high railings like animals.

Chapter 48

Diamond Clip and Sonja Henie

Oxford Street in the heart of London's West End is perhaps one of its most crowded thoroughfares. It is filled on both sides of the road with stores of every conceivable type, from boutiques to department stores. For this reason it is usually so jammed with shoppers, especially during the London season, that walking is sometimes almost impossible. Today these crowded sidewalks are filled with tourists and travelers from all quarters of the globe and foreign tongues are to be heard on all sides. Most of these pedestrians are quite well dressed, and one rarely sees anybody along the street who might be termed a hobo. One day in June, when the crowds were milling about, perhaps in greater numbers than usual, a policeman walking his beat noticed a particularly scrofulous-looking individual lying up against one of the windows of one of the department stores. He seemed to be fast asleep and was probably under the influence of drink.

The store manager was quite upset to see this man propped up against his window, feeling that he would keep customers away, so he stopped the policeman and asked him to get the man away. He said to the constable, "He is ruining our business."

The officer then endeavored to rouse the man, who was snoring very loudly in his sleep, but to no avail. He could not rouse the man.

Seeing this, the officer called his station house and asked that they send a wagon to pick up the vagrant.

It did not take too long for the police van to arrive, and very soon the man was taken away, still asleep in his drunken stupor.

Upon arrival at the police station, the man was formally charged with loitering, although at the time he was in no state to even know where he was or what was going on. After this he was taken into a room where he was deloused and cleaned up as well as possible.

In the course of this most unpleasant task it was necessary to remove all of the man's filthy clothing, and while doing so the officers had to go through his pockets to see whether perhaps he had his name written somewhere or other, so that at least they could ascertain his identity. On going through these pockets they found a very small amount of change, an odd piece of string, and a tiny pencil, but beyond these petty items they found at the bottom of one of the man's pants pockets, to their great astonishment, a very important-looking ruby and diamond clip pin, one obviously from a pair of the fashionable double clip pins of the twenties and thirties. It seemed to the officers who saw this that the jewel must be quite new, and they became quite excited, certain that the man could not possibly be the owner of such a piece. They then placed the clip pin together with the other things in a bag and placed it in their safe so that when the man woke up they could ask him some questions. The man was then put into a cell until, when sobered up, he could be questioned.

Some hours later the man awakened and, becoming a little more coherent, started to scream that they had no right to put him in a cell and lock him up. He said that he had done nothing wrong but had just been sleeping in the sun.

The policeman in charge, hearing the screams, had the man taken out of the cell and seated at a table in a side room and said that he would have to wait there until a detective arrived.

As soon as this detective came in, he said to the man, "Where did you get the brooch that we found last night in your pocket?

The man replied quite simply, "It's mine."

"If the brooch is yours where did you get it?" queried the detective.

The man then stated, "It is mine because I found it in the street yesterday."

"As you found the brooch in the street you should have reported its finding to the nearest police station immediately—that is the law—and having failed to do this you can be charged with stealing by finding, and this is a criminal offense," said the detective.

When the man heard this he became very perturbed. "I may be an old drunk, but I don't want any trouble, so I am reporting it to you now, and you can keep it."

249

The detective, not wishing to worry the poor man more than he had, said, "This report is now in order, and you will not be charged criminally."

Now whenever a jewel or any other valuable is lost or stolen it should be at once reported to the police, who list each item on a daily basis in what is known in London as the "Police List," sometimes called the "Bargain List" by unscrupulous dealers. Most of the jewelers and pawnbrokers receive this list every day, and most read it through religiously so that in the event they recognize any item that may have been or might be offered to them for sale they can report the matter to the authorities. Since this jewel was quite obviously a very valuable piece and had not been listed, it must not have been reported as missing by its owner.

The detective in charge was quite at a loss and decided that he would try to investigate the matter and see whether perhaps he could in some way trace the owner.

It so happened that I was at our London office at the time and was seated at a desk when the detective came in to see my brother Bertram, whom he knew. As over the years our office had appraised so many jewels of great value, the detective, knowing this, inquired whether my brother had ever seen the clip brooch that he held in his hand. He told my brother that he thought that possibly he might know who owned such a jewel.

My brother looked at the jewel and told the detective that he was quite positive that he had never seen it before. But my brother did tell him that it was quite positively a very recently made piece.

At that moment our man, Hughes, came through the office and my brother showed the jewel to him and asked him whether he had ever seen it. Hughes then studied this piece with his loupe and said that there was no doubt at all that the jewel had been made in England for some special order and after a few moments continued, "I do not know who made the brooch, but I do know that it has a very special type of pin at the back and that there are only three jewelers in London who do this work."

Now jewels have certain characteristics that readily establish where they were made, either London, Paris, or New York, much in the same way as a furrier can tell in which city a fur coat had been made.

Hughes then said to the detective, "If you will leave the pin with me I shall ask around, and I am sure that in a very short time I may be able to get you some definite information about it."

The detective told Hughes that he could certainly keep the jewel and also that if he had any information about the piece he would be delighted to hear from him.

As soon as the detective was out of the office, Hughes told my brother that he would go down to Hatton Garden to speak with the three jewelers he had mentioned and ask them whether one or other of them had made the pin and also for whom. Later that afternoon Hughes was back at the office with the clip and told my brother that the first two jewelers that he visited told him that they had never seen the piece, but when he showed it to the third, he said, "Yes, I recently made that pin together with its mate for a special customer and only delivered it to her yesterday."

Hughes then asked him to tell him the name of the customer, and the jeweler replied, "Don't be ridiculous. I am not going to disclose the name of my client to you or anybody else."

"All right," said Hughes. "This is a police matter, so I shall tell the detective in charge to come down and see you about it."

The jeweler, hearing that this was a police matter, became alarmed and at once told Hughes that the customer was Sonja Henie, the renowned skater who had been in London for a couple of weeks and had just returned to the States. Hughes then returned to the office and reported to my brother what he had discovered, and Bertram at once telephoned and spoke with the police station and was told that the detective had already left for the day, so he left a message for the detective asking that he telephone first thing next morning when he arrived.

Next morning the man was on the telephone and my brother told him what Hughes had discovered and asked that he come around and collect the jewel. An hour or so later the detective arrived and collected the clip and told my brother that he would call the lady in New York and tell her of the finding of her jewel.

Next day the detective told my brother that he had spoken with the lady, who told him that she was positive that she had her two clips in her vault at her bank, but she said that she would go down and look through her things, as she said that she might be mistaken.

251

A few hours after this conversation she telephoned back to say that there was only one of the clips in her vault box, and the detective told her that her clip had been found on Oxford Street and had been picked up by a man. She replied that she remembered shopping on Oxford Street when she said she must have dropped it. He told the lady that he would send the clip to her by airmail immediately, and she thanked him.

A week or two then passed and there was no word from the lady, either that she had received the clip or not, so the detective put through another call to New York to inquire. "Oh yes, I have it," she said and without another word hung up the telephone, without so much as a "Thank you."

The police were quite upset at this ungracious attitude on the lady's part, and the chief at the station house said, "I am really sorry that we didn't let the bum keep the piece."

However, as Sonja Henie passed away very shortly after this episode, the police concluded that at the time the lady must have been quite sick and in no mood to say, "Thank you," to anybody.

As the quotation goes, "De Mortuis nihil nisi bonum—of the dead nothing but good."

Chapter 49

Baroness De Reitzes and Admiral Harris

Over the many years that we had been interested in antique gold boxes, having over these years accumulated a great deal of information on the subject, my brother Henry and I decided to write a book on the subject, giving emphasis to the several centers where these lovely objects had been created over the past two centuries. Such a work had not previously been done. In this book we endeavored to concentrate not only on the raison d'être of such boxes, but also on the many aspects of history attached to some of them. Also in this work we attempted to make an analysis of the few of such boxes that had been produced over the years here in America.

When after several years of effort the book made its appearance, in a limited edition, it was an immediate success and almost an overnight sellout. Over the past few years and since its publication during the early fifties, we have on several occasions been asked to reprint it. But when we suggested this to the publisher we were told that during some removal of his business the original plates had been lost, and although they had searched all over the place, they were not to be found. Thus we were not able to do it.

During the early days of the infamous Nazi regime in Germany, there lived a very prominent banker named Hans Arnhold, who had escaped the menace quite early and arrived safely here in New York. Before leaving Germany, he later told us, he had found a copy of our book in the hands of a German bookseller and, having over the years been a lover and collector of these beautiful items, had bought it and brought it over with him, together with his collection. How he had managed to leave Germany and carry away with him his collection he would never say, and his collection was quite large. However, whenever the question arose he would always reply with a somewhat quizzical smile.

As soon as he was settled in his hotel he telephoned us to ask whether he could come over to our offices to see us. He said that he had taken a suite at the Hotel Pierre, where he would be very close to us.

We told him that he would be most welcome to continue his collection over here, where, he told us, he had been informed very fine specimens could be found from time to time. He also said that after reading our book he knew that we would be able to assist him in his hobby, as he called it.

We then discussed many of the boxes that he already owned, and he asked whether he could see what we had in our collection. We had these boxes brought out to him, and after going through each of the specimens, he selected and bought several fine ones.

After speaking with him for some little time, we suggested that as he wished to have us assist him in his collection, it would be best if we paid him a visit and saw what he already owned.

He said that he would be delighted to have us visit with him and take a drink while studying what he had.

A few days later, by appointment, we found ourselves at his hotel, where together with his wife he had arranged all of his boxes in a fine Louis XVI display table, where they looked resplendent. The collection ranged through the high period of Louis XV and Louis XVI of France and on through that of Napoleon Bonaparte. He had several by some of the great German masters and especially some of those by the renowned Neuber of Dresden, who specialized in creating boxes incorporating agates of all differing hues and whose boxes are today inordinately rare. In these boxes the master engraved a tiny numeral against each piece of stone, after which he inscribed all these in a very thin booklet, which he concealed in a tiny little drawer at one end. Here he gave the specific name to each piece of agate. Arnhold told us that he had been very fortunate indeed in having found these over the years.

While we were with him he inquired whether we might be interested in handling some other such collections that might be on the market for sale by other immigrants, some of whom had been as lucky as he was in getting their things out of Germany.

We told him that we would be most happy to assist anybody that he might care to introduce to us. We also said that for any such owners who might be in great need of immediate finance we could always promise very speedy action.

254

Next day he telephoned to tell us that a friend of his, an Austrian baroness, had just arrived and had brought over with her a superb collection of antique gold boxes and that she had specialized in very fine Louis specimens and she also had with her a superb collection of miniature portraits, many by masters of the high period of the seventeenth century, which were inordinately rare.

We told him that we would be happy to meet the baroness at her hotel, if she wished us to do so—she was similarly staying at the Hotel Pierre—so that we could discuss her things with her at leisure. He said that he thought that this would be an excellent idea and he would speak with the lady and call us back later. He told us that in the event that the lady were to call us herself her name was Baroness De Reitzes.

Later that same day he telephoned to say that the baroness would be very happy if we would come over to see her next morning and that she would then have all of her things available for us to study.

When we arrived and met the baroness, she told us something about her boxes and then took us into an anteroom where she had laid them all out on a table. When we saw them we knew that we were in the presence of one of the finest collections that we had ever seen outside of a museum; we knew that many of the boxes could easily be included in some of the great museum collections.

After we had looked over the group, she said that first of all she wanted our opinion and, second, our advice regarding a possible sale of all or some of the pieces. We then suggested that we take the entire collection back with us to our offices so that we could examine each box in great depth.

We also told the lady that while the boxes were in our possession they would be covered by insurance and that she would thus be spared the expense in this regard. She then told us that she would be delighted to have us take the entire collection with us as we suggested, and she also said that she was especially pleased that she would not have to pay any insurance premiums, adding, "I must tell you that the thought of selling any of these boxes is like a dagger in my heart."

We were not in the least surprised at this outburst of emotion, as Mr. Arnhold had already informed us that she had been much involved in the theater in her younger days.

After we had spent quite some time examining each of her specimens, we telephoned the lady and told her what prices we would propose placing upon each. After a few moments' thought she asked that we proceed with any possible sales as soon as possible.

Now it had been just a short while before the arrival of the baroness that we had shown our collection of boxes at the Armory antiques show, and while there we had shown them to a gentleman named Admiral Harris. At that time he had informed us that he did not think that he was in the market to buy, but he said that he would contact us later.

A few weeks had then passed, and he came up to see us. "You remember that I told you at the Armory show that I might consider starting a collection?"

I replied that I did recall our conversation.

"Now I have decided to go on with the idea, and I would like to see what you can show me so that I can make a selection of a few boxes as a starter."

Meanwhile he began discussing himself and told us that he had been a marine architect and that for his services during the war he had been given rank of Admiral, although he laughingly remarked, "This title means very little, as I do not go to sea." Despite this, he loved being called Admiral. He then explained that his wife had quite recently passed away and that this had left him very lonely indeed, and he said that he felt that if he had some interest such as the collecting of gold boxes, he would have dealers calling him and coming up to show him things and this might make life a little easier for him. At least he would have some people to speak with. He then drew us his check for his purchases, and after promising to advise him if anything special came out way, we shook hands and he left. This meeting with the admiral was only a short time before the Baroness De Reitzes collection came in to us for sale. As we had promised him we would do, we called and told him what we had just received and that we would be delighted to give him first sight.

He then suggested that we visit with him at his Park Avenue apartment, bringing the collection over with us to show the boxes to him.

We then made an appointment for the afternoon of the following day, and then taking all of the collection of boxes with us in two valises, we visited him. When we opened the two valises he was amazed at what he saw and told us that he had never even expected to be able to buy anything like some of these. He then went through each of the boxes and examined them with great care, and before very long he had purchased almost the entire De Reizes collection. He left out several of the minor specimens, as he told us he had already purchased several just like them and he did not wish to make any duplications.

After making this purchase, he at once wrote us his check. "Now I must open a very special bottle of champagne that I have been keeping for just such an occasion," he said, and going into the kitchen, he returned with the bottle. "Be prepared for a very loud pop as I open the bottle," he warned as he started to draw the cork. But alas, to his chagrin, the cork came out very quietly and without a sound.

He then poured out three glasses, but the wine was undrinkable. It had certainly been lying on his shelf for much too long and was now quite dead. We then laughed together over his disappointment.

"Next time you bring me another fine collection I shall see to it that the champagne is drinkable," he stated.

A few weeks then passed, and the admiral telephoned to tell us that he had been introduced to the baroness by a mutual friend of his, one of the Rothschilds, who happened at that time to be here in New York, and he told us that in conversation with the baroness she had told him about the sale by us of her collection of gold boxes. He then said that he told her that he had been the buyer, and she replied that she was delighted to hear this and that she hoped that he would enjoy them as much as she had done over the past many years. At the time, as the admiral had already told us, he was extremely lonely, and he then told us that he had invited the baroness to be his guest at dinner and also to the theater and she had accepted his invitation. The baroness was a very beautiful, if very buxom, lady, and the admiral was obviously

257

very flattered that a real live baroness would consent to go out with him.

After the first invitation with the lady the admiral was again up to see us, and then following this he was up on an almost daily basis and each time that he came he told us that he had been seeing the lady on many occasions. He told us that the lady was a great conversationalist and that he loved listening to her stories, all about her past glories in the theater in Vienna.

A week after his last visit to us, the admiral was again up in our offices, as he told us that he had to speak with somebody about his newfound friend. "If anything," he said, "I like the lady more than the boxes that I got through you."

I told him that I was very happy to hear that we had been instrumental in his having met the lady with whom he was having such a wonderful time. The very next day he was again up, but this time he seemed entirely rejuvenated. He had had his hair neatly cut, his nails nicely manicured, possibly for the first time in his life. He wore a new suit, new shoes, and a new tie and even sported a silk handkerchief in his breast pocket. He then confided to me that he was again meeting the baroness that day for lunch at the 21 Club and that at that time he was going to propose marriage to her. He then thought for a moment and continued, "From what I elicited from a conversation with the lady when we dined together last night, I am sure that she will not turn me down and that I shall shortly be inviting you to our wedding."

Then with a jaunty step he left, after I had told him that we all wished him success with his proposal and all the good luck in the world.

Next morning he was again up to see us, but this time he was entirely a changed man and he was dejected to a degree. He told us that she had said how flattered she was at his proposal, but she explained that she had to reject him as she was expecting the arrival of another suitor to whom she was already engaged. He said that he did not really believe this story after the way she had spoken the previous evening. As he spoke, the admiral seemed on the verge of tears. He was an entirely broken man.

Two weeks later the admiral passed away, either because of his intense disappointment or because of his age. Nobody, of course, could speak about this.

Included in the group of furnishings that were later disposed of at Parke-Bernet Galleries there was a superb Kelim rug that had been on the floor of his very large apartment and upon which I had remarked when selling him the De Reitzes boxes. At the time I required a large rug for my apartment and decided that I would try to buy it, if for no other reason than nostalgia. At the time the admiral had told me that it had cost him ten thousand dollars at auction. At the auction I attended the rug was knocked down to me for one thousand dollars, and when I had it laid on the floor it looked magnificent. When I later moved into a smaller apartment it was much too large for any of my floors and I did not have the heart to have it cut down to fit. I then resold it to a dealer for the same sum as I had paid for it. To this day I regret its sale, as since those days such rugs have skyrocketed in value.

The other objects that were included in the De Reitzes collection and which she subsequently consigned to us for disposal was her group of seventeenth-century miniature portraits. This collection was similarly superb, and in the group there were some of the rarest names.

It soon became known that we had this collection for sale, and we were introduced to a collector and his wife, people named Starr who came up from Cincinnati to see them. They were enamored of the group and at once acquired all, which they presented to their local museum and where they certainly are today on exhibition.

Chapter 50

The Nefertiti Ring

Reading through a catalog that he had received from Christie's, my brother read about an extraordinary collection of antique rings of all periods and types, and in the listing there were several of ancient Egyptian periods. A few days later the items were on view and he went to see what there might be in the group that we would wish to acquire. Knowing of our interest in all matters pertaining to ancient Egyptology, he found several items of Ptolomaic association, and with us in mind he studied these with special interest.

There would have been no time for us to receive a copy of this catalog in New York, and so he decided that he would rely entirely on his own judgment and buy whatever he thought we would want. There was in the group one particular ring that he knew would be a must as far as we were concerned. It was a gold ring of quite simple type, but on top there was a cartouche engraved in hieroglyphics with the name of Queen Nefertiti. As far as he could tell this was of the greatest rarity and a certainty for the collection of King Farouk of Egypt, who already owned an extensive collection of ancient Egyptian gold objects.

Bertram attended this auction sale and purchased quite a few ancient rings of many periods and types, many of which were fascinating to a degree, but his most important acquisition was this Nefertiti ring.

As soon as he had his buys back at his office, he cabled us and described in length all of the specimens that he had acquired, with special mention of this Nefertiti ring.

As soon as we received his cable we replied asking that he air-mail these items, as we were just at that time preparing a shipment to go out to Cairo and wished to include this particular ring.

Very soon after he received this cable the rings were in our hands and we found all in the collection as interesting as he had done. From what he had written in his accompanying letter, the entire collection came from the estate of an antiquarian who had always been particularly a collector of antique jewels.

Going through the rings now in our possession, we were amazed at the quality of each of them, with particular emphasis on this Nefertiti specimen, which we knew would be shining object for the royal collection.

The moment that we saw it we wrote a letter to King Farouk explaining how Bertram had purchased this collection, and we emphasized this particular ring; we also wrote that the collector had made a special feature of antique rings in his catalog. We mentioned this fact as we knew that the king always loved reading about other collectors.

Just as we had finished dictating this letter to the king, our secretary, Blanche, came into our private office and told us that there was a gentleman outside who said that he had to speak with us on a very special matter. I told her to ask the gentleman to come in.

As soon as he was seated at my desk, he began speaking. "I understand that your people in London have just purchased a Queen Nefertiti ring at Christie's, and I want very much to buy it from you."

I told him that his information was quite correct but that we could not sell him this particular ring for very private reasons.

The gentleman then began to beg us to sell him the ring, saying, "I don't care how much you want to charge me for it, but I have to have it."

I told him that the ring had just arrived from London and that although I could not let him have it, I would show it to him, but I reiterated that there was no way that he could buy it. Also I told him that the question of cost did not in any way apply.

After he had the ring in his hands for several moments he said, "Please let me tell you why I must have this ring. It is for my wife, as we are this week celebrating our tenth anniversary and my wife is the very image of Nefertiti, and this has over the past years always been remarked on by all who knew her."

The gentleman was so insistent that after a while I relented. After all, I thought to myself, we had not as yet mailed the letter

261

to the king, who could never know that we had purchased this particular ring.

May I say at this point that I am not quite sorry that I did not keep the ring for my own collection?

The gentleman, named Mr. Borchart, then at once wrote us his check and after thanking me most profusely put the ring in his pocket and left.

But before leaving as an after thought he said, "You have been so very kind to me that I shall be a client of yours for very many years."

We then changed our letter to Farouk and of course omitted any mention of this particular specimen.

It was indeed most fortunate for Mr. Borchart that the letter to the king had not as yet been mailed, as had it been, then no money on earth would have paid for it.

A few weeks then passed, and Mr. Borchart was in again to see me and tell me that he had presented the ring to his wife and that she was so enthralled at its beauty and rarity that she told him that now that it was on her finger she would never remove it under any circumstances. She also said that of all the gifts that he had ever given her this was the one that delighted her the most. Following this visit the lady herself came in to see me, to tell me that her husband had explained to her how he had managed to get the ring away from us and that she was delighted with it and she felt impelled to add her thanks.

For our part we were delighted that we had been the means of giving the lady so much pleasure. As far as we were concerned, that ended the episode of the Nefertiti ring.

But no, this was not to be the case, as some weeks later Mr. Borchart came in to see me again, and this time he seemed most distressed and told me, "Last night we were out to dinner with another couple of our friends at the Russian Tearoom on West 57th Street when the subject of our tenth anniversary was mentioned. My wife then told the other lady that her husband had given her the 'famous' Nefertiti cartouche ring as a gift and also how thrilled she had been." Mr. Borchart then continued, "My wife's friend then asked whether she could perhaps look at the ring in her fingers, and without a moment's hesitation my wife took the ring off her finger and handed it to the lady.

"After we had finished our dinner and were ready to leave the restaurant, my wife asked the lady to let her have her ring back, but the lady replied, 'I returned it to you a long time ago, and don't you remember that I then remarked how excited you must have been to be able to wear the ring that Queen Nefertiti, your lookalike, must have worn?'

" 'But I don't have it,' said my wife, and we then began to search the table to see whether perhaps it was still hidden under a plate or a pot, but without any success. We called the waiter and asked him to see whether perchance it had gone out with the dishes; he then checked in the kitchen, but again without any success.

"We then, all of us, emptied our pockets to see whether by any chance it had gotten into a pocket without anybody thinking, but no, it was nowhere there.

"The ladies both went through their handbags, but still it was not in either of these.

"We then had no alternative but to leave our name and telephone number with the maître d'hôtel, as we thought that perhaps it might turn up somewhere on the floor."

As far as I know this ring has never yet come to light, and it is well within the bounds of possibility that it is today in the collection of some Egyptologist, and if it is, then maybe he does not even know that it bears the name of Nefertiti.

Chapter 51

King Farouk and Hans Schulman

When the young Farouk of Egypt was about sixteen years of age and at school in England, his father, King Fuʻād, died, and the young prince was immediately proclaimed King Farouk I of Egypt. The young prince, knowing of his late father's great love of collecting, particularly in the area of coins, medals, and stamps, contacted a Dutch coin dealer named Hans Schulman, who was at that time a resident of New York City. Farouk knew that during his lifetime his father had dealt with Schulman's company in Amsterdam before they had been, to a great extent liquidated by the Nazis, when Hans's father was imprisoned and murdered. When Hans's father was arrested and liquidated, Hans managed to escape unharmed and settled over here in New York City.

Farouk, getting Hans's address in New York, wrote him that he wished to continue with his father's coin collection and asked him to make him any offers that would fit into the collection. From what King Fuʻād had told him, Farouk knew that Hans would be able to fill into this already great collection many items of interest.

When the young King Farouk came to see us in London, he told us all about this collection and told us that not only did he wish to continue his father's collections, but he himself wished to make collections in many other areas. He said that he was particularly interested in any fine objects that had some mechanical operation or anything pertaining to fine antique horology, but as he explained, he was primarily interested only in objects of gold. He also told us that he wished to collect anything of a military nature, such as guns, pistols, swords, and similar memorabilia.

Not only was the young king, despite his young age, a lover of fine things, but he was also a lover of beauty in all areas of applied art. The young man was a true collector of the highest order and had the finances to assist him; this inheritance had been left him by king Fu'ād, who had received an enormous sum from the British government when he had been crowned king of Egypt after the First World War. Later, one day in conversation, after he had been on the throne for several years, King Farouk confided in us, "You know, were it not for my interest in my collections, I would have nothing in my life to live for."

Many years then passed, during which years we had done very considerable business with Farouk, and one day on one of my crossings to London from New York, I found myself passing through Bond Street, and looking up at the bulletin board outside of Sotheby's auction rooms, I saw that a very notable collection of antique firearms of all types was just at that moment on the point of being offered. Actually, the sale was scheduled to commence about five minutes after I saw the notice outside.

I at once went into the office and got a catalog. I was of course too late to view any of the items before the auction, and all that I could do was glance very quickly as each of the lots was passed round the room by one of the porters. (It is in this manner that such auctions are conducted in London.)

However, I soon saw that each of the items was of such quality that together with the catalog description I would be able to buy without first having encountered them.

I soon knew that I was on safe ground with anything that I might buy.

Suffice it to say that I bought very heavily. As far as I now recall, some 50 lots fell to my bids out of the entire group of some 150 lots. Primarily the collection comprised firearms from many nations and of a quality that one doesn't often see outside of a museum.

Many of the items were of the early nineteenth century and others of the eighteenth—both periods that I knew the young Farouk loved to collect. The collector had made a special emphasis on the collections of firearms that had belonged to the emperor Napoleon Bonaparte, and of this group I acquired some thirty pieces that I was quite positive the king would want, as in previous conversations he had always said that this was a period that particularly interested him.

In this Napoleonic group was a superb pair of pistols that had surely been made especially for the emperor. They were of hardwood, and highly polished steel and inlaid with motifs in platinum, which incorporated the Imperial Bee motif. It is this bee that one finds so frequently in objects associated with Napoleon. These pistols were encased in a carrying case of superb craftsmanship similarly inlaid with the Bee. Beyond this pair of pistols there were several others in similar vein and obviously emanating from the Imperial Armory.

Of the other items there were several of French make, but each was by itself a masterpiece of craftsmanship.

As soon as I had made my purchases, I had all collected by our London shippers and transferred to New York. In about a week they were waiting for me at our offices when I had returned home.

We then studied each of the items in depth, something that I had not been able to do in London prior to shipping, when I soon realized that my purchases were of major interest. We then wrote a description of each of the items, and they were soon on their way to Washington, D.C., for transshipment to Cairo in the Egyptian government pouch as usual.

At the same time as we sent the pieces we mailed the king our letter setting out the details of each of the pistols, together with the way in which I had made the purchases.

As usual, the king thoroughly enjoyed the stories that we were able to spin round each of the items, especially as they were all of such magnificent quality. The king always loved these stories and had his secretaries record every detail in the palace records. The following week we received a letter from the king congratulating us on our "wonderful purchase" and advising us that he was buying every one of the pieces we had sent.

At this point it is interesting perhaps to note that when, after the king's ouster, there were the auctions of his collections in Cairo, none of these pieces were offered on the auction block, so one must presume that they were retained and included in the national Egyptian Armory.

Following upon this crossing, a few weeks later I was again in Paris, and as I was walking through the Faubourg Saint Honore, returning to my hotel, I met an old dealer friend of mine.

"Monsieur Hill, I was just at the moment thinking of you, and in fact I was about the leave a message at your hotel to tell you that I had found something that I know will intrigue you no end," he told me.

I asked him to tell me something about the item, but he refused to tell me anything.

"You must come to my shop to see it before I tell you anything about it."

"Well," I said, "what are we waiting for?"

And a few minutes later I was at the gentleman's shop, which was quite a close to my hotel.

As soon as we were there the dealer opened his safe and took from it a small leather *pochette* containing seven superb miniature rifles, each with its tiny bayonet. Together with this *pochette* there was an old letter explaining that each of these rifles was an exact replica of one of the rifles in the Royal Napoleonic Armory and that they had been created by a master armorer especially for presentation to the then minister of the army.

The dealer, seeing that my interest was aroused, said to me, "I see by the way you are looking at this item that you want to buy it, but before we go any further into the matter I must tell you that the only way in which I can sell it is for cash, no checks or any other methods."

As I had plenty of cash in my pocket at the time, I at once inquired how much he was asking for the rifles, and when he told me the cost I counted out the bills for him. I then asked how he had obtained the objects, and he told that he had received them in their *pochette* from an elderly man who stated that he was a direct descendant of the minister.

After paying, I at once pocketed the *pochette* and went straight back to my hotel to record what the dealer had told me about the rifles. He had said that the reason that I had to pay in cash was that the man who had sold the item had stated that he did not want any of his family to know that he had disposed of the rifles, as if they knew there would be great trouble in the family.

So delighted was I with this purchase that I at once invited the dealer and his wife to be my guests at dinner that same evening. But as his wife was a doctor and at the time on call at the hospital, she could not join us. However, the dealer, whose name was Monsieur Bernard, did join me.

Bernard over dinner told me that during the Nazi invasion of Paris he had been one of the heads of the Resistance, and he told me some hair-raising stories of the period, which I thoroughly enjoyed hearing direct from the horse's mouth.

When in due time we sent this *pochette* with its rifles to the king, together with the story of how I had purchased them, the king again wrote us how delighted he was to have them. As he stated, not only was he interested in the group because they were rifles, but he was similarly interested in the fact that they were miniatures. Again, after the king's exile I watched for this *pochette* of rifles at the auctions that were held at the Khoube Palace, but they were not included, so again I had to presume that they were held back for the national Armory. Actually, I had hoped to be able to buy them back for my own collection of miniature objects.

Chapter 52

Purchase of Miniature Objects

While I was in London on one of my travels I was approached by an old dealer friend of mine who told me that he had just acquired a group of miniature objects that literally beggared description. He wanted to know whether I might be interested in seeing them. I told him to tell me more about it.

"I am sorry, but I cannot begin to tell you anything, because whatever I tell you, you will not believe until you actually see the objects," was his reply.

I told him that as he knew of our interest in miniature objects of all types I would be more than interested in viewing the collection.

He then told me that he would telephone me later in the day to tell me when it would be convenient for us to get together and study the objects. Later that same day he called and we arranged to meet at his offices the next day.

When I arrived as arranged, I saw a glass-topped showcase standing on a side table, and inside it contained some thirty items, some of which at first glance I could not in truth believe.

When the dealer unlocked the case and began to remove the objects one by one, I saw that each was a most remarkable specimen, some of them I really could not believe.

The first item that I picked up was a real walnut that had been cut across its middle and hollowed out. These two sides had then been hinged together with tiny gold hinges at one side to form a sort of etui.

When the case was opened there lay inside on a bed of silk a pair of the tiniest gold pistols; they were in truth unbelievable. Next to them lay two of the tiniest gold bullets; these were so small that they could scarcely be seen with the naked eye. The dealer told me that according to a booklet description that accompanied the group, if it were possible to pick up these objects by hand the mechanism in the pistols was workable. He then handed me the booklet he had mentioned, in which each of the objects was described in fullest detail.

The next item that he took out of the showcase was a cherry stone that had similarly been hollowed out and then cut across its middle and hinged in gold, and when this was opened it disclosed another pair of tiny golden pistols of superb quality, but even smaller than the first pair.

After replacing these two items, he took out a fully operative diesel engine, made of silver and about the size overall of an average postage stamp, not one of the larger commemoratives, and with a movement of a tiny lever at one side he made the engine operate perfectly.

Beyond these there were two objects that were in truth quite unbelievable. They were constructed of human hair. One was a ship's mast of gold with its cross section of hair drawn through it and then another mast with two hairs, one drawn through the other. I do not at this time recall the precise nature of the second of these two "hair" items.

Replacing these two objects, he then withdrew another walnut that had been similarly handled as the previous one had been, and when opened it contained four tiny trays, one placed upon the other, each tray lined and containing knives, forks, spoons, and other utensils, making a total of a service of tableware for twelve. These items could not be touched by the hand.

Unfortunately, I do not recall the nature of the other tiny objects. Suffice it to say that each was of an unbelievable nature.

Together with the little booklet that he had given me, he handed me a folder of newspaper clippings of approximately a hundred years ago. In each of these there were stories of the remarkable nature of these miniatures. In the booklet it stated that the man who had created this fantastic collection had some very curious eye condition, and apparently his vision was such that everything that he saw was magnified twofold and it was through this condition that he had been able to make these tiny things. It also stated that the collection had been seen around the country and had collected money for charitable purposes, in much the same way as Queen Mary's dollhouse is today sent throughout the world. There was one report that this collection had been taken to Windsor so that Queen Victoria and her husband, the Prince Consort, could view it at their ease. The story in the paper went on to relate that when they saw the objects they became so excited at what they saw that they insisted that the creator be called to visit with them at the castle to explain how he had managed to make such things. The queen said that she was particularly fascinated by the items of human hair and said that she could really not believe her eyes.

Needless to say, I at once purchased the collection as it stood in its showcase. I then had a serious problem. How was I ever going to get the group over to New York without damage?

I pondered the matter for some time, and then I went over to see our fine arts packers and shippers and explained my problem to them.

When I had finished speaking, the director answered, "Mr Hill, don't you bother your head for one moment, I shall have the collection expertly packed, and it will arrive at your offices in New York without the slightest damage to any of the pieces." Then after looking over the items he jokingly remarked, "Not a hair will be damaged."

True to his word, he shipped the group with its glass showcase and all arrived at our offices in New York in perfect condition.

As soon as I was back and had the collection I had each piece photographed so that I could mail the photos to Egypt for King Farouk to study before making any shipments. For some reason or other best know to himself, the king at once ordered the golden firearms to be sent but said that he did not want any of the other items, although he wrote that they were all quite remarkable.

Naturally, I was a little upset at this, as I had not anticipated breaking this wonderful collection, despite the fact that I knew that we would have no difficulty in selling the remaining items. But a royal command is, after all, a royal command.

It did not take us very long to place the other pieces from this collection, and they are today spread far and wide across the States. As I write I know that it will be virtually impossible for any reader to appreciate the nature of these miniatures without viewing them.

Chapter 53

A Massive Egyptian Gold Ring

During the many years that I have spent searching the capitals of Europe for acquisitions that I felt would happily fit into the varied collections of the now deceased King Farouk of Egypt, I was naturally drawn to many of the auction sales that were always being held at Sotheby's or Christie's; similarly I attended many that were held at some of the smaller houses. While I was at one of these latter on one occasion, the objects being offered were not very exciting, but I did buy one or two objects of somewhat minor appeal.

However, just as I was at the door about to leave a dealer came over to me. "Mr. Hill, I know that you are always interested in items having ancient Egyptian appeal, and I wonder whether you might be interested in seeing a very large Egyptian gold ring, but one which is, unfortunately, quite modern," he said.

I replied that I would certainly like to see the ring.

The dealer then withdrew from his pocket what was to my mind a most beautiful and massive gold ring, the head of which was covered with a series of Egyptian hieroglyphics. Now although I was able to read some of the signs, I could not in any way decipher any that were engraved on this particular cartouche. Nevertheless, I decided to buy the ring, as it was indeed very beautiful, whether ancient or modern. But then I was by no means an expert Egyptologist.

Taking it back with me to my hotel, I studied it for quite a while and thought that definitely it looked quite new, as though it had just come from the hands of the jeweler who had made it, but I was not convinced that it might not be ancient. I knew from my experience that such objects were all from excavations from the ancient tombs, and I decided that in all possibility when it had been unearthed it had been at once placed in a cabinet and remained untouched. Pure gold, such as this ring was made of, would not in any way be changed by time, as many of the golden objects taken in such manner were kept aside in museums and collections where there was no way they could be changed in color or not look quite new. Thus I considered the matter and decided to leave my mind open until I was back in New York.

The day after my return to the States I lunched with Mr. Fahim Kouchaki, one of the New York's renowned Orientalists. It was he who had owned the great silver chalice purported to have been made at the time of Christ, which he sold to Mr. Rockefeller, who presented it to the Metropolitan Museum of New York. It was this same silver chalice that was the inspiration for the Thomas Costain book *The Silver Chalice*. Mr. Kouchaki studied the ring when I handed it to him and said that he was much intrigued by it, but he could not at the time make up his mind as to whether it was, in fact, ancient or modern. This was, of course, quite understandable.

Despite this he said, "Ancient or modern, I would love to buy it from you, even to wear on my own finger, so please quote me your lowest price."

I then told him the figure that I had in mind and he replied, "Much as I love it, I could not meet your price."

I then returned to my office and endeavored to try to decipher some of the hieroglyphics, but without any success, although there were several that I did understand. I decided that I would consult with the head of the Egyptology department at the Metropolitan Museum and see what he thought of the ring.

I telephoned the museum and spoke with the curator, who asked whether he could look at the ring in his own hands, and I told him that I would be delighted to bring it in to the museum. We then made an appointment for the following day at noon.

Next day, I arrived promptly at the museum and was at once shown into the curator's office, where he was seated at his desk awaiting me. Seating myself at the side of his desk, I handed him the ring.

As soon as it was in his hands, without a word he began to study it with his magnifying glass. He did not utter a single word, although he had it in his hands for quite some time.

Then he turned to me looking at me over his half-glasses. "I am sure," he said, "that you know that it is not old."

Naturally, I felt, after the time that he had taken in his study, that his opinion would have been quite different, but still I could well understand his thinking.

He then continued speaking. "No, it is not old; it is of the Saitic period."

This last stunned me somewhat, and I replied, "In that case it would date circa 600 B.C., and he replied, "Oh, yes, certainly, but it is not old."

I could not wait until I returned to my office, where I reported the gist of what the curator had said and we all had a good laugh. I knew full well that from the viewpoint of the Egyptologist anything dating after the great period of Tutankhamen was not old in an antiquarian sense. To my thinking it was indeed ancient.

At this point it is perhaps germane to mention that Egyptologists are able to read the hieroglyphics of this early period quite readily. Some can even read them as one might a newspaper, thanks to the discovery of the Rosetta stone, which is today housed in the British Museum in London. This stone was discovered in Egypt about a century ago and is engraved on its surface with three sets of writings that, as the great French savant of the period Champolion discovered, translated themselves, one to the other. The first is Greek, the second hieroglyphics, and the third Demotic. The Greek, being the language of the priests, was readily readable, and the others followed suit.

During the Saitic period the goldsmiths had extended their hieroglyphics by inventing new signs to make the reading more understandable to the populace, but unfortunately they left no dictionary, which would make these signs understandable and give us a clue to their meanings.

Knowing that King Farouk would be delighted to secure this rare ring for his great collection of ancient Egyptian gold, we wrote him a letter setting out the details of its purchase and how the curator had reacted at its examination, how he had looked at me over his spectacles with the words. "No, it is not old; it is of the Saitic period."

Next day the ring was on its way to Cairo, and in due course we received a letter from the king telling us how much he loved the ring and also stating that he had enjoyed reading about the episode at the museum almost as much as he enjoyed the ring.

The day following the dispatch of the ring to Cairo, I again met Mr. Kouchaki at lunch and he told me that since I had shown him the ring he had decided that he would like to buy it from us at our quoted figure. I then told him that it was no longer available, as it had already been shipped overseas. He was quite upset at not having taken it when he had seen it originally. He said that after he had left me he had done some research into its possible antiquity. But as he then remarked, "That is the antique business."

When I was at the auctions in Cairo after the king's abdication, I decided that I would again buy the ring back for myself, but it was not included in the objects offered for sale. I must only presume that it was held back for the National Museum collection of ancient Egyptology. It was, in fact, a very great rarity.

Chapter 54

Harvey Wheeler and the Haile Selassie Plates

Harvey Wheeler, an American gentleman to whom we had sold a series of Haile Selassie silver dinner plates, inset with gold and silver coins of various nationalities, was certainly one of the most colorful characters that one could ever meet anywhere. We became acquainted with him under some rather unusual circumstances. It was while we were still operating our store on London's Piccadilly that we acquired what must certainly, have been the most glamorous and interesting of all ladies belt buckles. This buckle had been brought out of Russia after the Revolution and had derived from the great personal collection of jewels belonging to the last czarina. It was of massive gold bordered with pale blue enamel, and this border held an enormous oval aquamarine of superb color. Overall the buckle measured about three inches in width and six inches across; it had almost certainly been a creation of the house of Fabergé.

Being very excited about this acquisition, we decided that it would make an admirable central feature for our window display, and when we did in fact set this up the result was fascinating to a degree. The buckle had not been in situ for a day when, just as we were on the point of closing for the night, our door opened and a very unkempt and rather disreputable-looking man came in—actually, he sidled in—and, speaking to one of our assistants, said, "Sir, could you please tell me the price of that aquamarine buckle that you have in the center of the window?"

The assistant, seeing how badly the man was dressed, was quite offhand with him and appeared almost prepared to ignore the question.

At the moment I was just on my way out for the day, but knowing from my experience that clothes do not make the customer, I told the assistant to take the jewel from the display and let the gentleman have it in his hands. Upon this the assistant took

The Berry store in Piccadilly, London.

the buckle out of the window and handed it to the man. I then told him that we were quoting the piece at four hundred pounds. At the time, that would have amounted to some two thousand dollars.

The moment that the man had it in his hands he remarked, "I think that this is certainly one of the most beautiful jewels that I have ever set my eyes on, and I would like to buy it from you."

I told him that it was available for sale and that if he wanted it he could buy it.

Without further ado he took a shilling out of his pocket. "I want to give you this shilling as an earnest, and I will be back at noon tomorrow to pay you the balance and collect the buckle from you."

I replied that as we were at the moment just on the point of closing we would put the buckle away in our safe overnight and that we did not require the shilling deposit.

But he was adamant. "No, I must give you this shilling as an earnest of my purchase." He then turned and left without even giving us his address.

A couple of minutes then passed, and he returned and said to me. "Would you be so kind as to give me back a sixpence out of the shilling that I gave you just now, as there is a man outside who says that he needs a sixpence to buy himself a cup of coffee."

Naturally, I at once gave the man a sixpence, and he left. We then concluded that we were indeed dealing with some sort of "nut," but after telling the assistant that one must never judge a customer by his costume or mannerisms, I laughingly placed the buckle in the safe and told the assistant that it was to be kept there next morning until noon.

Then, precisely at noon next day, the gentlemen was again in, as he had arranged to do, and handed me the cash less the sixpence, and then putting the jewel, unwrapped, into his waistcoat pocket, he was about the leave. Before he went we commenced a conversation with him, and he then began to talk and tell me about his life. "When I was a very young I sold newspapers on the street outside of Tiffany's when they had their store downtown in New York, and while there I always had my eyes glued to their window displays. On one occasion I saw three stickpins in a corner, each topped by a diamond of a different color. One stone was canary yellow, one was dark blue, and the third was greenish. At that moment I said to myself, *If and when I make my pile I am going to collect gems of color.* I became entirely fascinated by the thought of color."

As he spoke he opened his very old and dirty jacket and took out of one of his vest pockets one of the most important, as yet, unset pink diamonds of extraordinary quality. I had never previously seen anything to even approximate its beauty and brilliance. To say the least, I was amazed.

The man then replaced this gem in his pocket, and as he did so he drew out of another pocket a very large and superb blue diamond similar in size to the pink one. "How do you like these gems?"

And before I could even reply he took another very important sapphire from a third pocket. He was, as far as I could see, like a magician on the stage. By this time he commenced to be quite confidential and began to tell me something of his life and business operations. He told me that many years ago he had formed a company titled Initial Services and that they had supplied corporation washrooms with towels and soap. He said that this business had flourished and had spread all over the world. This was, of course, before the advent of the paper towel.

At this point he advised me to buy some stock in the company, and as I recall, I later did this and made some money out of the purchase.

After telling me all this, he told me that he had quite recently sold all of his interest and now had the wherewithal to buy almost anything that he wanted. "I am now able to satisfy to the full my lust for color," he said. He then proceeded to tell me that he had an estate on the Pacific Palisades in California where his wife lived. "I stay away from home as much as possible because my wife is enormously fat and I cannot even bear to look at her, let alone live with her."

He then continued talking. "About twenty years ago I was a strongman in a circus, and now I want you to take me into your private office so that I can get you to punch me in the belly, when you will see how strong I am, even at my age, which is in the seventies."

I did not like the idea of this at all, but to satisfy him we went into my office, where he undressed down to his waist.

"Now punch me as hard as you can," he told me.

Naturally, I am not in the habit of punching people in the stomach, particularly not elderly men, but he was insistent. Thus I did as he wanted and punched him.

"You call that a punch? Now please try again and use all of your strength."

I then hit him as hard as I could, and all that I got out of this was a very sore wrist; the man was as hard as a stone. It was like hitting a sheet of steel.

Actually, I was much more interested in the waistcoat with the wonderful gems that he had thrown onto the floor when undressing than his bared stomach. As he was about to leave—he had spent about three hours with me—I asked him the address where I might contact him in the event that we found another great jewel for his collection and also I told him that I would like to invite him to dine with us one evening.

He replied, "I am sorry that I cannot give you my address in London, as I never know from day to day where I might be spending the night, and I must explain why this is the case. I have thirty girls that I keep and support, and in exchange for their services I pay each of them weekly wages every Friday. I have made an arrangement with Mr. Edward Good, who owns the shop that I am sure you must know, Good's Cameo Corner, and he pays these girls for me on my behalf. I do this so that I always have a bed available to me, with one of these girls to keep me company. All that I ask and insist upon is that every evening they must be in their rooms waiting for my possible arrival. They know that at any time that I arrive at one of their apartments and find that the girl is not there, she is immediately out and I replace her."

He then left and after this Harvey Wheeler, for that was his name, became a regular caller at our store, from time to time making significant purchases from us.

It was just at about this time that King Edward VIII was about to be crowned, and the Coronation route had been announced. It was stated that the procession would pass through Piccadilly and would pass right in front of us.

As at the store we had our upstairs gallery with its wide window over the street, we decided that we would place chairs in this window so that anybody seated there could view the procession as though they were in loge seats at the theater.

I asked Harvey Wheeler whether he would care to be our guest and watch this parade, and he replied that he would be overjoyed to come. He then asked my permission to bring along one of his "girls." I told him that he could do so with pleasure.

We then arranged that we would have three tables set up in our window where we would serve a luncheon of chicken salad and champagne.

I told Harvey that he would have to be at our place no later than five o'clock on the morning, as otherwise the street would be quite impassable, this despite the fact that the procession was not slated to pass before eleven o'clock.

On the day Harvey, accompanied by his "girl," arrived precisely on the dot of five, and we all took our seats in the window at the tables. As we told him that they would be, the streets soon filled up, and it was this that seemed to impress him almost as much as the eventual procession.

When the procession commenced it was most colorful, and loving color as Harvey did, he was immensely pleased. There were detachments of soldiers all polished up and wearing their ceremonial uniforms, these men having been drawn from four of the greatly renowned British regiments.

Following the wake of these detachments came a long series of open carriages, all filled with royalty and other notables, followed by the royal coach in which were seated Queen Mary and other members of her royal household.

Behind this royal coach came the King's horse, all beautifully groomed and carrying on his back a large blanket upon which rested the Royal Crown of England, which was to be placed on Edward's head at the Coronation ceremony. As the procession passed our window we saw the crown topple slightly, but this was soon righted without any damage. We then pondered whether this might be any sort of omen for the future. Naturally, we did not know that within the year Edward would be abdicating the throne for the "woman I love."

As far as I recall, the president of the United States was not present, but the ambassador came in his stead. As the ceremony took place in the spring, the weather was beautiful and clear, and the cheering of the crowds was tremendous.

Later, after this visit, Harvey called to thank us for inviting him and said, "This is one experience that I shall never forget, and I must thank you from the bottom of my heart for inviting me."

After this Harvey continued to call in to see us, each time with one or other of his "girls" on his arm. Never once did we see him with the same girl twice.

It is perhaps interesting to mention that each of these girls followed a similar pattern. They were none of them taller than he, and he was quite short. It seemed that he never wanted to have a girl tower over him. Each was a blond; none of them were what one might call beautiful, though they were all fairly good-looking. I suppose that if one lined them all up in a row, they would look like the chorus line at a cheapish vaudeville theater. They none of them looked or dressed like hookers, although they may well have been.

As I write these words I am reminded that shortly after this ceremony I had occasion to visit with Mr. Edward Good on some business matter and when I arrived I saw him standing at his door wearing a long purple caftan and a pair of Oriental slippers on his feet. Round his neck he wore several long gold chains, and at his waist he had a wide girdle of gold cloth. On his chains he had large gold pendants. After we had discussed Harvey Wheeler's visit and his "girls," we began to discuss the business that I had called to see him about.

For some reason or other, at this time he was calling himself by his Hebraic name of Moise Ovid; having written several books on philosophy, for which reason he considered himself a great savant, he apparently dressed himself for the part.

Before we could continue talking about our business, he commenced telling me some stories about Queen Mary, who was a customer of his and also a very frequent visitor. By the time that he had finished telling me these stories the time was running late and I had to leave, as I had another very important appointment for which I could not be late.

Just at this juncture the door opened and in strode, or should I say stomped, a very tall and quite heavy man who carried in his hand a heavily gnarled walking cane with a massive gold finial on top. As soon as Mr. Good saw this gentleman, he fell on his knees and kissed the hem of the man's coat as though perhaps the man were the pope having his ring kissed. After this, to me, very amusing ceremony, Mr. Good rose to his full height of some five feet as though spellbound and, calling his visitor "Master," proceeded to introduce him to me, saying, "You are now in the presence of the greatest living Yiddish writer of all time."

Whether the man was himself amused by this entire performance or not is a moot point; he hadn't spoken a single word since entering the shop, nor did he appear to have moved an eyelid. Maybe, I thought to myself, he was accustomed to this adulation.

Seeing that Mr. Good was by this time in no mood to further discuss any business with me and as I was in a hurry, I left without a further word.

Chapter 55

Duveen

A book was written some few years ago by S.N. Behrman titled *The Days of Duveen*. Lord Duveen was one of the great international art dealers of several decades ago. It was he, perhaps more than any other of the world's great art dealers, who had advised and assisted the late Andrew Mellon in the acquisition of many of the great masterpieces that went into the formation of the National Gallery collection in Washington, D.C. As an art dealer, Duveen, later to become Lord Duveen when he was raised to the Peerage, was accepted far and wide for his knowledge and acumen in the fields both of fine art and antiquity, with perhaps the important period of the Italian Renaissance as the high point of his career. Beyond being a great art dealer, he was a superb salesman, and it was he who had employed the highly regarded art historian Bernard Behrenson in his operations both in Europe and in the States. To so high an eminence had he grown in the international art world that the words *a Duveen* denoted a great work of art.

One beautiful afternoon in the spring while I was sunning myself on a seat in Central Park, an old acquaintance of mine, Lord Duveen's nephew, happened by. Seeing me seated, he asked me whether he could join me and chat awhile. I was certainly delighted to have his company and talk about the art news of the day. This gentleman was quite short, with a slightly bulging waistline, and sported a Vandyke, which in many respects made him look like the great seventeenth-century Dutch artist Frans Hals. So much so was this the case that he was affectionately known as Frans Hals, and as he was an art dealer himself, this name fell happily on many dealers' tongues.

As we sat and chatted, I mentioned to him the Behrman book that had just at that time been published about his uncle. I asked him whether he had as yet read it.

"But certainly I have," he replied, adding that he had found the contents quite absorbing. "Yes" he continued, "I found it most

284

interesting, particularly for some of the interesting affairs that Behrman did not mention."

I then inquired what affairs he was referring to.

"If you have the time, I can tell you some stories that were omitted but which are to my mind most fascinating."

I told him that I had all the time in the world and would love to hear what he had to tell.

He then recounted the following story.

"Among my uncle's millionaire clients was Jules Bache, the renowned stockbroker," and as an aside he said, "My uncle was only interested in millionaires."

He continued, "Bache was a great lover of fine art and antiquity and quite an aesthete, and one day he telephoned my uncle. 'Joe,' he said, 'I have just today acquired what must be the most exquisite ancient Grecian vase that has ever come on the market, and I would dearly love to have you see it and give me your opinion.'

"My uncle replied, 'Certainly I would be delighted to visit with you and see the vase, but I am engaged for this evening, and if it would be convenient, I would love to come around to see you tomorrow evening.'

"Bache then said, 'Fine. Why don't you come to dinner tomorrow evening at, say, seven o'clock, when we can have a drink and you can see my wonderful vase?'

"My uncle replied, 'That will be fine and I shall be round at your apartment on the dot of seven.'

"Bache then added, 'I hope that you will stay and dine with me.'

"My uncle accepted. Next evening, as arranged, my uncle arrived at seven and was greeted by Bache, who at once ushered him into his library, where they had a drink together.

" 'I am afraid that the drink will have to be a very quick one, as I cannot wait to have you see my prize,' Bache said. They then put down their glasses and went into the living room, where Bache had had the vase placed in the center of his mantelpiece.

" 'Well, Joe, there stands my treasure. What do you think of it. Am I right when I say that it is possibly the greatest example of its kind ever to come onto the market?' Bache asked.

" 'Jules,' my uncle replied after a short inspection of the vase, 'I consider it to be certainly an extremely fine and rare specimen and, as you rightly say, possibly the finest of its type ever to come onto the market.'

"Having this report from the great Joe Duveen was for Basche just too wonderful, and brimming over with joy, he led Uncle into the dining room, where they partook of a dinner that was, in truth, an epicurean's delight. While dining, their conversation was centered around the great art of ancient Greece, and my uncle began telling Bache about some of his great acquisitions, stories that Bache much enjoyed hearing.

"After they had been talking for a couple of hours, my uncle looked at his watch. Jules, you know it is getting quite late and I have a very important appointment tomorrow morning. Also I am sure that you will be wanting to be at your office early, so perhaps we had better call it a day. Saying this, my uncle rose to leave, and Bache was so delighted at what my uncle had told him about the vase he went out into the foyer with him and insisted on helping him on with his coat. While he was holding his coat he heard a noise like tsk-tsk' coming from my uncle's mouth.

"Being somewhat intrigued by this, he inquired, 'Joe, what are you "tsk-tsking" about?'

"My uncle then replied, 'I was just thinking to myself what a pity it is that such great beauty as your Grecian vase should have been used for the purpose for which it was created.'

" 'What do you mean?' asked Bache.

"My uncle then replied, 'Didn't you know that such a thing was not a vase, but an urn used to hold the ashes of the dear departed?'

"Bache blanched visibly when he heard this. 'No, I thought that they were just beautiful adornments for the home.'

"As are so many stockbrokers, Jules Bache was a very superstitious man, and no sooner had my uncle left the apartment when he called his butler and said to him, 'Take the goddamned vase out of my sight and hide it somewhere in the kitchen. I never want to look at it again.'

"Then a very saddened man, Bache went up to bed, but all night long he tossed and turned and could not get to sleep. He could scarcely wait for morning to call the dealer from whom he had purchased the vase to tell him the following: 'Get your man up here as soon as possible and get that god-awful vase out of my apartment. I cannot sleep knowing that it is in one of my rooms.'

"The dealer was thunderstruck at this outburst, but what could he do but tell Bache that he would get his trucker to pick it up as soon as he possibly could? After all, Bache was too good a customer and he did not wish to upset him more than, seemingly, he had already done."

My friend then continued, "That was just one example of my uncle's great talent for damning with faint praise anything that came from a competing dealer. He could always try to instill a little poison if he could spoil another's deal. My uncle had not 'knocked' the vase—on the contrary, he had praised its beauty—but similarly he had muddied the other dealer's waters."

I told my friend that I loved the story.

"I have another wonderful tale that I can tell you if you have the time to sit and listen."

"Yes, please tell me your other story and I have plenty of time and I think that your story is much better than anything in the Behrman book."

He then laughed and continued talking. "Many years ago, before the 1917 Revolution in Russia was even thought of, my uncle had been created a Peer of the Realm by the king after he had presented London's National Gallery what had become known as the Sargent Room, which he filled with the collection of portraits of members of the Wertheim family, all painted by Sargent. Because of this great gift, my uncle's name became known throughout the international art world. At his gallery he also had in his safes one of the greatest collection of fine antique gold snuff boxes in the hands of any dealer and actually at that period probably as fine as any such collection in any of the world's great museums.

"One morning a gentleman came into the gallery whom my uncle did not know. By the man's dress my uncle had to assume that he was somebody, as he was attired in the finest that Savile Row could supply.

"My uncle then asked the gentleman his name, and the man replied in a very imperious tone, 'I am a Russian grand duke and I am staying at the Ritz and I am informed that you have a great collection of antique gold boxes of the Louis XV and Louis XVI periods and, if my information is correct, I want you to show me what you have. Please do this right away, as I am in London only until tomorrow.'

"My uncle at once called an assistant and asked him to bring all of the gold box collection out of the safes. In very short time the assistant returned with six trays filled with gold boxes, which he placed on a side table in one of the gallery rooms. As he did this the grand duke did not utter a single word, nor did he look at anything else until the assistant told my uncle, 'This is the entire collection.'

"As soon as the trays were in situ, my uncle asked the assistant to leave the room, whereupon the grand duke, again in a very imperious tone, said, 'I want you, Duveen, to leave the room as well so that I can examine these boxes undisturbed. When I have finished my study I shall ask you to come back in.'

"My uncle then had no alternative but to leave the room, and then he commenced to pace back and forth outside waiting for the grand duke's call back.

"Some two or three hours then passed and the door opened and the grand duke asked my uncle to come in. My uncle immediately entered, and the duke, pointing to three trays, said, 'Please send this group that I have selected to me at the Ritz together with your bill, and I will have my secretary draw you a check immediately. Please do this at once, as I am returning to Russia tomorrow. You don't have to tell me the prices, as I have seen these tiny parchment tags that are enclosed in each of them,' and without a further word the grand duke said good-bye and left.

"Now my uncle was in somewhat of a quandary. The numbers that the duke had seen and noted on the tags were the inventory numbers and bore no relation whatsoever to the actual cost. The prices themselves were all in code of three or four digits, while the inventory numerals were all of them in five and some six digits. Now the grand duke had said to him that he had seen the prices, so presumably that was what he expected to pay, and this being the case, my uncle had his accountant write up a bill using these inventory numbers as the prices and sent the bill together with the collection to the Ritz that same afternoon by messenger. Next day he received a check for the enormously exaggerated amount. The total figure was, in truth, staggering, but that was what the grand duke has asked for, and that is what he had been given. And as this was in the days when the pound sterling was the pound sterling and the income tax was purely nominal, it was quite fantastic."

I then discussed with my friend what may have happened to the collection that the grand duke had bought, and as the Revolution had followed some years after the purchase had been made, we decided that it was highly probable that the Bolsheviks, who had taken most of the treasures from the royal palaces when they took over, got them. It may be reasonably assumed that the boxes today have gone into the fabulous collection now on view in the Hermitage museum in Moscow.

After my friend had finished telling me this fascinating story, he said that he had recently heard a very amusing joke about his uncle that he would love to tell me, but which could not possibly be true. "It seems that when Lord Duveen died, he at once went straight up to Heaven, where he was greeted by Saint Peter at the Pearly Gates. Saint Peter inquired whether there might be anybody special that he would like to meet. Duveen said he would like to meet the great Raphael. Saint Peter replied, 'That will not present any problem, and I shall arrange a meeting for you tomorrow.'

"True to his word, Saint Peter next day introduced Raphael to my uncle, and he told him that he had heard much about him and also that he was delighted to meet him. My uncle then said, 'The reason that I asked to meet with you was that several years ago I sold a large circular painting to the National Gallery in Washington, one of the type known as a tondo, and at the time I attributed the work to your hand. Now my question to you is, Did you paint it?'

"Raphael then thought for a few moments and replied, 'You know, if I painted it that would have been over four hundred years ago, and really I don't remember, but why don't you ask Bernard Behrenson, who worked for you? He would surely know.'"

At this point my friend said that, unfortunately, he had to leave me, but he hoped that we might get together again soon, when he could tell me some more stories about his uncle. I am indeed sorry that he was not able to tell me some more stories about Lord Duveen's operations and his carryings-on, as I am sure that they would have been worth recording and retelling.

Chapter 56

The Eastern Potentate and His Jewels

There is a very amusing story told, the veracity of which I cannot in any way vouch for, except that it was told me by a person attached to one of the embassies, for which reason I tend to accept it as possibly true. It appears that an Eastern potentate decided that he wished to have created for his family and especially for his empress, an entire set of Crown Jewels. The Shah, having been introduced to a Belgian jeweler by an intermediary, contacted him by cable and inquired whether he could undertake so important an assignment. Could he? Of course he could, and the jeweler, who resided in Brussels, became very excited at the prospect of what he knew must be an enormous commission. He at once replied by cable that he was prepared to meet with the Shah and discuss the details in great depth with his Majesty.

He could scarcely wait for the Shah's reply, until a few days later he received a formal invitation to present himself at the palace. He was also informed that he would have no trouble at the Customs upon arrival, as they were being alerted to expect him. Upon receipt of this invitation the jeweler immediately called his team of designers together and instructed them to prepare a complete series of sketches of all manner of jewels, from crowns to tiaras to rings to bracelets and so forth. He told his men to prepare as many drawings as they could of any type of jewel they considered might be incorporated in such a collection of Crown Jewels.

It took these designers about two weeks to prepare a highly significant series of designs, all painted in high color, and the next day the jeweler was en route, after having cabled that he would arriving the next day. Arriving at the palace, he was at once shown into the royal presence, where he found the Shah awaiting him.

Receiving a very warm welcome from the Shah, the jeweler proceeded to spread all of his sketches out on a long table for the

291

Shah's inspection. The Shah passed by each of these sketches with scarcely a word, and then, after just a cursory glance at each, he told the jeweler that he would like every one of the jewels made for him as speedily as possible. The jeweler was quite taken aback at this speed and promised to proceed as quickly as possible. He then left to return home, clutching this great order to his breast.

Next morning he arrived home in Brussels and at once called his craftsmen into his office and explained to them the magnitude of the commission. He promised to double their wages if they would work overtime and get all ready for delivery in the greatest of haste. The men all promised him that they would do their utmost to please both him and the Shah and that they would work as quickly as possible so that not a moment would be lost. The men also promised to work nights on some occasions if they felt that this was called for.

It took the men about six weeks for the entire completion of the commission, and as soon as this was accomplished the jeweler cabled the Shah that he had the entire group of jewels all ready for delivery and also that upon hearing from the Shah he was holding ready to fly over and personally deliver the collection.

The next day he received a cable from the Shah inviting him to come to the palace as soon as he possibly could, again reiterating that there would be no problem at the Customs.

Upon receipt of this cable, the jeweler at once made his arrangements to fly over the following day, carrying all of the jewels with him. He also paid for an extra seat on the plane so that he could have his valise with the jewels at his side during the crossing. He did not wish there to be the slightest risk of loss or damage.

Immediately upon landing, he went directly to the palace, where he was at once ushered into the royal presence and proceeded to lay out the entire collection on a side table. There were crowns, tiaras, brooches, earrings, necklaces and rings together with some other items of lesser importance.

When all was laid out, the jewels presented a most impressive array. The Shah just glanced at the jewels, which he at once approved, and called his secretary into the salon and asked the jeweler to present his bill, also asking him how he would like payment to be made. The jeweler, being somewhat allergic to paying taxes of any kind, said that he would prefer to have a check drawn to his numbered Swiss banking account. The Shah was not in the least put out by this and instructed the secretary to do just as the jeweler had suggested. The Shah then told the jeweler that he was more than delighted with what had been created for him and, taking a long red sash from a drawer in a side cabinet, placed it over the jeweler's shoulder and then attached to it a star inset with a series of the worst possible quality of diamonds.

As he did this the Shah told the jeweler he was very pleased with the work done that he was decorating him with his Royal Order of the Third Class.

The jeweler was quite overcome by this great honor and, armed with his check, which was for an enormous sum, and with his Royal Decoration, could not wait to return home to Brussels and tell all of his good news.

The moment that he was back in his office, the jeweler had all of the terrible-quality diamonds removed from the star and replaced with the finest quality of diamonds that money could buy.

He was so intensely proud of this new honor that he decided that he would wear his decoration at any function where evening dress was called for. Especially after the new diamonds had been set into the star, the whole was most resplendent. A few months then passed, and one morning he received another cable from the Shah advising him that he wished to order some additional jewels, including a very important crown, and he again invited the jeweler to prepare for him another series of sketches.

The jeweler then replied that he would put his designers to work immediately and that as soon as they were ready he would advise the Shah and make further arrangements with him.

It was just about two weeks later that the jeweler cabled the Shah that all was ready and that upon hearing from him he was prepared to fly over with the sketches for his approval.

Next day he received a cable inviting him to come immediately, and the following day the jeweler was en route.

Upon arrival at the palace he was once again ushered into the royal presence, as he had previously been, and the Shah, after a very cursory glance, again said that he thought that all of the sketches looked wonderful and told the jeweler to proceed with all speed with every one of the pieces.

The jeweler then returned to Brussels in a very happy mood, as this second commission was even larger than the first had been, and again called his craftsmen into his office and gave them instructions to proceed with the order with all possible speed. They, knowing that they would be receiving double wages as previously, were delighted at this prospect, and they again said that they would work nights whenever necessary.

Thus, in due course, the new collection of jewels was ready for delivery and the jeweler again cabled the Shah that everything was in readiness for delivery and that he would again await the Shah's invitation to present himself at the palace with all speed. Next day he received a cable, and that same day he was off with the jewels in his valise as previously. As soon as he was in the royal presence the jeweler had all laid out as he had done previously, when the Shah glanced them over and told the jeweler that he was delighted with what he saw.

Apparently the Shah had a very good memory, because he called his secretary into the salon and instructed him to draw a check for the jeweler similarly on his Swiss numbered account.

The question of cost had never once entered into any of the discussions. Now, before entering the Royal presence the jeweler had placed the silk sash with its diamond star over the shoulder of his cutaway suit that he had deemed suitable for the occasion. And now the jeweled star looked very much more resplendent with the fine diamonds that he had set into it. Without a glance the Shah removed the star from the sash and, telling the jeweler that he was so happy with what he had done for him, added that he was raising him to the order of the second class, and as he did this he replaced the star with a somewhat larger version of the first, similarly inset with the terrible-quality diamonds.

What could the jeweler do but thank the Shah for this greater honor. All the while he did not know whether to laugh or cry.

Then, returning home to Brussels armed with his enormous check, he at once decided to replace the diamonds as he had done previously, but he also told himself that if he should ever again be invited to visit the Shah at the palace he would never again wear his decoration.

Chapter 57

Meeting Agathon Fabergé in Paris

I was informed by a friend in Paris that one of Fabergé's sons, Agathon, was at the time living in Paris, but under the humblest of circumstances. I at once decided that I would visit him and if possible buy some Fabergé pieces from him.

Getting his address, I found where he lived and went to see him. I knew that after the Revolution his father, Karl, had returned to his native Alsace and that another brother had gone to Finland, but other than that until this moment, I had no further information about Agathon. The dealer who had given me Agathon's address warned me that I would find him living in the humblest of circumstances.

After quite some difficulty, I did manage to locate the house in a very poor part of Paris, a neighborhood to which I had never previously been and where after this visit I vowed never again to set foot. I did find Agathon living here in a very squalid garret. There was no elevator in the house, and I had to walk up seven flights of stairs, which were the most rickety of any that I could ever have imagined.

When I arrived, somewhat out of breath, at the top floor, I saw a door on which had been pinned an old card reading "Agathon Fabergé."

As there was no bell that I could find, I knocked on the door, but I heard nothing. I then knocked again a little more loudly when I heard somebody moving about. I then heard a chain being moved, and the door was opened very gingerly. He had left the chain in place and then in very quiet tones asked me what I wanted. As he spoke he seemed to be quite frightened at the thought of receiving anybody.

I told him who I was. He then withdrew a chain and invited me in.

In the room I noticed that he had the scantiest and bleakest of furnishings! There was only one old wood chair, which he asked me to sit on while he stood. There was against one wall a sort of bed, no carpeting on the floor, which was just bare wood, and old broken table in the center of the room, and against a wall an old cabinet.

I was here faced with the remnants of what certainly had been one of the wealthiest and most prodigious of all European jewelers of old Russia.

Agathon spoke to me very quietly in cultured French, since he knew that I would in all probability not understand Russian, and in this surmise he was quite correct.

Although he was living in the direst of poverty, yet he was still a most elegant gentleman.

There is an Arab proverb told to me by Fahim Kouchaki, the antiquarian, that aptly described the situation. It says, "When a rich man loses his money he remains rich for forty years, and when a poor man makes money he remains poor for forty years." Agathon proved the veracity of this old saying. When Agathon spoke I could scarcely hear what he said; it seemed as though he were afraid that he might be overheard. If ever I saw a man cowed by circumstances then this was he.

I told him about our interest in the creations of his old establishment in Russia and how I had been introduced to Mr. Bowen, who had been their manager at their shop in London.

When he heard me mention Mr. Bowen's name he seemed to light up; he said that he had the fondest remembrances of this gentleman, with whom he had spent so much time in London in his many visits there in years gone by. I then filled him in on Mr. Bowen and told him that he was now quite prosperous and doing business with some of the clients whom he had known from his years at the old Fabergé shop, and Agathon told me that he was overjoyed to hear this about his old friend. We then discussed his father's great creations and especially the fabulous Easter eggs that he had produced for the czar and his family, and when I told Agathon that these were being collected and that some of them either were or would be in the collections of some of the world's great museums, this information appeared to gratify him enormously; he said that if his father were still alive this would similarly please him greatly. I then mentioned the connection of Malcom Forbes, the great publishing tycoon, whose collection of Fabergé was on display at his offices in New York City. I also told him about the great collection at the Metropolitan Museum in New York City that had come to them from Mr. Lansdell Christie.

We then spoke about some of the great buyers who had been among the Fabergé customers at their various establishments in old Russia, and he seemed delighted to speak with me about them. We then discussed the collection that had been formed by the late Mr. Henry Walters of Baltimore during his travels through Russia, and when I told Agathon that this was presently on display at Walter's Art Gallery in that city, of which he was the founder, he appeared overjoyed.

He then told me that he would have loved to be able to travel to America and see some of the things that we were talking about before he died, but that this thought must ever remain just a thought.

He also seemed to be very pleased to speak with me about the various ateliers in Russia and the so-called workmasters who operated them in Moscow, Odessa, Kiev, and Saint Petersburg; he refused to refer to this latter as Leningrad. He told me that as far as he could discover, several of the workmasters had been able to get out of Russia and some of them might at the time actually be living in Paris, but he said that he had no idea where they might be found, if, in fact, his information was factual. He then thought for some little time.

"You know, Mr. Hill, speaking with you today is to me like returning to my old home in Russia."

I then mentioned Lady Zia Werner, who had been a princess in old Russia and who was then living in London, where she owned a fine collection of Fabergé's creations, some of which she had been able to smuggle out of Russia and many that she had acquired after her marriage to a very wealthy man in England. I told him that I saw her quite often and that she always looked very well indeed and was always dressed in the utmost chic. This pleased him enormously, and he told me that when they were children they used to play together and had almost grown up as brother and sister. We then spoke of the many lovely pieces that Queen Mary had in the royal collection at Buckingham Palace, and he said that he remembered the palace very well and that he had often visited there in the "good old days," as he called them.

We then discussed the Rothschilds and the many wonderful things that his father had made for them, and I told him that one of the younger Rothschilds had presented my late brother, Bertram, with a piece that I still have in my apartment. It is a ball-shaped match holder with an opening at the top surrounded by a collar of blue and yellow enamel interspersed with tiny diamonds, the blue and yellow being the Rothschilds' racing colors. Agathon told me that he recalled that these colors were incorporated in many of the Rothschilds' things. We then chatted a little about the delightful little animals, which he said had been among his father's favorites. He explained that in making these little gems the craftsmen had always endeavored to match the colorations of the stones with the actual colors of the animals' skins or pelts. For instance, he told me about the gray stone named *troitsk*, which they used for many of their little elephants, and which stone almost matched the color of an actual elephant hide.

We then discussed the little dogs, cats, birds, ostriches, and monkeys that they had created and I also told him that many people were making collections of these, and this seemed to please him enormously. He said that the tiny little rock crystal flowerpots with their tiny flowers were similarly among his father's favorites. Agathon then described how his father always discussed these little pieces with the craftsmen involved in their making, explaining to them just where he wanted them to place the tiny jeweling, little diamonds, rubies, or sapphires; he also said that his father would often speak with the enamelers and tell them precisely what color he wanted used on any given subject. Then, warming to the subject of these various hardstones and crystals, he began to describe to me many of the really wonderful things that they had made for some of the very wealthy maharajas who, he explained, mostly loved large objects in clear rock crystal. I told him that some of these items appear today on the auction blocks in both London and Paris, and he said that he was not at all surprised, as they were in truth very exquisite works of art. I then recounted the very amusing story about the Honorable Mrs. Bruce, a lady who he said he thought he remembered, the story told earlier in this book about her naming her elephants, particularly when she named a rather broad-beamed specimen after my brother Henry.

When I related this little story to Agathon he laughed quite loudly. It was the first time that he had laughed while I was with him, and possibly the first time in many a year.

I then told Agathon about the book that had been coauthored by myself and my brother Henry on the subject of antique gold boxes and that we had included a chapter on those made by Fabergé because we had considered that their creations were as fine as anything that had emanated from the hands of the great craftsmen of the eighteenth and nineteenth centuries. He was so delighted to hear this that he said he had to write his brother in Finland and tell him about it. I then asked him whether perhaps he still had anything that I could buy from him, and he told me that every piece that he had managed to take with him from Russia had long ago been sold.

As I asked him this, I could sense that he was in direst need of cash.

"I still have one item that I will never sell," he admitted. In fact, when I asked him to show it to me, he said that he did not even want to let me see it, as he knew I would want to buy it from him and he was afraid that I might be disappointed.

"Please let me see it, and I promise that I will not even try to buy it from you," I pleaded with him.

Then reluctantly he opened a drawer in his cabinet and took out a small flat leather *pochette*, maybe four inches across and wafer-thin. He then opened this very carefully, and inside I saw a complete series of tiny plaques, each enameled with one of the colors that had formed the Fabergé palette, and against each was a very tiny numeral, which the craftsmen knew at once when his father mentioned the number he required for any piece.

"My father always carried this little *pochette* in his breast pocket, and it is for that reason that I shall never part with it in my lifetime," Agathon said.

I thanked him for having shown it to me, and as I had promised, I never even suggested that I might want to buy it from him. As he showed it to me I could visualize a dozen collectors who would have given their eyeteeth to possess it.

By this time it was midday and I invited him to be my guest at lunch, but after thanking me profusely, he refused. I really think that he was afraid to be seen on the street, as he felt that he might be arrested. Now, in the manner of all flesh, he has surely passed on, and the *pochette* has certainly been disposed of. I am sure that it must be in the possession of some collector of Fabergé, but I have no idea where it might be. Whoever does, in fact, own it is the lucky possessor of a great Fabergé gem, certainly quite unique, and may not know the story behind it.

Chapter 58

Bermuda and Mr. Ball of Berlin

It was some few months after the usual agonizing and frustrating period before any divorce is finalized that I was called by my attorney, who told me that the final decree was due to come through at any time and that to all intents and purposes I could actually feel that I was free, again.

It was just at this juncture that two very good friends of mine were leaving for a vacation in Bermuda, where they intended passing the entire summer, and they told me that they had engaged the entire suite on top of the Castle Harbour Hotel.

I knew this suite very well indeed, having seen it when I had spent some time on the island a few years back. Knowing of my impending "freedom," they insisted I join them there, and they told me that there was an extra room in the suite that they would not be using, which they wanted me to have as their guest. They also told me that the room faced out to sea and that the breezes emanating from it would be truly delightful.

Although I was much tempted to accept their very kind offer, I refused to take advantage of it; I had never enjoyed being a guest at anybody's house away from home. Despite my refusal they were most insistent, and after several telephone conversations reconsidering the matter, I decided to accept. A few days later I was on the plane, in a very happy mood, expecting to receive word from my attorney very shortly.

Upon my arrival at the airport in Bermuda, there were my friends awaiting me with their limousine to take me back with them to the hotel. They could not possibly have been any kinder.

The moment that we were back at the hotel and I was in the room that had been set aside for me, it did not take me very long to change my city clothes and get myself into a bathing outfit.

All three of us then went out onto the patio to chat and out came a bottle of champagne in my honor. They also said that they wanted to discuss my future plans as a free man.

The Bob Kriendlers of the famed 21 Club in New York had a house on the island where they passed their summers and where they were at the moment already in residence. Being friends and hearing about my impending divorce, they said that they wanted to throw me a "divorce party" luncheon as soon as I received word from my attorney in New York.

A couple of days later I received this information and at once telephoned the Kriendlers and thanked them for their thoughtfulness and told them that I could not wait to be their guest.

Bob Kriendler told me that they had an old Bermudan cook and that as I had once been a Britisher he was going to have her prepare a true old-fashioned Bermudan meal, which he said he thought would be most appropriate. They then set a date for the following day, and I must have been very intrigued at the time, because even to this day I recall with clarity most of the menu that was served at my "divorce" luncheon party.

We commenced with fried bananas, followed by kippered herring with scrambled eggs, and this was followed by some chicken dish and we ended with a melon for dessert.

As soon as lunch was over we all sat out on their patio and chatted, primarily how I was going to change my life style from married bliss to bachelordom. I listened very carefully to all that they said. They were all very free with their advice, and for possible reference I mentally pigeonholed all for possible future use. At the time I did not, in truth, feel that I needed any advice.

After this we returned to our hotel suite, where for the next two weeks I thoroughly enjoyed a life of extreme *dolce far niente*, the sweetness of doing nothing. A few days later my hosts were invited to a dinner at the governor general's mansion, and they told me that I had been included in the invitation. The thought of visiting at this historic house was for me, an antiquarian, a true delight, and in my own mind I decided that while there I would find some way to get myself taken through its rooms.

The dinner was quite unusual as far as I was concerned and rather amusing. It was like no other that I had ever attended.

There must have been some three hundred guests, and we were all invited to seat ourselves on large rugs that had been spread out over the very spacious lawns that surround the mansion. The waiters were all men dressed in starched whites who marched around as though they were marines on duty, which they in all probability were. The amusing part of the dinner was the fact that straightforward American hot dogs, all nicely lined up on silver platters, were served; there was nothing else.

While seated on my rug, I was quite fortunate to have as my companion the son of the governor, who in the course of conversation asked me what my business or profession might be.

I told him that I was an antiquarian and also an art dealer, and he then said, "In that case you must let me show you through the house and point out to you our great collection of antiques and memorabilia."

I replied, telling him that this was one of the things that I had hoped to see while there, and it was then arranged that as soon as dinner was over we could go into the mansion and see what the various rooms contained.

Thus in due course, we left our rugs and he took me into the house, and as he did this he pointed out many of the items of historic interest that were contained in showcases or which were hung on the walls. The house was a virtual storehouse of history pertaining to the island of Bermuda.

After we had ended our most interesting tour and were about to leave through the front door, he pointed out to me a very high white marble slab that extended from floor to ceiling. On this slab there were incised in gold lettering the names and birth and death dates of all the preceding governors general, starting with the first and dating from the beginning of the colony. At the foot of this list was the name of the present governor general Sir Alexander Hood, with his birth date to one side and space left open for his eventual death date.

At this point, seeing that I was looking down this list of names, my host made what was to me a very humorous remark. "Well," he remarked, "I don't suppose that it will be too long now before dear old Dad's death date is added up there," and as he spoke he pointed out the obvious empty space.

After the dinner ended, we returned to the hotel suite, where life proceeded normally until about six weeks had passed and I found that doing the same thing day in and day out was becoming utterly monotonous: down to the beach in the morning, back to the hotel for lunch, and then, after an afternoon siesta, back to the beach and back again for dinner. The only break in this monotony was an occasional dinner at one or another of the then few good restaurants. At this time I would dearly have loved to be back home in my apartment in the city, but I found myself in somewhat of a difficult situation. My host was leaving the island with ever increasing frequency, and I was being left with his wife as a sort of guardian.

Neither I nor his wife appreciated this behavior one little bit, and I decided that I had to find some way to extricate myself from what was becoming a rather unpleasant entanglement.

I then began to realize that his comings and goings were to be with a woman that he eventually married after his divorce.

Finding a telephone at some distance from the suite in the hotel, I placed a call to my secretary in New York and asked her to send me a cable reading: "Please return as soon as possible as a very important deal is pending with King Farouk that requires your attention."

Later that same afternoon I received the cable and, after showing it to my hosts, told them that I had to leave at once, and then thanking them for their great hospitality to me, I packed my bags and was off on the next flight.

All that I recall of this flight back to New York was an intense feeling of relief.

The day following my return to the city, while walking along Fifth Avenue I was approached by a gentleman who called me by name. "Mr. Hill," he said as I turned around. "Don't you remember me? We met on the beach at Biarritz some time ago, when you were there with a very pretty young lady and we were lying on the sands behind the hotel?"

In some sort of vague way I did recall him.

He then continued, "I am Mr. Ball, the auctioneer from Berlin."

As soon as he said this I did remember that we had done some considerable business with his firm in years gone by. As I looked at him I did remember our meeting on the beach, and in my mind's eye I saw a very elegant gentleman wearing a pale blue silk dressing gown with his initials embroidered on his breast in gold thread and at his side a beautiful blond. In the old days

before the war his firm had been one of the principal art auctioneers in Berlin, dealing with all types of fine art, paintings and
sculpture, furniture, and so forth. His firm could be compared
with the great firms of Christie's of London and Sotheby Parke-
Bernet of London and New York.

He then said to me, "Mr. Hill, would you do me the great
favor and come and take coffee with me, as I have to speak to
somebody, particularly with an old friend, as I have a story to tell
that I am sure you will find most fascinating."

I told him that I would join him with pleasure, and as we
were outside the St. Regis Hotel, we went into the bar for our
drink.

As soon as we were seated at the hotel he began to speak.
"After leaving Biarritz, where we met, I went straight back to my
home in Berlin, and as soon as I arrived I could sense a terrible
feeling of unease and insecurity with the rapidly rising tide of
anti-Semitism, with violent incidents increasing daily. I felt this
and, speaking with my brother and mother, told them of my
feelings and that, in my opinion, we should get away from Germany as soon as possible. I felt that this was an absolute necessity,
as I had a young daughter. The four of us were the only members
of our family, and beyond them I had no responsibility to anybody. Both my brother and mother agreed that this was the
proper thing for us to do, and without telling anybody of our
plans, we collected together as many of the smaller valuables as
we could carry, as well as a quantity of foreign exchange that we
always kept on hand in our vaults.

"My mother took her wonderful collection of antique jewels
from her personal vault, and taking all in several valises, we left
as soon as we could for Paris. The moment that we arrived there
we went to a bank and secured all of our valuables in one of their
vaults. We then sent my daughter off to school in Switzerland,
and as it transpired, I was correct in paying for her several years
in advance. Why I was prompted to do this at the time I will never
know.

"We then commenced to trade quite successfully in Paris,
where we had many fine contacts and were very well known
throughout the art and antiquarian world. However, this was not
to last very long, as after we had been in Paris for what seemed

305

to me to be a very short time, the Nazi menace was in fullest spate and we were beginning to congratulate ourselves on what we had done, then, with a suddenness, France was invaded by the Nazis and we were all arrested. My mother was taken away from us and we were never able to discover what happened to her, as we never saw her again. In all probability, as she was quite elderly, she must have been among the first to be liquidated.

"My brother and I were immediately shipped off to North Africa, where we were made to work on the road across the desert. The Nazis required this road for their panzer divisions under Rommel.

"How we survived this work under the broiling sun I shall never know, but after the defeat of the Nazis we found ourselves free again.

"As soon as we were liberated we went at once to the bank, where we had deposited all of our valuables, but found that the Germans had removed all of the safe deposit boxes and taken them back to Germany. We were penniless, but together with the assistance of some friends in America, we were able to get passage over and in due course arrived here in New York. We then, upon arrival, began trading a little, although at the time we were, both of us, in a very poor state of health, and besides, we hated the thought that we were being supported by friends. After we had been in New York for about three months, we received a cable from the bank in Paris advising us that all of the safety deposit boxes had been returned to them and that as far as they could tell nothing had been disturbed or removed from the contents. Hearing this, we at once crossed to Paris and when we arrived went at once to the bank, where, to our amazement, we found the contents of our boxes intact. We also found that the Germans had placed a meticulous list of every piece in each of the boxes, together with the amounts of various foreign currencies. We were rich again and returned to New York, where we at once started to trade, and we had the great pleasure of being able to repay all of our friends who had financed us in our period of dire need.

"I at once sent for my daughter to come to New York, soon we saw standing before us a very beautiful young lady. She told me that she had been worried about us while she was at school, but although she endeavored to contact us in Paris she could never find out anything about us. She did tell us that while there she had studied for the stage, as she wished to become an actress. I told her that she was free to do anything that she wished and that she could go on to the stage with my blessing. Unfortunately, my brother was so broken by the terrible experience we had lived through that he was never able to take advantage of our regained fortune and soon passed away.

"Now you can see why I had to stop you, as you are one of the old friends of mine that I have not seen in so many years, and now I hope that we can continue to do business together again."

I told him how happy I was to have heard his story and how I was sure that we would soon be doing considerable business together again. On that we parted, but I have not seen him since.

Chapter 59

Renaissance Jewels

As antiquarians my brothers and I were always interested in antique jewels, particularly those wonderful creations in gold and enamel by the great master jewelers of the Italian Renaissance such objects as emanated from the ateliers of such men as Cellini and others of his period.

In this regard we were approached one day by a fellow dealer inquiring as to whether we might be interested in handling what he termed "a fabulous group of wonderful Renaissance jewels."

Such items did interest us very much indeed, and it was arranged that he bring the collection up to our offices next morning, when he would leave the things with us for study.

In due course next morning, the gentleman arrived and placed on our table one of the greatest collections of antique jewels of this period that we had ever seen. Each piece was magnificent. Actually, we never thought that we would be in a position of acquiring such a fantastic group. In the collection there were about twenty items. Coincidentally, with this dealer's call to us about this group we had received a telephone call from Dr. Berliner, the then curator of fine arts at the Rhode Island School of Design. In this call he advised us that he had been commissioned by one of their very wealthy donors who wanted to acquire for them a collection of fine Renaissance jewels. At the time that he called we told him that we had nothing that we could suggest for her, but if anything were offered we would at once be in touch with him. At the time he told us that the lady in question was enormously wealthy and that the amount of money involved would be of absolutely no consequence.

Now that this group that had been brought in to us was available, we at once telephoned the doctor and told him about it. We also told him that we had just at that moment the entire collection in our hands. We described some of the pieces to him in detail, and he again told us that the amount of money involved was of no consequence. He then asked that we hold the collection for his further instructions and that we were to hold the items for his eyes only, and also that he would contact the lady at once and then be in further touch with us.

Later that same afternoon he called again to tell us that he had spoken with his donor and that he had arranged with her to come up to New York the next day to study the collection.

Next morning when I arrived at our offices they were waiting outside our door. I then invited them in, and after they were seated at my desk I brought the collection out of our safe and laid each of the jewels onto a table. In situ they looked fantastic.

When the lady saw what we had placed in front of them she became quite excited and exclaimed, "I never even hoped to be able to get such a wonderful collection for the museum!" She then continued, "I don't care how much this is going to cost me; I just must have them." She then wanted to write out her check on the spot, although the question of cost had up to that time not even been mentioned.

In the meantime, the doctor had not said a word, but all that he did was look very closely at each of the pieces. Then, in his very thick German accent, he said, "Can you perhaps give me ze provenance of zis wonderful collection?"

I replied that at that moment I could not, but that I knew that were they to be interested in its acquisition this would certainly be forthcoming, provided together with a detailed documentation of each of the pieces.

The doctor then, in his very German accent, again spoke. "You know zat I have been America now for several years and since ze time zat I had to leave my native Germany, courtesy of Hitler, when I was curator of one of Germany's great art and historical museums. So I know a great deal about zuch jewels, and zis group is ze collection zat vas in the Brandenburg Museum, and I zink zat zey should go back to the museum where zey belong. Don't you zink that I am right?" He then after a moment continued. "Do you mind if I tell ze FBI about zis?"

I replied that he could certainly do as he wished, and I also told him that if what he said was fact, we would not wish under any circumstances to handle the collection. At that time there was much that had been brought back to the States by returning soldiers after the war.

When the doctor spoke, the lady appeared to be most distressed, as she knew then that she was not going to be able to buy the collection. She was almost in tears. They then left the gallery after thanking me for giving them even the opportunity to buy.

No sooner were they out of the gallery that I telephoned our dealer friend and told him that we had to see him as soon as possible, and he promised that he would be round next day. Next morning he arrived and as soon as we were seated at my desk I told him about our visit by Dr. Berliner and his donor. He said that he knew the doctor very well. I told him that the doctor had asked for the fullest documentation of provenance.

And my friend then recounted the following story. "It appears," he said, "that following the cessation of hostilities in Germany, when it was overrun by Allied troups, the American and Russian armies made contact with each other in Berlin. And as a result two American and two Russian generals befriended each other. They decided that they would enjoy a game of poker together, and they made a date to meet at one of the hotels where the Russians were staying.

"Next evening they met there and, as arranged, sat down to commence playing, and as they played they joked and drank and were having a glorious time. After they had been playing for several hours, the Americans decided that they were rather tired and that they had played long enough and they then decided that they would play one last hand.

"The Russians similarly stated that they were rather tired and thought that this was an excellent idea. When this final hand was ended the Americans told the Russians that they owed them about five thousand dollars.

"The Russians then began to laugh and one roared, 'Five thousand dollars! We don't even have five thousand rubles between us!'

"The Americans were in no mood for fun at this point and explained that had they been the losers, they would have had to pay. They then suggested that unless they were paid they would knock the Russians' blocks off; they were, incidentally, much bigger and heavier men than the Russians.

"Seeing that the Americans were in no mood to be played with and that they were very incensed, the Russians pointed across the hotel room where several boxes lay on the carpet, which the Americans saw were filled to the brim with gold objects of some sort or another.

" 'Look, please take five handfuls of each of these things out of these boxes in lieu of the five thousand dollars that you say we owe you,' one Russian said.

"The Americans, seeing that they were not going to get any cash, agreed to do as the Russians suggested, and what you see here is the collection that they took out of the boxes"

I told my friend that this was a quite a story, and he replied, "I know that the whole thing sounds quite ridiculous, but I can show you a letter which I have in my pocket, a letter signed by General Eisenhower, in which it stated quite succinctly that the collection of jewels held by the two American generals was properly owned by them that they were free to deal with them in anyway that they pleased."

As soon as I had finished reading this letter I telephoned Dr. Berliner and told him that in light of what this Eisenhower letter stated we were obviously free to handle the collection and sell it to his donor if he still wished to go ahead with the purchase. He then said that he would be in again the next morning to further discuss the matter.

When he arrived the next day he said to me, "I must tell you at once zat I am very well acquainted with zis collection of Renaissance jewels and zat I zink zat zey should all be returned to the Museum of Brandenburg." He then continued, "Even if zey don't go back to ze museum we could not possibly acquire zem for our museum."

He then left the gallery, and I telephoned my dealer friend and told him regretfully that he would have to take the jewels away, and I also told him what the doctor had said regarding the FBI.

The dealer said that he understood our position very well indeed and that he would be in the next day to collect the collection from us.

A few weeks then passed, and I had almost forgotten all about the collection when one afternoon a man called to see us. He told our secretary that he had to speak with one of our principals on a very private matter and asked her to tell us that he was waiting outside.

Our girl then came into our private office and gave me the message and I told her to show the man in.

As soon as he was seated at my desk, he showed me his credentials as an agent of the FBI and began to interrogate me. "Do you," he asked, "handle Renaissance jewels from time to time?"

The moment that I heard these words I recalled that Dr. Berliner had suggested that he would inform the FBI about the collection that we had shown him. I replied to the agent, telling him that we did. "I presume that you are seeking information about a collection of such jewels that we showed Dr. Berliner of the Rhode Island School of Design," I then added.

He replied that he was.

I then said to him. "If you promise me that you will not laugh at what I can tell you, I will tell you a story that is, to my thinking, quite fantastic." I then waited for his reply.

"Please tell me all that you can about the matter, and I promise that I will not laugh at you."

I then recounted the story of the collection and also all about the Eisenhower letter.

He then said, "I am not laughing at you because what you have just told me is perfectly true in every detail." He then left the gallery.

Some few months then passed and I again saw my dealer friend and asked him what transpired with the collection and he told me that as far as he understood it the government had in some way taken over the jewels from the two generals involved and that they had been returned to Brandenburg, where they naturally belonged.

Of a certainty there must be many stories of fine antiquities that were taken by the troops out of Europe after the war, and as I recall, so much so was this the case that an ordinance was passed that suggested that ownership of anything under one thousand dollars in value was in order, but that valuables totaling more than this sum were to be considered as loot and would be confiscated from the holder and returned to the original owner wherever this was possible.

I have not yet been to the Brandenburg Museum to see the collection in situ but I am sure that anyone interested in seeing exceptional jewels of this great period of the Renaissance could do worse than visit at the museum, where I am quite sure they are displayed today.

Chapter 60

John Wayne

During the many years that I was crossing the Atlantic, first by boat and later by air, in my never ending search for rare and exotic objects of art that I felt would fit happily into the very many and varied collections being formed by the late King Farouk of Egypt, I never bothered about weather conditions, whether it be summer, winter, spring, or fall. I always traveled on the theory that if the boat or plane crossed then that was good enough for me.

During the early forties the journey by plane from New York to London or Paris took approximately twenty hours or there-abouts, ever depending on weather conditions.

It was one day during the depths of winter that I was informed that a very special item was to be offered for sale in Paris, which, according to my informant, was something that I should not fail to acquire. I at once decided to fly to Paris.

In those days I always traveled on Pan American, where the planes had an underbelly that housed a cocktail bar and on which travel was most comfortable.

On this particular flight there were, as it was in winter, just a small handful of passengers.

After he had been airborne for several hours, the captain announced that he was having some problems with the operation of the aircraft and that would have to set down in Nova Scotia, where he said the plane could be handled by local ground staff. He then jokingly said, I thought, "I don't wish to take any undue risks flying over the Atlantic." All of us on board heartily agreed with his thinking.

Very soon after he had made his announcement we set down at Goose Bay, in those days about as isolated and uninviting a spot as one could ever possibly imagine. Maybe in summertime it looked better, but in winter it was awful. The ground was piled high with snow, which was swirling all around, and as we left the aircraft the cold was so intense that none of the passengers thought that they would ever make it to a sort of Quonset hut that stood out on the ground. We seemed to be in the middle of nowhere.

Naturally, we went as speedily as we could manage into this hut, where we felt that it would take us some hours to thaw out. However, when we entered we saw that centering the hut there was a most welcome potbellied stove blazing with flame and there were several wood chairs set all around it. We at once sat down and began to warm ourselves. Precisely, we were about seven or eight on board, and we at once introduced ourselves, the one to the other. To my great delight, John Wayne was traveling with several very pretty young girls and two similarly very pretty boys, all traveling over to Ireland for the filming of some movie or other, probably *The Quiet Man*, that they were doing. Their destination was Shannon.

Being an art dealer and knowing the reputation held by the Duke as a great collector of American art, I at once commenced a conversation with him. He told me that he owned an important collection of Western bronzes by the great American painter and sculptor Frederic Remington, and I told him that on the market of the day what he owned would be worth a veritable king's ransom. If I recall this conversation, he told me that he owned *The Rattlesnake*, which is perhaps the rarest of all.

We then discussed the question of where American art and particularly Western American art was going pricewise, and I told him that in my opinion such art had only just begun to scratch the surface and that its value would increase enormously with the passage of time. How right I was. My prediction was obviously very well founded, as today the value of any fine American Western art, be it in oil, watercolor, or bronze, has ascended to enormous heights and is continuing to do so daily.

This conversation around the stove was for me most interesting, but something began to occur that was for all of us very amusing.

As soon as the ground crew realized that the great John Wayne was seated by the fire, the men began to enter to get his autograph. As the door would open the men would enter with

315

the snow swirling around them and quickly close the door against the cold. All were dressed in heavy parkas, and it seemed that they wore several of each, one over the other. The amusing part was watching the men opening these to get at pieces of paper on which John Wayne could write.

As each of the men received his autograph—there must have been about ten men in all—they thanked him and stated that they would treasure theirs as a great memento of so great a personality.

I am sure by the way John Wayne laughed that he enjoyed this episode more than anybody else, and as the men left he turned to me and said, "During the very many years of my film career I have signed literally thousands of autographs, but these that I have just signed I shall never forget."

Basically, this flight would have been a veritable nightmare, but because of my meeting with John Wayne as my traveling companion it turned out to be one of my most memorable crossings.

The prospect of sitting round the fire for almost an entire night on hardwood chairs was not too pleasant. However, after a short while, what with the heat of the fire, we all began to doze and were soon asleep.

When eventually we were aroused and told that we could reenter the plane, I continued my chat with john Wayne and he began to talk about some of the movie stars that he knew. He told me about the young star Judy Holliday, who had at the time recently passed away at a very young age, and he said that she had been among his favorites, not only because she was a wonderful actress, but also as a person. He told me that she had confided to him that she missed her early life in Israel and also that it was in Israel that she had hoped to end her days. He said that when he had first met her he had had no idea that she was a Sabra.

The following morning the plane landed at Shannon in Ireland, and here John Wayne and his party left me. He asked me to keep in touch with him and not to fail to visit him whenever I found myself out on the coast. I promised that I would do that. Unfortunately, with all my crossings to Europe I never made the coast, so that now all that is left me of my meeting with the Duke is a happy memory.

Chapter 61

Farouk Abdicates

After my return to New York from this crossing I decided that if at all possible I would endeavor to remain in the States before I started again my transatlantic flights, particularly as my two boys were at the time preparing to go off to camp in the spring. I am quite sure that most parents send their offspring to camps as much for their own sakes as that of the children. Be that at it may, in due time my boys were off to their camp in New Hampshire. I had sent them there because I had visited in that State so many times and always felt welcome and happy there and I knew that the climate would be ideal for the boys.

There was a small inn at Lebanon, New Hampshire, where I had always stopped and had always been very well received and which was quite close to the camp. After the boys had been up at the camp for about a month, I decided that I would make my formal visit to see how they were faring. I knew well from previous experiences that when I arrived I would be showered with a volley of complaints. But I knew that this was par for the course.

When I arrived at the inn on a Friday I arranged to have a car take me to the camp the following morning. Promptly next morning the car arrived, and it did not take me too long to get to the camp. As soon as I saw my boys and despite the fact that they welcomed me with stories of mistreatment, which I had expected to hear, they were both soon off to some activity or other. With the usual "Hi, Dad" and "Good-bye, Dad," they were off. One was off canoeing and the other to play some ball game or other. Being satisfied that their complaints had meant nothing and that both of them were looking exceedingly well, I felt that I had nothing more to stay for, so I returned to the inn.

Arriving back at the inn just before they were ready to serve lunch, I decided to sit out on the lawn and relax a little with the *New York Times* that had just been delivered. As I opened the

317

paper I saw the headlines "Farouk abdicates" in large type right across the top of the front page. I was momentarily stunned and all thought of lunch left me. I then recalled that several years prior to this we had taken out a very large life insurance policy on Farouk's life, thinking that assassination was ever a possibility, but unfortunately, and for no reason I could recall, we had omitted the question of possible abdication, so that in this regard we were out in the cold moneywise. At that moment our twenty-odd years of almost daily association with the king and the palace in Cairo paraded through my mind. I knew that we had lost a very important client and over the years we had allowed ourselves to be lulled into placing virtually all of our eggs into one basket. We were now in a very difficult situation, and I at once began to plan our next move.

Having read in the *Times* report that after his abdication Farouk had been taken by boat to Capri and knowing that at that moment my brother Henry was vacationing in Italy, I put through a call to him. Fortunately, when I called he was still in his room, and when I spoke with him he was as perturbed as was I at the news. I suggested that as he was in Venice, it might be a good idea to fly to Capri and meet with Farouk and see if there was anything that he could do. The press had stated that Farouk was stopping at the Quisisana Hotel in Capri.

Henry said that he would fly there immediately, and he also said that he would telephone the king at once to see whether he would be received.

When he spoke with me on the telephone later, Henry told me that when he had contacted Farouk, the now ex-king said that he would be delighted to see and speak with him. The king also said that his visit would be most welcome. During all the many years that we had been working with Farouk, our bills had always been sent one day and almost immediately funds had been passed to our bankers in New York, but for some reason that at the time we could not understand, a few weeks prior to the abdication, moneys had been quite slow in arriving, and at this point there was an enormous sum owing us. When Henry saw the king, he told my brother not to worry about the debt, because the State would be responsible for any debts that he had left unpaid. He then told my brother, "According to the law of the Koran, as soon as you prove that the money is due you, it will be paid."

At that time we did not know that several years were to pass before we would be paid; neither did we know that in the ensuing years we were to hear the same refrain about the law of the Koran.

Then Farouk went on to tell Henry that when he was ordered out of his bed very early in the morning by a troop of soldiers they had ordered him to dress himself very quickly despite the fact that he had gone to bed very late the night before and was very tired. He also told Henry that he had decided to stay in bed all that morning. But he said that the soldiers were waiting with their guns pointed ominously directly at him and he had little alternative but to comply. He also said that just at the moment when he was half-dressed the American ambassador, Mr. Caffery, having been informed of the events, came in to see him and that had it not been for his arrival, the king was positive that he would not have left the palace alive. He said that he had been expecting a bullet at any moment.

Farouk then told Henry that the soldiers had allowed him to take with him only one change of clothing, which the soldiers had literally thrown at him.

Some months after the abdication the Egyptian government established a consortium of twelve colonels who took over control of the country, and about a year later the consortium decided that they would hold a series of auction sales in Egypt, where they would dispose of all of the collections that remained in the various palaces. Thus a series of auctions lasting about two weeks was announced for the spring of 1953, which was in their opinion a most propitious time for any such sales in Egypt.

Sotheby's of London was given the commission to conduct these sales, and when they commenced cataloging the thousands of items they saw that very many of the pieces still had our small parchment tags affixed to each. Seeing this, they consulted with Colonel Gafar, one of the consortium, who contacted us by mail and who asked whether I would be agreeable to come to Cairo to assist with the work.

Thinking that perhaps if I did this it would speed up settlement of our bill, I consented to fly out. I at once cabled the colonel and told him to expect me in a couple of days, so that I would be there well in advance of any of the scheduled auctions. At this point it is perhaps interesting to mention that the international press had reported that when he left, the king had transported with him most of his great collections, but these reports were categorically without the slightest foundation whatsoever, as was proved by the eventual sales of almost all.

The auctions were slated to extend over a two-week period, with sessions both in the morning and in the afternoon. As soon as I arrived in Cairo and had settled at my hotel that had been arranged for me by a friend, I met with Colonel Gafar, and at this meeting discussed with him the question of our account that was as yet unpaid and he replied, "According to the law of the Koran, as soon as you establish that the money is due you, you will be paid in full."

At the time that I arrived in Cairo I found the city in a state of turmoil. It was a city gone quite mad. Every available hotel room was at a premium, and the city was jumping with dealers and collectors from every corner of the globe, all wanting to acquire pieces from the various royal collections. There were, in fact, many of the objects that we had acquired for the Farouk collections that were quite exceptional and some pieces quite unique. So crowded was the city that even Farouk's yacht tied up at one side of the Nile had been quickly converted into a floating hotel and was at once fully occupied.

Three days then passed and I again called Farouk's secretary as promised, but this time I invited him to be my guest at a restaurant in the city and he said that he was delighted to accept, especially as I said that I would like to be his guest at his home a little later. I thought that perhaps in private conversation with him I might be able to get some information from him about our due bill.

At the restaurant I asked him about the financial situation in Egypt at that moment, but other than the same response about the law of the Koran, I could get no further information from him. Either he was afraid to discuss the financial situation in Egypt, which was obviously very bad at the time, or he did not know. As we glanced over the menu he saw that the most expensive item listed was shrimp, and he at once asked whether he could have them. I told him that he certainly could and ordered shrimps for both of us.

We then continued our dinner and talked about the forth-coming auction sales, but I soon began to tire after my long flight, and as I was feeling quite exhausted, I told him that I wanted to get to bed as soon as possible. We then finished dinner very quickly and I left him, again promising to be his guest when I would call him in a few days.

On arrival back at my hotel room I was soon in bed and fast asleep, but at about four in the morning I awoke with the most violent stomach pains that I had ever suffered. There was, how-ever, nothing that I could do but lie in bed and writhe while telling myself that there should be a large sign outside every Cairo restaurant reading: DON'T EAT THE SHRIMP.

Next morning I told my friend what had happened and he gave me some pills that he said he always carried for just such an emergency. These pills alleviated my pains, and then I spoke with a doctor at the hotel who advised that I eat only eggs and rice. This then became my regular diet for all of the two weeks that I was in Egypt.

Now as an adviser to the government I had to be present at the Khoube Palace for most of the sessions there. The Khoube Palace was Farouk's summer palace and lay about half an hour's drive from the city. It lay in a most beautiful setting, with a large expanse of lawns all round. Going back and forth to the palace was agonizing, and I was extremely miserable, particularly, as can well be imagined; toilet conditions in the desert are nonexistent. How I managed to survive I shall never know, but survive I did.

The series of auctions was held every one of the seven days of the week. As Friday is the Arab day of rest, no Arabs attended; Saturday being the Jewish day of rest, similarly no Jews were in evidence; Sunday being the Christian day of rest, I regret to say that they were all there and at work, day of rest nonwithstanding. At the commencement of each session, the auctioneer would an-nounce the number of each lot in English, followed by French and then Arabic. The auctioneer had announced at the opening session that they would offer anything in any other language that might be called for. Fortunately, the audience appeared satisfied with these three tongues. He would offer the lots as Number One, then Un, and then Aleph and so on with utter monotony.

As far as the government was concerned, the sales went extraordinarily well, and enormous profits were realized over the original sums that had been paid by Farouk.

After one of the afternoon sessions had ended, Colonel Gafar invited me to have coffee with him in one of the great salons at the palace. By this time we had become bosom friends, particularly as I had advised him about the least that the auctioneer should accept for some of the more important pieces, and even these sums had been superseded.

As we sat in this enormous salon, seemingly filled with gilded chairs and sofas, I felt very small indeed against this backdrop. We chatted about the auctions and other matters pertaining to the situation in Egypt at the time, and he explained how everything was going to be very rosy in a very short period. At this moment one of the Arabs arrived with our coffee.

The colonel could not stop telling me how happy his government was with the outcome of the auctions, and I told him how happy I was to be of assistance, hoping that this might speed up the settlement of our account. For some reason best known to himself, he insisted on calling me Dr. Hill. Why, I could not understand. Incidentally, at this point I would have welcomed the arrival of any doctor of medicine.

Suddenly the colonel spoke. "Do you know, Dr. Hill, how we could solve all of the world's problems and troubles?"

I must say that I was quite astonished at this remark and responded, "Colonel, I do not know, but I would dearly love to hear what you have to say."

He then responded quite simply, "If the whole world embraced Mohammedanism then this would be the solution." He appeared to be quite serious, but when I heard what he had said my mental reaction was the thought that if the entire world became Sioux Indian we all might achieve a similar result.

The day following our meeting in the salon we were all invited to an alfresco luncheon to be served on the lawns surrounding the palace. Large tables were set up and shaded from the intense sun by large and very colorful umbrellas. The entire scene was resplendent with color, and as the setting was against the azure sky, entirely unclouded, the scene seemed to be like one of the Hollywood spectaculars of a decade or so ago. The food that was served was of the finest and according to all who were able to partake of it was as fine as anything that they had ever eaten. For my part I could only sit and watch.

Despite the fact that this was a Mohammedan country, every type of liquor was available at the bar.

Despite my intense discomfort I was determined to try in any way that I could to get a line on the question of the settlement of our account, and at this luncheon I again spoke with the colonel, but all that I could get from him was the usual response about the law of the Koran.

During the time that I was in Cairo I was in continual touch with our local attorney, a Dr. Hanafi, and after I saw this gentleman one morning he told me that I would have to go to the Hall of Justice to get a certain document sworn. As he spoke he handed me a long paper that he said had to be sworn by me alone and added he could not send anybody else, but he said that after this swearing the question of settlement of our account could be soon arranged. He then told me that although the document was written entirely in Arabic, I would have to swear to it. He again reiterated the fact that only I, as a principal, could do the swearing.

I was not too happy about this; as far as I could tell, this document might have been a death warrant. I was in no way able to see or judge the contents of the document. Nevertheless, I presented myself at the Hall of Justice, which appeared to be swarming with Arabs, all robed in their native galabias or caftans. They seemed to me to be running helter skelter all over the place and up and down a very wide staircase. All seemed to be like frightened mice. In retrospect the scene was extraordinarily funny.

Now I had to find the proper room where I could get the swearing done, but as I could not speak Arabic, I could not ask anybody where I had to go.

Fortunately, there was one gentleman who by his dress I thought might be able to answer me, and fortunately for me he spoke a little English and was able to direct me to the correct room upstairs.

In this room, by dint of some sign language, I managed to get the paper signed and sworn to.

The moment that I had the document in my hands I went directly to my attorney's office and handed it to him.

He appeared to be very pleased indeed. "Now that I have this sworn document in my hands I can go right to work and get the settlement of your account." He then said that he would very much like me to be his guest at dinner that evening so that we could celebrate.

I thanked him for his kind invitation and accepted. However, I informed him of my stomach problem and he told me that he would tell his wife of my situation regarding food—just eggs and rice.

As arranged, I arrived at the apartment that evening, and after I was introduced to Madame Hanafi we were soon seated at table.

In all there were twelve at the table, and as I was supposedly the guest of honor, I was seated at my hostess's side; fortunately for me, Madame Hanafi spoke some French, as nobody else spoke anything but Arabic. At this point I would have enjoyed a Scotch or at least a glass of wine, But as this was an Arab household no strong liquor was anywhere in evidence. Madame Hanafi, having been informed by her husband of the very delicate state of my stomach, served me my rice and eggs.

The Hanafi's occupied what would be the equivalent of a New York six-room apartment; they had no children. But during the meal I counted about a dozen Arabs who did the serving; all were dressed in long white robes and wore red and white turbans on their heads. Having nothing that I could think of to speak with my hostess about I asked her whether these Arabs were her regular help.

"Oh, yes," she replied.

I then inquired where they slept at night after work, and she stated quite simply that they wrapped themselves in their blankets and slept on the sidewalk outside the apartment house. It was naturally quite obvious that they could not have been accommodated in the apartment. As she spoke I began to visualize such a situation in New York City and became amused at my thoughts.

After dinner had ended, I again spoke with Dr. Hanafi and inquired what he considered might be the outcome now that the document, duly sworn was in his hands. He replied that we would be getting satisfactory action very shortly.

I then returned to my hotel with a feeling that I was getting somewhere and congratulating myself that I had been on the scene in Cairo to swear to this important document.

The following day I again called to ex–private secretary of the king and told him that I would very much like to accept his kind invitation at his home and be his guest. He appeared to be overjoyed by my call, and it was arranged that I dine with him and his family that same evening. Promptly at seven o'clock I arrived and he greeted me at the door, when he introduced me to his wife and mother-in-law. Fortunately, they all spoke English and also some French. At his side I saw his young son, a boy of maybe five or six years of age. The child was one of the most beautiful children that I had ever seen, with a lean face that could only be compared to those pictures on the tombs of Fayoum, which date back to the period of the pharaohs.

As a slight gesture I handed the boy a crisp American dollar bill and he was delighted to accept it and, speaking in excellent English, said, "Thank you, Mr. Hill. This is going to be the first money towards the fortune that I know I am going to make when I grow up."

The secretary then told the child to go to bed, which he did at once, and we then sat down at the table. The wife and mother-in-law did not sit with us but commenced serving, this apparently in accord with Moslem custom.

Here again, as this was a Moslem household, no strong liquor was served. The two ladies, having been informed of my diet, began to serve me heaped plates of eggs and rice and when I managed to eat most of the food insisted that I eat more, although by this time I could scarcely even look at either rice or eggs.

As soon as the meal had ended, the private secretary came over to me and, speaking with a hushed voice, said, "Mr. Hill, would you be so kind as to come with me into my private office, where we can have our coffee and dessert, as I have something very important to speak with you about."

The moment that I heard this I could not wait to get into his office, thinking to myself that he must have something quite confidential to tell me about our account. But in this I was quite wrong.

As soon as we were seated he commenced to speak. "Mr. Hill, I must tell you that I am not a Moslem, although nobody, not even the members of my family, knows this. I am a Christian, but should any of the powers that be ever hear about this I would at once be out of a job."

Why he was telling me all this I could not fathom. As far as I was concerned, he could have been a Hottentot, but I very soon discovered his reason for his confidence.

"As you know, my king is out, and since this is the case, I can see no future here in Egypt for me and certainly not for my little son. I want to give him to you to take back to America with you and to raise him as your own."

As he spoke I could sense a terrible wrench going on in his body, as I am quite sure that this little boy was his whole life. I was quite taken back, and although I told him that I was extremely honored at the confidence that he placed in me, I could see no possible way in which I could accede to his request. First, I explained that I would have to smuggle the child out of Egypt and that as the country was at the time under virtual martial law I could see no way of doing this, especially as at the airport the place was alive with soldiers. Second, even if I could manage to get him out with me, I could never bring him into the United States without a proper passport and certainly not without proper papers. Then finally I explained to him that I was at the time living alone as a bachelor and that even were the first two imponderables to be overcome I could see no way in which I could care for the boy.

As I finished all that I had to say, he replied, "I, of course, knew quite well what your answer was going to be, but I felt that if I did not even make the attempt I would not be able to live with myself."

So many years have now passed since that evening that I have completely forgotten the secretary's name and, in fact, where he lived, but I would dearly love to know what exactly happened to the little boy, by now obviously grown to manhood.

Shortly after this evening I returned to New York, and curiously, the stomach pains appeared to cease immediately and I had no further problems and I at once ceased eating eggs and rice. Actually, I had almost forgotten all about these pains until one day many years later while walking through our galleries I suddenly felt a stabbing at my insides, but soon the pain stopped and I ignored the matter. Next day at about the same time as on the previous day I had a recurrence of the pains, and then I decided that something must be wrong and I called my doctor and made an appointment to see him the next day.

When I was seated at his desk after explaining to him what had occured, he asked me, "Have you ever had dysentery?"

I replied that I was sure that I had not, and as I spoke I recalled my problem when in Cairo, and I then told him about this.

He then asked me how long ago this might have been, and then, thinking back, I told him that it must have been about seven years ago.

"You know, amoebic dysentery has a curious habit of recurring in seven-year cycles and I would like to have my secretary call and make an appointment for you at the laboratory for you to have your stomach examined and I want her to be sure that this is done without delay."

Next day, after she had made the date, I was at Dr. Katz's laboratory and had my stomach examined.

Later that day my doctor telephoned me. "Mr. Hill," he said, "I would like you to come to my office at once, as you have a hundred percent case of amoebic dysentery."

I was soon in his office, and he prescribed some pills that I was to take daily for one month. After I had done this, the situated appeared to be cured. I have never since had any further problem.

It was maybe some ten years that passed after my return from Cairo, and we had almost forgotten all about the debt outstanding, despite what my attorney had said, when, seated across my desk with my brother one Saturday morning, I looked desultorily at some mail that had arrived. The entire pile of mail seemed to be the usual lot of advertisements and also some letters from banks that were always arriving asking for our account. However, fortunately for us, I have a rule that I never discard any piece of mail, be it junk or otherwise, without first opening it. From one of the envelopes from a bank fell a check drawn on Cairo for the exact amount of our bill down to the last cent. There had been no interest added after all these years. Apparently according to the law of the Koran no interest is ever charged or paid. As we saw this check, and it was for a very large sum of money, we both looked at each other across our desk and started to laugh. After all these years that had passed we had almost forgotten the entire matter and had virtually given it up for lost.

We then decided that we would close our office and go to a restaurant for lunch and break a bottle of champagne. As I have already stated, the press had been filled with stories that when Farouk had been exiled he had taken away with him most of his valuable collections, together with a vast amount of liquor. This was, of course, quite untrue, as he never touched a drop; at least he did not while he was still on the throne. Proof of the false press reports was the auction sales. In the collections were included some fabulous pieces of Lalique and Gallé glass.

In the cellar under the Khoube Palace there existed what they called "Farouk's Pornographic Museum," and anybody who attended the auctions and spent a sizable amount of money was invited, if he wished to do so, to visit and view his museum. I then recalled at the time Colonel Gafar had asked me whether I would care to visit the museum, in which case he could take me down. I had told him that I would be interested in seeing the museum.

Descending a very long flight of stairs, we went to the palace cellar area. There, right across the room, was a series of high steel gates with soldiers standing at attention at each side. As we approached, these soldiers saluted the colonel and at once unlocked the gates so that we could enter.

What I saw there was to my mind a lot of arrant nonsense. There were several sheets torn from old copies of the French magazine *La Vie Parisienne*, which, in view of such magazines of *Playboy, Playgirl, Hustler, Oui*, and so many others, one might construe as suitable reading for little children. There were several sets of candelabra of nudes in bronze holding in their outstretched arms candles; they were such objects as one might see in the shop of any average interior decorator. There was one book opened at a page with the work "Fuck" printed in the text, and this word had been circled in red ink. Alongside this book was a printed card in English, French, German, Italian, and Arabic stating that this book opened at this page was taken from the bed table of the queen at the time that Farouk had gone into exile. The entire matter was utterly ridiculous.

Chapter 62

The Cairo Museum Tutankhamen Collection

Some few years ago some of the great finds from the tombs of Tutankhamen were placed on display at the Metropolitan Museum in New York City and at several other museum across America. I went to view these at the Metropolitan Museum and then realized how fortunate I had been to have visited the museum in Cairo when I was there to attend the Farouk auction sales. At that time the then director was kind enough to take me round and explain to me many of the finds in greatest detail.

On the day when I was there, the museum was almost empty. Today I understand it was usually so very crowded because of the tourist traffic that serious viewing was almost an impossibility. When there I saw the enormous rooms with their walls lined with sheets of gold and inscribed with what are known as writings from the *Book of the Dead*. These rooms are so vast and fantastic that they virtually beggar description.

While in the museum, I saw a contingent of soldiers being marched through the various galleries under the leadership of an officer. At the time it seemed to me that they were there to smoke as many cigarettes as they possibly could; they did not seem to be in the slightest interested in their great heritage.

Talking with one of the guardians who spoke some English, I asked him what the soldiers were doing there, and he replied, "Our government has inaugurated a policy that the army is to be indoctrinated in the great art of Egypt, and these men are here for this purpose."

It was to me an utter farce; in fact, it was one of the only things that I found in any way amusing during my entire stay in the country.

When I had spent sufficient time going through the various galleries, as I approached the exit the guard who had spoken to me in English about the soldiers accompanied me to the door. When we were just outside he turned to me.

"Did you, by any chance, notice the bushes outside when you came in?"

I told him that I supposed I had seen them, but I had not in any way taken notice of them particularly. I told him that as far as I was concerned, they were just bushes.

He then replied, "But no, you are quite wrong, because they are something quite unique and quite special." He then continued in almost a reverential tone of voice, "At the time that Lord Carnarvon and Mr. Carter were taking the fabulous things that you have just seen out of the Tutankhamen tomb, they found on opening one of the drawers in one of the cabinets a bag of seeds. As the tomb was perfectly dry, for some reason or other they planted some of these seeds outside in the museum grounds, and these bushes are the result of that planting. As far as is known there is no other vegetation anywhere in the world that is in any way comparable to this."

Whether what he told me is fact or fiction I have never yet been able to discover; it may well have been entirely a figment of his imagination. On the contrary, however, it may be fact.

Chapter 63

Leona

For several years, maybe five or six, after the finalization of my divorce decree I found myself living the life of a man-about-town. I was accepting all sorts of dates from all sides. Some of these engagements I enjoyed, some I detested, and some I accepted as just agreeable.

While I was attending a Sunday party at a country club on Long Island, a lady who was the widow of an old friend of mine asked me whether I would be her escort at another country club on the following Sunday. Remembering that as yet I had made no commitment for that particular day, I accepted, and then she said that we could spend the day together at the pool relaxing and swimming.

Thus the next Sunday, as arranged, I picked her up at her apartment and we drove out to the club; the day was obviously going to be very hot, and the thought of the pool was most enticing.

After we had spent several hours at poolside she suggested lunch, and after changing in her cabana into more acceptable clothes for the restaurant we were soon on our way to lunch. As we passed the bar I suggested a drink before eating, and she said that the idea was most appealing. So perched on our stools up at the bar we both ordered martinis, extra dry to be sure, as I have always had a particular fondness for this drink. With our drinks in our hands we began chatting about all manner of things, and the first martini led to a second and after that to a third.

Suddenly after the third and while my date was by now somewhat under the influence, she asked, "Do you like blind dates?"

I replied that I loved them because, I jokingly said, there is always a measure of challenge or possible intrigue. I also recall telling her that such dates reminded me a little of the stock market gambles, and she replied that in this she agreed with me.

"I asked you this question because I have a young lady friend of mine whom—I think you would find most interesting." She then continued sipping her martini. "You being in the art world and she being associated with graphic arts, should have much in common. You will be quite safe with her, as there is no question of marriage, since she is living apart from her husband, who lives in Little Rock, where she refuses to join him, and he has always refused to give her a divorce, and as far as I know, divorced or not, she will never go out to live with him there. If you would like to meet her I can give you her telephone number so that you can call her when you feel like it."

The following day, Monday, having nothing planned for that evening, I called the lady in question and spoke with her. Hearing my English accent, she later told me, she concluded that somebody was playing a joke on her. Nevertheless, as she was just on the point of leaving for a short vacation, she suggested that I might call her in a couple of weeks, when she would again be home. I replied that I would make a note in my diary. As I spoke I mentally suggested to myself that I would do this unless something more appealing might turn up. The next couple of weeks seemed to fly by, and then going through my engagement book I saw the entry that I had made so I called her. She told me that she had just returned home and suggested that I drop by her apartment at about seven that evening and have a drink with her. I accepted her invitation, but at the time there was no mention made of any date for dinner after the drink. After all, it was a blind date and we might have considered each other complete "dogs."

So promptly at seven I arrived at her apartment, and when I introduced myself I noticed that she appeared to be very nervous about something. I could not possibly have known that just on that same day she had broken up with a boyfriend.

We then sat in her living room and she asked me what I would care to drink and I told her that I would love a Scotch on the rocks. In her nervous state she filled a highball glass almost to the rim with Scotch and handed it to me. I could not tell whether this was done to get me drunk or because of her upset state.

Realizing at this point that my accent was indeed genuine enough, she became a little friendlier, and I mentally decided that it had not been her intention to get me drunk. As I had, only a few weeks prior to this meeting, returned from Cairo after the ending of the Farouk auctions, I commenced telling her something of my experiences out there in Egypt and she said that she was most fascinated with anything pertaining to that country.

After speaking for some short while she said that she was delighted that I had called her, and we then began to enjoy each other's company. At this point I suggested that she be my guest at dinner and she said that she would be delighted to accept.

I then suggested taking her to the old Barbary Room, and she told me that she loved that restaurant and that it was, in fact, one of her favorites in the entire city. When we arrived we were both greeted at the door by Carlos, the maître d'hôtel, who knew us both quite well but seemed quite surprised to see us together. She told me that she loved the twinkling lights set in the ceiling, and I told her that I was most partial to their very comfortable chairs.

At dinner, after I had exhausted the story of my stay in Cairo, I asked her in what way she was associated with the graphic arts and she told me that she was executive vice president of the Sterling Advertising Agency, at that time the most important in the field of fashion. It was her work at this agency that brought her into contact with the graphic arts.

During our conversation she told me how she had employed Andy Warhol to do some work for her to be used in some of her shoe advertisements, and she also told me that she had commissioned Salvador Dali to do an advertisement for the American Silk Association, one of her other accounts. After eating and drinking and talking, we suddenly realized that we were all alone in the restaurant, so calling for my check, I paid, and we left.

As it was a beautiful night, she suggested that we walk a little. This was in those wonderful days of long ago when one was quite safe walking the streets at night. We then walked and we talked until we arrived at the door of her apartment house where, it being two o'clock by then, I left her, saying that I would call her to make another date. She replied that she would be delighted if I did.

From the first moment that I set my eyes on her I was entirely smitten, and apparently she similarly enjoyed my company. So during the few weeks following this initial meeting we spent more and more time together.

At that time she had a very beautiful black maid in her employ who, she later told me, had said to her, "That man is for you; don't let him slip through your fingers."

Then after we had been seeing each other fairly frequently she called me on the telephone, saying, "The lady who introduced us has just called me on the telephone and she is most insistent that I visit with her and go to see a fortune-teller and she said that it is most important that I come."

Leona, for that was her name, told me that she replied that she did not wish to visit any fortune-tellers because she never believed them nor trusted them, but, she continued, "Our friend was so insistent that I agreed to join her." A couple of days later she went with the lady to visit the fortune-teller, and as we arranged to be together that same evening, she told me all about her visit, and she seemed to be very upset at what she had been told.

I asked her to tell me what the matter was and why she was so upset, and she said, "The fortune-teller told me that I was going out with a man whose initials are S.H. and that I must not see him again, and she also said that the man in question was in the art world. She then told things about myself that were quite true, and I got really scared. And now I don't understand how she could have been so positive about both of us and also that we were seeing each other so much."

The moment that she finished talking, I said to her, "Don't you realize what has happened? The lady who gave me your name was under the influence of the third martini and is a widow, and she is now heartily sorry that she introduced us, and she is also very jealous, as she herself would have liked to have a husband, but under the influence she had not realized what she might be doing to herself, so she got herself a fortune-teller and told her what to say to you and that is how she knew so much about us both and also that we were seeing so much of each other."

Leona, realizing that what I had told her was quite true, began to laugh, and we then went to dinner in a very jovial mood.

After this we continued seeing each other with ever increasing frequency until I proposed marriage. Leona then explained to me that she would be delighted to accept but that she was still married to her husband, who had refused to give her a divorce. She said that he had always said to her, "I live for the day when we can get together again and live as man and wife."

In conversation one day Leona had informed me that her husband was a high-ranking Freemason, and as I myself was similarly such a one, I told her that I would write him a letter as from Brother to Brother and that in my opinion he would be very hard pressed to refuse and that he would in all probability agree to divorce. Then returning to my apartment, I at once composed and wrote him a long letter. I sent it to the address that Leona had given me, and later that same week I received back a reply saying that he would not deny her the divorce that she so badly wanted.

The following day I showed his letter to Leona, and following on its heels, or so it seemed, she was on her way to Mexico to get her divorce and in a few days she was free to marry me.

To my utter regret I hadn't kept a carbon of the letter that I had written, as many of my friends, being in a similar state of matrimony, were offering me all sorts of enducements to let them see a carbon, but none did exist.

May I at this point say that it is now almost thirty years that have come and gone since the divorce and subsequent marriage and these years have given us both long years of intense happiness? To such an extent is this the case that the renowned columnist Liz Smith once wrote: "Sidney and Leona Hill are two people who give marriage a good name."

It was just prior to my first meeting with Leona that a friend had taken her to the shop of an antiquarian named Baron Waleski and that at the time had bought for her as a gift an eye of Horus charm, or *uchat*, as it is called, and the baron had told her, "This is going to bring you a lot of good luck." As I had been telling Leona all about my experiences in Egypt she felt quite positive that this Egyptian eye of Horus had been the catalyst that had brought us together. Leona then asked me whether I could perhaps find some more such ancient Egyptian *uchats,* and as it happened, I at the moment had a small collection of these and I told her that she could have them with the greatest of pleasure.

She at once gave one to her late sister Hortense, who had just at that moment been widowed and who proceeded as soon as she had received her "eye" to get herself married. Unfortunately, this marriage did not last very long and she was soon divorced.

Leona then gave another to a very dear friend of hers, Evelyn Pearson, who had been for many years an important client of her old agency. This lady was so intrigued with her *uchat* that she vowed that she would never take it out of her handbag. A few months later she similarly became engaged and married to a gentleman, as fine a person as it has ever been my privilege to know. This latter marriage lasted for the better part of a quarter of a century and ended with his passing a few years back. To this very day Evelyn never moves without her little amulet snug in her handbag.

When all is said and done, these happenings tend to suggest that perhaps the idea of the three-martini lunch is not such a bad one.

Chapter 64

Portrait of George Washington

People frequently do things for curious and sometimes very unusual reasons. And so it was that just as my brother and I were on the point of vacating our premises on East 57th Street to relocate on Fifth Avenue, in a much more commodious location, we received a telephone call from, by her voice, a very young lady.

"I read in the press that you are art dealers located on 57th Street at Fifth Avenue, and I am calling to inquire whether you might be interested in buying from me my porthole Portrait of George Washington?" she asked.

Were we interested? You bet we were.

She then proceeded to explain her reason for calling us. "I was born at my family's home on East 57th Street, precisely at number 1, and I lived in that house until it was pulled down and rebuilt for business purposes and where I see that you are presently located." She then continued after I told her that she was quite right that we were at number 1, "I have grown up with this portrait all of my life and have always admired looking at it, but unfortunately for me, I am now in the process of moving my residence to a much smaller apartment where it could never possibly be hung. The apartment is much too small for any such painting and I am simply heartbroken at the thought of parting with it, but I have to, so I felt that if you would buy it from me at least it would return to be on the site where it had always been for so many years. That in some sort of way would satisfy me."

She then gave me her name; she was a Miss Havemeyer and a daughter of one of New York's great families. I then arranged with her to have our truckers collect the portrait and bring it up to our galleries so that we could study it and then advise her all about it and how much we could pay her for it.

She told me that the portrait was still held in its original frame, which was quite large and heavy and very fragile, and she

338

Porthole Portrait of George Washington, 1795, by Rembrandt Peale (reprinted courtesy of the Butler Institute of American Art).

suggested that we ask our men to be very careful in handling it. I thanked her for telling me this, and all was arranged for the following day.

The so-named Porthole Portrait of George Washington is something that is quite special in the realms of American art, and it depicts the president in an oval reserve seemingly cut out of a surrounding brick wall and peering through it. The artist of this portrait was the great Rembrandt Peale, son of Charles Willson Peale, one of American art greats. It was Charles Willson Peale who painted the now famous portrait of George Washington from life, his son Rembrandt accompanying him while he did this portrait. While Charles was at work the young man made a series of sketches of the president, and which he later used to translate into this Porthole Portrait. It is perhaps interesting to note that George Washington was a very difficult sitter, as he detested the whole idea of having his portrait painted, but for the young Rembrandt this was an opportunity not to be missed. It is still as of today unrecorded actually how many replicas of the Porthole Portrait Rembrandt painted, but one thing is positive—he must have done a number of them. It is a pity that he did not keep any records of this.

In due course we had the portrait in our galleries, and as soon as it was unpacked we saw that it was about as superb an example as one could ever conceive. I was quite positive that it had never been touched by a conservator or cleaned since its painting or if, in fact, it had been cleaned, it must have been done at least a hundred years ago. To find a painting in such original state and apparently untouched is an art dealer's dream.

The portrait was held, as Miss Havemeyer had informed us, in a very massive gilt frame. When we saw it we realized it was in itself a tour de force. The entire surface was covered with attributes of a military nature. There were guns, swords, cannonballs, and cannons, all carried out in very high relief, and the entire frame was interwoven with flags.

As we moved the portrait around in our galleries, we soon realized that pieces of the frame would fall away at every move that we made with it, so we decided to reframe it in a more manageable manner. While we were having this new frame made we had the portrait cleaned by our conservator. The old-period frame was, however, not discarded but at our request was given to the Metropolitan Museum of New York by our conservator so that the museum could use it on a similar portrait that they owned. Today such Porthole Portraits are inordinately rare, and whenever any one appears on the market it is quickly competed for.

A short while after the portrait had been returned to us by our conservator and reframed, it looked simply magnificent, and this being the case, we advertised it for sale. At about this time we had placed an advertisement in the *New York Times* asking for offers of American paintings, and although we received several responses, there was nothing offered us that we wished to buy.

But one morning we received a letter from a gentleman who wrote: "While flying over the Swiss Alps I read in the *New York Times* about your wish to buy American art, and I write to inquire what you might have that you could offer us for our collection." The gentleman was Mr. Joseph Butler, the director of the famed Butler Institute of American Art in Youngstown, Ohio. We at once replied to him, telling him about this delightful portrait of George Washington.

As soon as he was back in Youngstown, with our letter in his hands, he telephoned us and told me that he wished to buy the portrait. I told him that we would be happy to ship it out to the institute so that they could see it before committing themselves to its acquisition.

Mr. Butler then replied, "If you tell me that it is so beautiful then I can buy it unseen."

To this day this Porthole Portrait hangs at this institute, where they have what is probably the greatest and finest collection of American art in America and where it is considered by them to be one of the crowning jewels in their collection.

Chapter 65

Epstein; Charles Dana Gibson

There are across the country many so-called antique shops, or should I say "shoppes," that do sell objects of all kinds, although in many of these establishments their merchandise could not in the true sense of the word come into the category of "antiques." Many of their objects on sale may be oldish or shopworn, but not to any connoisseur's minds antiques.

And so it was that while lunching at a small inn in Silvermine, Connecticut, one day I noticed that there was attached at the side of the restaurant an antiques shoppe. On that particular day I had been spending some time visiting at the Silvermine Art Gallery, where they had on display a bronze bust of George Bernard Shaw that had, at that time been recently acquired from our galleries and presented to it by a donor. This bust was a great example from the hands of the great Anglo-American sculptor Sir Jacop Epstein.

I then suggested to my wife, that after we had ended our lunch we would go into this shoppe and see what they might have on display that would possibly be of interest to me. From my experience I knew that one could never tell where something good might be lurking. Over the years we had known of many great rarities that had been discovered in some of the smallest antique shops, although not so often here in the States as in Europe.

When we entered this shoppe we saw there the usual collection of pieces of bric-a-brac and all sorts of ceramic items, things with broken handles, and much Victoriana of minor interest. There were china chamber pots, such as were used overnight and kept hidden under the bed, little china teapots, and other tea appurtenances and so forth.

Suddenly my eyes spotted a very attractive pile of green glass objects that seemed to be rather out of the ordinary. They had

Bust of George Bernard Shaw, by Sir Jacob Epstein.

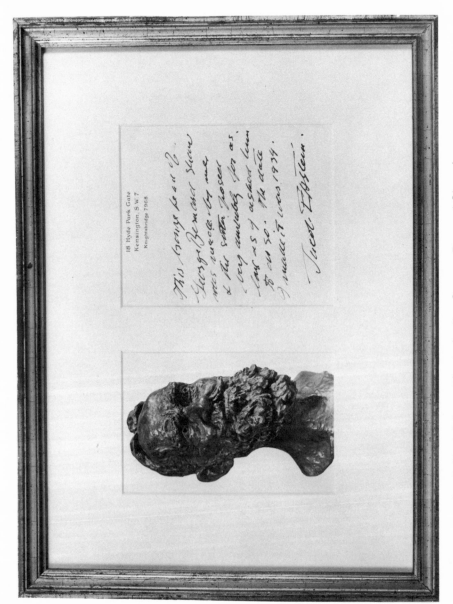

Jacob Epstein's certificate for the George Bernard Shaw bronze.

been placed on a side table in a sort of pyramid, and to their side had been placed a card reading in large type: *Exceptionally rare set of twelve royal salt cellars of the period of Louis XV of France.* This sign intrigued me, as when I looked closer I saw that they were a set of green glass coasters such as one puts under the legs of a full grand piano. Certainly they were not royal in any sense of the word, nor were they saltcellars, although French they may have been.

Being much amused at what I had seen written on the card, I called the young lady assistant over and inquired of her the cost that they were asking for the set, and she then replied, "We are asking twelve thousand dollars for them." She then went on to expatiate on their extreme beauty and also their unique rarity. When she had finished her spiel I thanked her and left. There was nothing else in the store that could be buyable for me. However, I have often pondered the thought as to whether the set had ever been sold to a collector and if so for how much.

Shortly after leaving the inn, I met an old friend of mine who was the son of the late Charles Dana Gibson, the great American illustrator of the late nineteenth and early twentieth century. While I was chatting with him he inquired whether we might be interested in handling the paintings and illustrations that had formed part of his late father's estate, which were at the time being held in a safe deposit room in the city, where they had been ever since his father's passing. We then discussed his father's work and I told him that I would be happy to go to see the things in storage together with my brother so that we could get some idea of what might be available. I arranged a mutually convenient date with him for the following day.

Meeting with him as arranged, we saw standing up against a wall in the storage room quite a number of original oil paintings together with a large pile of original pen and ink drawings that had been used for illustrations in various magazines for which Charles Dana Gibson had worked. The moment that we saw the items we knew that an exhibition of the works would be a great success, and the son then gave us a free hand to do whatever we felt best with regard to their disposition.

We arranged to have our truckers collect a large portion of the material and had all delivered to our galleries. After going through the pieces, we decided to commence with an exhibition of the oils. There were some thirty canvases in the group. Many of these paintings were of interiors that had been done up in Maine, where Gibson had lived, and in many of these there were portraits of some of the artist's friends and neighbors. He had loved doing this sort of thing. Several of these oils depicted what have today become known as "Gibson girls;" these had all been executed during the early twenties. As an artist, Gibson loved beauty in all of its forms, and it had been his custom to ask his daughter, at the time a student, of Bryn Mawr College, to invite as many of the prettiest girls there to come to his studio and have their portraits painted by him; he promised these girls that he would present them with their paintings when they were dry. Most of the girls invited accepted with alacrity and in due course received their portraits.

However, when going through the storage we saw a number of these "girl" paintings standing unframed against a wall. Obviously they had not been given the girls for one reason or other. Glancing at the backs of these canvases, as most art dealers do so frequently, I did notice that some were inscribed in pencil on the back of the stretchers. I must say that I noticed these with blind eyes.

As soon as we had decided upon the exhibition, we began to hang the paintings and at the same time arranged for some advertisements, particularly in the *Magazine Antiques,* where we had been advertising for practically half a century.

A few weeks after this issue of the magazine appeared, we received a telephone call from a gentleman living out on the West Coast. The gentleman told me, "I have just received my copy of *Magazine Antiques* and see that you are announcing a forthcoming exhibition of the works of Charles Dana Gibson, and I have to tell you that when my wife was an alumna at Bryn Mawr she was painted by the artist, who promised her the canvas after completion, but so far she has never received it and I am wondering whether by an chance you may have seen it in his storage."

I then asked him what his wife's maiden name was and said that next time we were in the storage we would look and see whether a portrait with her name written on the back might be there. While speaking with the gentleman I seemed to recall that this name was one on the back of one of the portraits. I did not tell the gentleman this, as I did not wish to disappoint him in the event that I was in error.

Next week I was again at the storage and there, sure enough, was the lady's portrait, and a very beautiful one it was; the lady must have been a ravishing beauty as a girl. As soon as I returned to our galleries I called the gentleman and told him that we had the portrait available for him. He replied that he was delighted and wanted to know how much he would have to pay for it, and I told him that I would have to ask the estate.

When I told Mr. Gibson's son about this, he told me that he knew quite well that his father had promised to give these portraits to the girls and would not allow the gentleman to pay a single penny for it and he asked that we ship the portrait out to the West all expenses paid, on his behalf. He told me, "In doing this I know that I will be carrying out my father's wishes."

Next day the portrait was duly shipped to the gentleman, and a week or so later we received a letter from the gentleman stating that he had received the "lovely painting" and that it would now hang in their dining room as its central feature and that after his death it would go to one of his children and remain a family treasure. Actually, painting in oils was the artist's hobby, as he loved doing this more than the illustrative work upon which he was always employed. But as he was so involved with his pen and inks for the *Saturday Evening Post* and several other magazines, he had little time to devote to them, except when he was vacationing with his family up at his home on Seven Hundred Acre Mountain in Maine. It was here that he had built for himself an atelier studio especially suited for this purpose.

Here at his home he was surrounded by masses of colorfully beautiful flowers, and it was for just this reason that he incorporated many floral subjects into his canvases. In his interiors he frequently incorporated old-fashioned washing machines, sewing machines, telephones, heating stoves, and such, and in so doing he created what we today term *Americana* in the true sense of the word. Gibson was a notoriously bad speller, and he frequently liked to paint titles into some of his subject matter; this proved to be very amusing, as in one instance he painted "Inseperable" for "Inseparable" on a canvas. This bad spelling was not in its way too important, but in retrospect it does add a modicum of charm to some of his works.

Among the other paintings there were several incorporating tabletops with flowers, some very much in the manner of the great French Impressionists of their period, some in the manner of the great Bonnard.

While I was discussing this aspect of Gibson's works one day with his son, he told me that he would tell me an interesting story concerning those with the tabletops with vases of flowers. "My mother loved flowers and was forever chiding my father that he never thought to bring home for her some flowers, as some other people's husbands do. After receiving this complaint one day, my father left the family room and went straight to his studio and proceeded to paint two large canvasses of tabletops with vases filled to the brim with large peonies. He painted very rapidly and as soon as these were finished he returned to the house with both of these two paintings, one in each hand, and said to my mother, 'Be careful not to touch these yet, as they are quite wet.' And he then continued speaking, saying, 'I hope that you are now satisfied. Other men bring home flowers to their wives that die very soon, but these that I am giving you will last forever.' "

Our exhibition was a great success and was a virtual sellout. So successful, in fact, was the exhibition that we at once began to prepare for a follow-up show of illustrations, some of which were in colored wash. Here again, as soon as our exhibition was announced we were literally inundated with callers wanting to view and acquire the Gibson illustrations. Especially did we receive many art directors from the many advertising agencies that abound on Madison Avenue, who came in droves, many of them missing their lunches to view the works of this great master. Many of these men actually went down on their knees the better to study the master's pen and ink strokes. It seemed as though they were bowing to that great master of American illustration.

To this day there is a constant call for any of this master's works, mostly for any that incorporate the "Gibson girl" with her upswept hairdo. These latter are great favorites with people in the fashion business.

It was during this second exhibition that there occurred one episode that was most pathetic. During the show a very dirty

"Flowers on a Table," by Charles Dana Gibson.

and scrofulous-looking elderly man came up to view the things. Though he was very poorly dressed, by his bearing he appeared to have seen better days. He was, as a matter of fact, quite smelly, and for this reason we would have been very happy to see him leave. He was certainly no ornament. But smelly or not, he was just as entitled as the next man to view the exhibit and to spend as much time there as he wished.

After he had been in the galleries for some little time, he came over to speak with me and told me that he had known Charles Dana Gibson many years before and when he himself had been entirely wiped out during the stock market crash of '29. Just as he had finished speaking with me, I was called away by an assistant to speak with another gentleman, and while in conversation with this other client I was again called away to speak with another gentleman.

This latter gentleman stood waiting for me to come over to him, and I noticed that he was most elegantly attired and polished to a degree that one does not often see these days. I knew this gentleman by sight as the president of one of our great banking institutions, and I recalled that I had seen his portrait that had been painted by Gibson some many years before.

Just as soon as I had finished speaking with my first gentleman, I went straight over to speak with the banker, and when I arrived he was just about to speak with me about some matter of business when the first man, the dirty one, looked over at us and, visibly trembling, darted across the gallery and, flinging his arms around the banker's neck with all his might, said, "How wonderful to see you again after all these years, and looking at the works of our old mutual friend, Charles Dana Gibson."

The banker was not at all pleased and quickly disentangled himself and agreed that it was nice seeing him again and then, as quickly as he could, left the gallery, saying that he had a very important meeting to attend and could not be late.

What it was the banker wanted to see us about I never discovered; suffice it to say that he never returned to our galleries.

Chapter 66

White House Restoration

It was shortly after the inauguration of John F. Kennedy as president of the United States that, at the instigation of Jacqueline Kennedy, it was proposed that the White House be entirely refurbished with paintings and other furnishings that would as nearly as possible correspond with those at the White House at the time of its founding, with special emphasis on the middle of the nineteenth century. It was under the aegis of Clement Conger that a committee was formed especially for this purpose.

Clement Conger was a very fine and knowledgeable gentleman and ideally suited for this purpose, as he had been for many years associated with American arts and antiquities and had been instrumental in the furnishing of Blair House in the nation's capital, where visiting notables and dignitaries are usually put up during their visits.

It was rightly held by the committee that practically every nation, be it large or small, has its royal palace or presidential mansion, which in most cases are furnished with paintings and other attributes commensurate with the building's importance as national shrines. In this regard the White House was in the opinion of the committee one of the only great houses of a nation of the world where this did not apply. The committee under Conger's sponsorship comprised a small group of ladies and gentlemen, all of whom were well versed in various aspects of history and Americana. At one of their first meetings their first thoughts were in the acquisition of suitable paintings, sculpture, and furniture that they considered would reflect their period.

The late Mr. Forsberg, himself a superb painter, was one of the principal members of the committee, and he was placed in charge of the purchase of the several American oil paintings of the midnineteenth century. In a conversation including his wife, Mrs. Forsberg, herself a member of the committee and a great connoisseur of art, the committee decided to call at our galleries to outline to us the project.

Mrs. Forsberg had been known to us for many years and was aware of our interest in this particular period of American art. She knew from her experience with us that we would be able to comply with the requirements of the committee.

Following his wife's advice, the next day found Mr. Forsberg at our galleries, when he explained to us in precise detail what was required and stated that they had decided that as a starter they wished to have two specific canvases. One was to be a still life with fruits and wine by the German-American artist Severin Roesen. It was this artist who had specialized in the type of paintings known as "Nature's Bounty," in which he incorporated table-tops piled high with fruit, including many varieties of grapes. Some of these compositions incorporated fruit piled on two tiers, one on top of the other; also frequently there was also a tall glass of white wine, and sometimes this was accompanied by a bottle.

We told Mr. Forsberg that we were acquainted with this type of canvas very well indeed, particularly as over the years we had been supplying such to the Stouffer Restaurants. However, just at that moment we did not have one that would be suitable, but we promised him that as soon as we were offered one we would buy it and make him the first offer for their consideration.

The second painting on their list was to be a landscape of the so-called Hudson Valley School. It was held that this type of canvas, perhaps more than any other, personified the Eastern American landscape. Here again we told Mr. Forsberg that we had nothing of suitable quality that we could suggest, but similarly we told him that we were quite sure that something would come in in very short order and we again promised that as soon as we had what we considered suitable we would advise him. He then left.

By one of those curious quirks that do sometimes occur, he had not been gone from the galleries for more than maybe an hour when a runner came up to see us with several photographs of paintings suitable for sale, and in their number were two canvases that answered Mr. Forsberg's requirements in every possible detail. We at once purchased these paintings, unseen, on the basis of these photographs, despite the fact that these can often be terrible liars. Nevertheless, in this case it turned out we were justified, as when the paintings were delivered to us we saw that they were both superb.

Not only was the Severin Roesen signed; it was also dated 1850, precisely the date called for.

The moment that we had these we telephoned Mr. Forsberg and told him what had occurred and he arranged to be in to see them in a couple of days. From what we told him he asked that they be reserved for him until he arrived. He said that he was as excited as were we. A couple of days later he was in again and was delighted with what we showed him, as he stated they were precisely what the committee had in mind. He then said that he would report his findings to the other members of the committee and would advise us shortly. He again requested that we hold the paintings for the time being. He then explained that the White House had a rule that nothing could be accepted for inclusion there until it had been formally seen by the president and accepted by him; Mr. Forsberg also stated that this was a mere formality. Next day Mr. Forsberg called advising us that they wished the two canvases sent down to Washington, and they also said that they would send the White House truck to collect them for us. The White House had a small white truck that they used for all such purposes. As soon as the paintings arrived in Washington they were taken to the White House, where they were hung so that they could be inspected by the other committee members, who were very pleased with what they saw. It was then arranged that they would be acquired for the national collection in due course.

A few months then passed, and we received another call from Mr. Forsberg, who said that the Saltinstall Foundation of Boston was desirous of presenting to the White House a painting that pertained to the city of Boston by an American artist of the mid-nineteenth century, and he inquired whether we either had or knew of such a canvas. It so happened that we had quite recently purchased together with another dealer friend a canvas that answered this request in all details. It was a painting by the great American artist of the period, Fitzhugh Lane, and depicted Boston harbor, with much shipping offshore and also much activity along the shore itself.

We told Mr. Forsberg of this painting, and next day he asked that it be sent down to Washington for hanging so that it could be viewed by the president together with the first two paintings before the actual acquisitions were made. Both Mr. and Mrs. Kennedy then saw the paintings hanging and expressed their pleasure at what the canvases represented. Sad to relate, very soon after the viewing they left the White House for Dallas, where, on that fateful journey, the president was assassinated.

Thus we had the privilege of being associated with the acquisition of both the first and the last paintings acquired by the White House during the Kennedy administration. The Alpha and the Omega!

In the interim there was also a painting owned by a friend of ours titled *An American Beauty Rose,* also by another eminent artist of the period, Martin J. Heade, a specialist in paintings of flowers, especially roses. We suggested to the owner that this American canvas would be a magnificent addition to the White House collection, especially as we already had a First Lady resident there known as an "American beauty." Our friend at once agreed to our suggestion, and we made the presentation on his behalf.

When we proposed this painting to the committee all were very pleased to accept and it was at once hung in the White House. We were not at the time able to discover where it was placed, but have always presumed that it hung in the private apartments. It is highly probable that it still hangs where it had been placed, and when next at the White House, I hope to see it again hanging there in situ.

Chapter 67

Chinnery

Some few years ago my brother Henry and I became especially interested in the paintings of the various ports on the China coast, with special emphasis on the so-called Treaty Ports of Canton, Whampoa, Macoa, and Hong Kong. It was at these Treaty Ports, notably the one at Canton, that the British, American, Scandinavian, Portuguese, and later French merchants were wont to foregather to work and trade under their respective flags, which were flown over their buildings, which were known as the "Hongs."

These paintings were being eagerly sought by merchants and collectors alike, with special demand always for those depicting Canton with its Hongs during the eighteen-thirties and the early eighteen-forties.

We were particularly drawn to this subject because our old records showed that during the eighteen-hundreds Lord Macartney, who had been appointed by King George III to be his ambassador to the court of the Chinese emperor Kien Loung, on his first trip there had carried with him many gifts of great beauty for presentation to the emperor and some of these had been created for him by the early forebears of our firm, Frederick Berry of London.

Records exist that show that this embassy was unsuccessful, as Chinese protocol demanded that Lord Macartney would be required to kowtow to the emperor, which he emphatically refused to do.

These international Hongs at Canton where the merchants were located were situated on a very narrow strip of land along the shore; they were not permitted to penetrate any farther inland. Naturally, life for these men became utterly boring and tedious and they had virtually nothing to occupy their leisure hours after their day's work had ended.

Beyond this, they were never allowed to have their wives or girls out with them on the coast, nor were these womenfolk ever allowed to even visit with them there. According to the Chinese philosophy, China had all the women that they needed already, and it was also similarly their philosophy that nothing good ever came to them from the sea.

There was one English artist named George Chinnery who, after running away from India, where he had accumulated an enormous amount of debts, had established himself in an atelier in Canton, and it was to this studio that many of the merchants and bankers working there came to sit to have their "likenesses" painted. It may be assumed that many of these paintings were executed for these men as an escape from their intense boredom.

Chinnery, whose name, incidentally, had nothing whatsoever to do with the fact that he worked in China, had several assistants working for him. The chief of these was a man named Lam Qua, who later established his own atelier in competition with the master. The name "Qua" is the equivalent of our "Mr." It was this Lam Qua together with his assistants who also painted many of the coastal scenes with their buildings depicted with their flags waving in the breeze.

It may also be assumed that many of the sitters purchased these paintings to send home to their families in their respective native countries to show where they worked.

Having dealt with these China coast paintings and portraits for many years and having built up many important collections of them for some of our clients, we decided, at the request of many of them, to write an illustrated volume on the subject of the artist Chinnery and his works.

We did this and the day that the book made its appearance it was an immediate sellout, and we were then prompted to commence a further work. As these two works were published in limited editions, they were both very soon acquired by museum and art libraries and by various universities, where in many cases they were placed on their rare-book shelves.

Over the past years there has been a constant demand from collectors for these books, whether new or secondhand, and today they are so rare that they are in many cases rarer than the paintings that they describe and illustrate.

These volumes naturally had to be considered labors of love, as the time and effort that went into their writing could never be covered by the royalties that derived from their sale.

356

It was during the research that we had made into the life and works of George Chinnery while he was in India that we discovered that he had been appointed painter to the rajah of Oudh, one of India's princely states. We also discovered that the artist had painted many important portraits of local British and Hindu celebrities of the day and that he had also painted many portraits of other rajahs and their ranis.

However, during our research we discovered that Chinnery had executed one very important full-length portrait of a judge of the High Court sitting at Delhi, and we thought that if at all possible we would endeavor to find out where this portrait might be, if in fact it still existed. We felt that it would make an admirable addition to our group of photographic material.

But where does one search for the proverbial needle in a haystack? Obviously we felt that the place would be India, and so with this in mind we wrote to the commercial counselor at the American embassy in New Delhi and outlined our problem to him. At the same time we told him something about the work that we were doing, which was at the time almost ready for the printing press.

Upon receipt of our letter he at once replied to say how interested he was to read about our project and that he had spoken with the editor of the local newspaper and outlined to him the purpose of our work and asked him for his advice.

He then wrote us that the editor had suggested that we write him a letter addressed at the newspaper and marked "For Publication." He said that everybody in New Delhi of any importance read his paper and that in his opinion we might obtain from this source some interesting leads to the painting.

When we received this reply I recall speaking with my brother and telling him that in my opinion we were about to waste the cost of a postage stamp. Nevertheless, we did write a suitable letter and mailed it.

Several months then passed and one day we received a letter from a gentleman in New Delhi; at the time we had almost forgotten all about the portrait. In this letter the gentleman wrote that he had seen our letter in the local newspaper and that he knew the portrait very well indeed. He wrote that he had been a very high officer of the court for over forty years and had sat facing the portrait over all those years. He wrote that not only was it a very highly colored painting of the judge, it was, as far as he knew, still hanging in situ. He then went on to say that it depicted the judge seated in his ceremonial robes and was indeed very beautiful. He also wrote that if we wished him to do so, he would consult with the powers that be and inquire whether they would be willing to have photographs in color taken for illustration in the book.

We at once replied to him to say how happy we were to hear from him and also how grateful we would be for his assistance in obtaining good color photographs for us.

In due time we did receive a superb set of color photos, from which we were able to select one eminently suitable for our purpose.

As soon as we received these photographs we wrote and thanked the authorities for their cooperation, and they replied that they had done the work with their compliments and with great pleasure.

Curious coincidences seem to occur with irregular regularity in the art business, as I suppose they often do in other fields of endeavor. Later that same month we saw mentioned in an auction catalog that a portrait of a China Coast merchant, actually signed by George Chinnery, was to be offered for sale. We at once made a note in our diary to attend this auction and buy the painting. We were particularly interested because the artist very rarely signed any of his works. It so happened that just on the day of this auction we were particularly busy and missed going to the sale and making the purchase.

When later that day we realized that we had missed the auction, we at once telephoned the auction house and asked them to tell us the name of the buyer. When items are sold privately the auction houses will not disclose the names of any buyers, but in this instance the buyer was a dealer in Connecticut and they did have his address, which they gave us. We at once telephoned to offer the dealer a profit on his purchase, but there was no reply on the phone. We then continued calling his number over several days, but always without receiving any response.

This being the case, we wrote him, but still we received no reply to our letter. Thus regretfully we had to abandon our attempt to purchase the painting from him.

Now it had been our custom, as it is with most dealers, to send consignments of paintings to be offered for sale at auction when such paintings were not considered of sufficient importance for them to be held in their collections. Thus about six months after this incident we sent a dozen paintings to the auction house for sale, and in due course we received from them a catalog in which our paintings were listed, and each of these was annotated at the side with a check mark, and there sandwiched in the center of our group was the Chinnery portrait that we had missed. The dealer who had made the purchase had passed away almost immediately after he had made the purchase, and it was then being reoffered for sale by his estate. It was as though the finger of fate were pointing out to us that the portrait was available. This time we were present and bought the painting, and today it is included in one of the greatest collections of China coast paintings.

Chapter 68

Uriah Phillips Levy

It was back in the fifties that my brother Henry and I had collaborated to author a volume on the subject of antique gold boxes; at that time this was the only work that had ever been published on this particular subject. Because of this fact it proved an instant success, and the limited edition was sold out within a very few weeks. At the time of its publication copies were purchased by many museums for their library collections on applied art, and it was similarly sold to many collectors.

Actually, the book had a readership that penetrated the four quarters of the globe and was at that time considered "Bible" on the subject. After the book was published, whenever the origin of an antique gold box was in question, our book was invariably used as the obvious source for information.

One morning we received a telephone call from a gentleman who said that he would like to come up to our offices to discuss a box with us, and we arranged a mutually convenient appointment.

Next day, when seated at my desk he outlined the reason for his visit. He told us that he had just arrived from San Francisco, where he had inquired of the museum there for information about a gold box that he had and he was advised by the director that we were the only people who would be able to advise him on such an object. While he spoke he placed the gold box in question on the desk and proceeded to explain that it had been inherited by four sisters, two of whom were very wealthy and two of whom were in quite humble circumstances. The two wealthy ladies wished to retain the box, but the other two insisted that they needed the cash urgently and wished it sold. As I opened the box I saw that it had a very important-looking inscription on the inside of the lid, and I was at once taken aback by what I read. The inscription stated that the box had been presented to Uriah Phillips Levy, commandant of the U.S. fleet in the Mediterranean, by the city of New York during the early eighteen-forties

After I had seen this inscription, I handed the box to my brother Henry and asked him to read the inscription, after which he became as excited as I had been. We felt that such an object belonged in the great collection of Hebraica at the Jewish Museum in New York on two counts: first, because of its historical association, and second, because it had been made by a goldsmith in New York and this of itself was quite a rarity. As a matter of interest, there had been very few gold boxes ever made in America during either the eighteenth or nineteenth century, the concept existing quite erroneously that it was only in Europe, in France, England, or Germany, that any such fine boxes could be made, despite the fact that there were quite a few consummate craftsmen over here in the States capable of making the finest of such items. In this regard it is perhaps interesting to mention that when a gold snuff box was required for presentation to our first president, George Washington, such a one was imported especially from Paris for the purpose.

As neither of us had ever heard of Uriah Phillips Levy, so very obviously a Jew and, as a Jew, to our minds, an almost impossibility as a commandant in the U.S. fleet, we were astonished. Yet here it was in front of us. Naturally we knew of the traditional anti-Semitism in the world's navies, with the only exception today that of Israel.

We told the gentleman that we wanted to buy the box from him, and we explained to him that if the two wealthy sisters would agree to a sale to us, we would undertake that it would never be resold unless for presentation to the Jewish Museum.

The gentleman then telephone the ladies in San Francisco and explained our proposition to them, and upon hearing that we were prepared to guarantee that the box would never be sold away from the museum, they agreed to allow him to make the sale.

At the gentleman's request we then drew four checks, one to each of the sisters, so that there would be no question that one or other of them might be receiving more than the others.

As soon as the box was in our possession we decided to research the life of Uriah Phillips Levy and then discovered that his family had come to Philadelphia during the late eighteen-hundreds from Tortola, where they had been established for very many years. The fact that the family must have been very wealthy can readily be judged by the fact that Uriah's parents had left America and gone to Europe, where they had planned to make a grand tour. When they left we discovered that they carried with them letters of introduction to many people in high places.

So much was this the case that they were invited when in England to attend a soiree given by the Prince Regent, who later became King George IV. Mrs. Levy must have been a lady of great beauty and charm, as she was singled out at this soiree by the prince, who declared her to be "an American beauty." Whether or not this name was the forerunner of the "American Beauty rose" must ever remain, as far as I am concerned, a moot point.

When the young Uriah was a boy of thirteen, presumably not wishing to go through the traditional bar mitzvah ceremony, ran away to sea, signing on as a cabin boy on one of the innumerable ships then in port in Philadelphia.

After he had been in this position for some short time, proving himself an able seaman, he took service in the U.S. Navy, later to find himself in the Mediterranean during the War of 1812. It was during this service that Uriah was promoted to the high rank of Commandant, much to the disgust and chagrin of his fellow officers. It may reasonably be assumed that he was promoted to this high rank through the influences of President Monroe, who had been and was at the time a great friend of Uriah's family. The records that we unearthed disclosed that his fellow officers trumped up many charges leveled against him, most of which were quite ridiculous and for which he was court-martialed no fewer than seven times. At every one of these trials Uriah was entirely exonerated and always at the behest of President Monroe.

Uriah had one idol, and that was Thomas Jefferson, whom he literally worshiped. To such an extent was this the case that he decided to buy the Jefferson estate of Monticello and at his death bequeath it to the "People of the United States."

After he had made this purchase, he commissioned the renowned sculptor David to create two statues of Jefferson, and upon their completion Uriah had presented one to the city of Angers in France, the native town of the artist, and the other to the city of New York. It was because of this presentation of the statue to the city that the gold box had been presented to him.

362

Uriah had never married, but when quite advanced in age he married his niece, a very young and pretty girl, presumably so that she could inherit his wealth.

Until this marriage Uriah had remained a seaman all through his life. After his passing, when his will was in the process of probate, an uncle, seeing that the Jefferson estate had been bequeathed to the "People of the United States," protested the will, declaring that there was no cohesive whole such as the "People of the United States."

Thus when the matter came before the judge, the court held in his favor and the estate was turned over to the uncle.

However, in the fullness of time the uncle passed away and the estate was purchased by the U.S. government, and so Uriah's desire that the estate belong to the People of the United States was fulfilled.

As we had promised to do, we refused all offers to sell the box until one day it was acquired by a Mr. Katz of Pittsburgh, who, as a most generous gesture, did present it to the Jewish Museum, where it was held as one of their crowning glories.

While writing this story I have been informed by the curator at the museum that this gold box together with several other important memorabilia, all of gold, had been stolen from their collection. Since this box and the other pieces were of gold, it may be assumed that they were melted down by the vandals for the value of their gold content. As far as the Jewish Museum is concerned, this was a tragedy of the greatest importance, as it is highly doubtful whether another such gold box with such impressive Jewish interest exists anywhere.

Chapter 69
Sacha Gack and His Chagall

Leona and I counted among our dearest friends a small coterie of Russians living in New York, including Marjorie and Heinz Metz. Of this small group we were particularly friendly with Jacobo and Georgette Eisenberg; she is today perhaps better known as Georgette Klinger, famed international cosmetician. Jacobo was known by his Spanish name, as after leaving his native Russia shortly after the Revolution he settled in Caracas, Venezuela, after which becoming more Spanish than Russian. Then after his marriage to Georgette he spent his days virtually commuting between South America and New York.

For many years we were very frequent guests at each other's homes, and while at their home Leona and I often met another émigré from Russia named Sacha Gack, who similarly had left Russia at about the same time as had Jacobo; they had been great friends from their earliest days in Russia.

Sacha had been a member of the Russian Intelligence Corps during the First World War, and because of this he had managed to leave Russia, carrying away with him his small collection of paintings, some of which were, although quite small, in their way very fine.

Sacha always enjoyed telling stories of his life and experiences in Russia with particular emphasis on his work as a Russian intelligence agent, and in the course of one of these chats he mentioned that he was very friendly with Marc Chagall, with whom he had gone to school; both of them had lived in Vitebsk.

One day while visiting with Sasha and his wife at their apartment, I was interested to see some of his small collection round his walls, of which he was quite proud. While looking at these various canvases I noticed a very fine landscape in purest academic style, signed by Marc Chagall in Russian characters. Never before having seen, nor for that matter ever having heard of

364

Chagall painting in this vein, I was much impressed by it and remarked to Sacha that in my opinion it was a most interesting adjunct to the entire Marc Chagall story. I was naturally quite familiar with Chagall's oeuvre in his distinctive "fauve" manner, with his little men wearing green hats and other amusing features, such as lying on tree branches in mauve trees and other similar poses. I had in my mind's eye those two fabulous masterpieces that flank the entrance to New York's Metropolitan Opera House at Lincoln Center.

I then asked Sacha how he came to have this little Chagall gem, and he replied, "If you like I will tell you a little story about it." I told him that I would love to hear his story, and this is what he told me.

"When I was a little boy, maybe five or six years of age, I lived with my parents in Vitebsk and there went to the local school. Among the other pupils was a boy of similar age named Marc Chagall, and we became fast friends. We often went for long walks together and, as we lived quite close to each other, were frequently in each other's homes.

"Even at this young age I loved looking at paintings, and one afternoon while at Marc's house I saw this landscape hanging up on a wall in their living room. I suppose that I must have been quite impressed by it, because I recall asking him to tell me something about it, and he then replied to me, 'My teacher at school has seen some of my sketches and has suggested to me that when I grow up I should consider become a professional artist,' and I remember answering him and telling him that I thought that he would make a very fine artist, but that for myself I wanted to go into business when I grew up.

"Seeing that I liked the landscape, Marc said to me, 'Sacha, please take it home with you as a little gift,' and taking it home with me, I hung it in my bedroom together with several other small paintings that my mother had given me, and I also told Marc that I would always treasure it."

In further conversation my friend said, "I don't ever want to sell it, but in the event that I did, what do you think it might be worth?"

I told him that I had no idea, as I had never seen any other work of Chagall in this vein, neither had I ever seen such a one recorded anywhere, but that the best way to find out would be to offer it at auction, where everybody interested in Chagall would be bound to see it and I was sure that a collector would want to buy it. On this note I left his apartment.

Some two years or so then passed, and Sacha became very sick and took to his bed, from which he never again rose. He passed away, and this painting, together with his other things, remained as part of his estate.

After his death his estate was in the process of probate, and his wife telephoned me one morning and asked me about the value of their Chagall painting. As I had previously told Sacha, I suggested to her that she consign it to Parke-Bernet Galleries and have it offered at auction and that as a result of this auction it would be sold at its value. She then thanked me for my advice and said that she thought that she would do as I suggested. However, not heeding my advise, she wrote a letter directly to Marc Chagall at his home in Paris, told him about the landscape that he had given to her husband, and asked him what he thought that it might fetch in today's market. Upon receipt of this letter Marc passed it over to his wife, who replied saying that my friend should ship the painting over to Paris out of its frame for Marc to study and that after examination he would be able to give her a suitable reply.

Then unbeknown to me she at once had the painting taken out of its frame and mailed it off to Paris.

She did not have very long to wait for her reply, and almost within days she received it back with "Ce n'est pas de moi" (This is not my work) written across its back in indelible ink.

She then called me again and told me what had happened, and then I explained to the lady that I considered that in its present state it would be quite worthless, as under no circumstances would anybody now accept it as a genuine Chagall, despite any story that she might tell about how she got it originally.

Little did the lady know that it is not at all uncommon for any artist to disavow some of his very early work. Particularly would this be the case when the work differed so radically from his recognized work. Here then was a classic example, as I am positive that the story that Sacha told was true in every degree.

Chapter 70

The Terre Haute Museum

I received a telephone call one morning from Dr. Howard Wooden, one of the great exponents of American art and, at the time, director of the Museum of Fine Arts in Terre Haute, Indiana. He told me that he was calling me at the request of Mary Hulman to ask whether I would be the keynote speaker at a supper that she was in the process of arranging at the museum to raise funds for the new gallery that they were at that moment proposing to erect. Mary was the wife of Tony Hulman, the owner and director of the famed Indianapolis 500. Together they virtually owned the entire town of Terre Haute.

It was proposed that this new gallery become part of the University of Indiana, whose campus was very close to the present location of their gallery. Both of the Hulmans were very art-conscious, and for this reason they were both of them most anxious, or so it appears on the surface, that the function be as rewarding as possible in regard to raising funds.

I told the doctor that I was most flattered that Mary Hulman should have chosen me to be this speaker, but that just at that moment I was preparing to go to Europe. But that I would go through my schedule very carefully to see whether I could manage to be there for the date that they suggested. He thanked me and said that he would await hearing further from me. Later that afternoon I called the doctor and told him that I would rearrange matters and that I would be available for the date mentioned by Mary. In discussion with Dr. Wooden I told him that in my opinion the Hulmans together with the museum owned a collection of some very fine canvases that were almost lost to sight in their present location and that the new gallery would be a very important asset for the town and also for the university.

It was then arranged that I would fly out to Terre Haute accompanied by my wife, Leona, and he said that we would be received at the airport by a lady who—they had put in charge of public relations.

On the day arranged we duly arrived and were greeted by the young lady, who told me that on the way to our hotel we would be stopping off at the local television station, where I was to be interviewed. She then said she was sure I would not mind her having arranged for this. I replied that I was happy to do anything that I could to further assist the museum. We then shortly after this conversation arrived at the television station, and I was then informed that a special broadcast had been planned for my interview at six o'clock that same evening to coincide with the supper that they had arranged at the museum.

At the station I was asked to sit and await the arrival of the interviewer, but after being seated for a short while I was taken into another room and seated with a microphone and asked to "talk." It appeared that the interviewer had not arrived. I was quite dumbfounded and being so unprepared for this did not, in truth, quite know what I was supposed to talk about.

But speak I did, and to this day I have no idea what I said. I do recall giving some background of our own gallery in New York City and also stating that this was the reason that I had been chosen as the keynote speaker at the supper that evening.

After I had ended my broadcast, I told Leona that as we were not expected at the museum before six-thirty we would be able to listen to the six o'clock news and find out what I had spoken about. However, just before six o'clock the lady arrived at our hotel and told me that the arrangement had been changed and that we were expected at the museum in a few minutes, so I never got to hear my broadcast. Upon our arrival at the museum all members of the committee were there awaiting my arrival and everyone asked me to take a cocktail with them. They all had their drinks, but not I, as from previous experience I knew that one drink leads to another and I had to remain absolutely sober if I was to make a speech.

I must say that all at the Museum were most cordial and did all in their power to make our stay agreeable. They could not have been nicer to us.

After this reception ended, we were all ushered into a large dining room where the supper was to be served and where I was asked to sit up on the dais next to Mary Hulman, with Dr. Wooden at my right. There were tables set up all over the floor, and some three hundred guests, all of whom had paid for their invitations, were seated at them.

Leona was seated at a large table set just in front of the raised dais, and I was able to look down on her from my elevated position. I saw that she had been seated next to Tony Hulman, who was to be her supper companion. Tony had ever been a very large supporter of the museum.

All went like clockwork and after the supper had ended the doctor rose and introduced me as the speaker. During the supper I had refrained from taking even one glass of wine, for the same reason that I had refrained from taking any cocktails. I was afraid that if I imbibed I might be a little too garrulous. I had been asked to speak for some ten minutes, but when I get started on a subject that is very dear to my heart, and here I refer to American art, specifically of the eighteenth and nineteenth centuries, I can go on for hours.

After I had been speaking for quite some time, certainly much beyond my allotted ten minutes, I was getting ready to end my speech, but seeing that the audience was apparently enjoying my words, I continued on a little longer.

Now Tony Hulman, who was seated next to my wife, was much more interested in the prospect of a date that he had arranged for that evening than in what I was talking about. He whispered into her ear, "If you can tell that fella to shut up and stop talking so that I can get up and leave, I will add another fifty thousand dollars to my already substantial gift."

Leona for her part would have been delighted to oblige, but she could not get my eye, as whenever I speak publicly at any function I always set my eyes on somebody seated toward the back of the auditorium. Similarly she would have been delighted to oblige, as Tony Hulman had spent most of the time pinching her thighs and she was getting utterly bored with his attentions.

The supper, as it turned out, was a great success financially and later I was congratulated on all sides for my talk and I was informed that an enormous sum had been realized through my efforts.

Seeing that he could not get his way and leave for his date, Tony decided to stay through to the end. Then becoming very friendly with Leona, he invited us to be his guests in his box for the forthcoming Indy 500, which was slated to take place the following week. But as we were off to Europe at the time and as she felt that I would not be too interested in the automobile race, she thanked him and declined his kind invitation and also explained why we had to refuse.

When later I told my son about the invitation he said, "You should have your heads examined refusing such an invitation. It is like being invited to a private dinner party at Buckingham Palace as a guest of the Royal Family."

As we heard later, this race was involved with more fatal crashes than at any previous one, and we were not sorry that we had not been spectators at this very tragic event.

Unfortunately, Tony has now passed on and the new building is still up in the air. However, I have been credibly informed that the matter may very shortly be revived and the university will have its art gallery on campus.

Chapter 71

A Jackson Pollock Show

During the past several decades, no artist's name has perhaps more intrigued the imagination of the American art scene than that of Jackson Pollock. The terrible motorcycle accident during 1956 on Long Island that culminated in his death at the very early age of forty-four has made him a veritable legend in the entire realm of American art history. As a man he was often beset with severe and violent periods of emotional crises that culminated in eccentricities and which in some measure contributed to his complete breakdown and subsequent visits to Dr. Joseph Henderson, a psychiatrist. It seems that during these sessions on Dr. Henderson's couch Jackson Pollock found it impossible to speak of his innermost emotional conflicts. This being the case, he decided, together with the doctor, to create a series of pen and ink drawings, which he sometimes did in water color and one of which he would leave on the doctor's desk for his study after each visit. It was hoped by both of them that through this medium the doctor would be able to analyze and elucidate some of Pollock's problems. They thought that after such study the doctor might be able to help in some way.

Whether the doctor did, in fact, find anything that would enable him to make any suggestions or not must now forever remain a mystery. Suffice it to say that after each of his visits to the doctor's office Pollock did indeed leave one of his sketches on the doctor's desk. It is quite impossible to decide whether or not the doctor was able to find anything of interest to him medically in any of these drawings, nor can one decide whether the doctor considered these drawings might be works of art. Whatever the doctor thought of these drawings, it appears that after each session he threw the sheet into a closet in his office and forgot all about it.

Thus after a while a small pile of these drawings accumulated in the closet. It was shortly after Jackson Pollock's demise that the doctor's wife while doing some spring cleaning came upon this pile in the closet, and she, being somewhat art-minded, seemed to find them of interest. Showing the pile of drawings to her husband, she said to him, "These drawings look to me as though they must have some value as works of art."

The doctor then replied, "If you want them, then you can have them for yourself."

In the pile there were some eighty-three drawings.

Some years then passed after Pollock's death, and in some way the Whitney Museum of Art in New York City became aware of the existence of this group and rightly decided to mount an exhibition devoted entirely to them. So highly did they esteem these drawings at the time that they had each of them nicely framed for hanging and they were then hung around a special gallery at the museum. At the same time as they hung these drawings they had a special catalog illustrating each of the works, many being shown in color. This catalog became even more than such; it was practically a Bible of Jackson Pollock's works on paper.

After the exhibition was announced in the press, enormous crowds swarmed through the museum and everybody seemed to be similarly impressed with the quality of the drawings.

I recall quite clearly that I was among the very first visitors to the museum to see this exhibit and that I was entirely enthralled by what I saw, although I must confess that I could not in any way understand any one of them. It appears that most of the viewers had a similar opinion.

It was either before or after this exhibition that the group of drawings was acquired by the Maxwell Galleries of San Francisco. After Mr. Maxwell had these in his possession, he decided that he would never sell them. But despite this, after his death a relative who inherited the galleries decided that perhaps he would sell them.

It was just at about this juncture that one of my sons, happening on this San Francisco Gallery, saw the group and was similarly impressed by them and suggested that perhaps we would mount an exhibition for sale at our galleries in New York City.

After this first sight and some further discussion and negotiation, each of the drawings was priced separately for sale and dispatched to us, with the exception of several that were retained.

As soon as we had the group in our hands we announced that we were about to mount an exhibition for sale, and as several of the drawings had been done on both sides of a sheet, we had a special stand made where these could be hung and viewed in the round.

What was indeed very fortunate for us was that we did not need to print any special catalogs; we were sent all of those that had remained unsold at the Whitney.

It was arranged that the exhibition would open with a cocktail party just before Christmas, and special guests were invited to attend. All awaited this opening with intense excitement.

The day that the exhibition was slated to open had the worst snowstorm that New York City had experienced in many, many years, and all through the day the snow continued falling unabated, accompanied with heavy rain.

Seeing that the weather was so terribly bad, we decided that nobody in his right mind would venture forth for the show, and we were inclined to temporarily cancel the entire exhibit. But in this thinking we were quite wrong, and fortunately, we did not cancel, as despite the weather, our galleries were soon crowded. The name of Jackson Pollock was magic.

Within a very short time many sales were consummated and the buyers were congratulating themselves on having come to the show despite the inclement weather.

As most of the visitors arrived wearing heavy snow boots, we had to request that these be removed and placed in a rear gallery before they walked all over the carpets. Thus as each viewer arrived he was ushered into the rear for this purpose, and then the boots were lined up all the way through the gallery. The sight of these boots caused many people to remark that they looked like a certain painting by Van Gogh.

So great was the interest in this show that we were requested to extend it from its originally announced two weeks. Many called on the phone to say that they were arriving from Europe and did not wish to miss the exhibition. There were even callers from several European museums who came to view the exhibition, and all agreed that the drawings were of major art interest. With further regard to the exhibition, there has always been a question of whether or not the sale of these drawings by the doctor had violated medical ethics, as the works might be considered confidential material between doctor and patient. This then is an unanswered question that can never now be concluded one way or the other.

Chapter 72

Autographed Copy of Book

In the normal course of our business as art and antique dealers during the years we always made it a point to be present at the many art and antique shows that abound in the city. At these shows we usually walk around and view the exhibits and meet with many of our dealer friends displaying their wares, always hoping to find some rarity that we want to acquire.

On one of these occasions I was walking through the antiques show held at that Armory on Park Avenue, accompanied by my wife, Leona, and while I was studying a painting she was browsing through the shelves of an antiquarian bookseller, who had in his collection some out-of-print and hard-to-find volumes. While there, she saw on one of the shelves a copy of the book *Antique Gold Boxes, Their Lore and Their Lure,* which I had coauthored with my brother Henry many years ago. More in fun than anything else, she felt that she might buy it for me, as she knew that many of our friends wished to have a copy, the book being now long out-of-print.

Leona then asked the bookseller how much he was asking for the volume, and he, taking it very carefully down from the shelf, quoted her forty-five dollars. Leona knew that when the book had been first published the price had been twelve and a half dollars and told the dealer so. She also told him that she thought that the price was too high.

Hearing this, the dealer replied, "Oh, yes, I know, but this book is actually autographed by the author."

Much amused by this reply and knowing that I would be similarly amused, she asked to see the flyleaf; at least, she thought, she should know to whom it was inscribed. Turning to this page she saw that I had written "with all my love" over my signature, but there was no other indication of who the recipient might have been. To this day I still ponder for whom I had inscribed the book and who, despite the "my love," had seen fit to dispose of it. Or it might be that the lady had passed on and the book was sold by her estate. I shall never know.